THE IDEA OF EUROPE

Its Common Heritage *and* Future

THE IDEA OF EUROPE

Its Common Heritage *and* Future

Edited by
C. David Gruender and
Evanghelos Moutsopoulos

Proceedings of PWPA Conference
Held in Yugoslavia
October 1–5, 1987

PROFESSORS WORLD PEACE ACADEMY

Published in the United States by
The Professors World Peace Academy
4 West 43 Street
New York, New York 10036

Copyright © 1992 by Professors World Peace Academy

All rights reserved. Except for use in review, no part of this publication may be reproduced, stored in a retrieval system, or transmitted in any form or by any means, electronic, mechanical, or otherwise, without the prior consent of the publisher.

The Professors World Peace Academy (PWPA) is an international association of professors, scholars, and academics from diverse backgrounds, devoted to issues concerning world peace. PWPA sustains a program of conferences and publications on topics in peace studies, area and cultural studies, national and international development, education, economics, and international relations.

Library of Congress Cataloging-in-Publication Data

The idea of Europe: its common heritage and future / edited by C. David Gruender and Evanghelos A. Moutsopoulos
    352 p.
    "A PWPA book."
    ISBN 0-943852-54-4
    1. Europe—Civilization—Congresses. 2. Europe—Civilization—1945- —Congresses. I. Gruender, C. David, 1927-. II Moutsopoulos, E., 1930- .
CB203.I33 1991
940—dc20   91-29764
                                                      CIP

CONTENTS

Preface	*(Gordon Anderson)*	vii
Welcoming Address	*(Thomas Cromwell)*	ix
	(Evanghelos A. Moutsopoulos)	xi
List of Participants		xiv
Notes on Contributors		xvi

1. The Evolution of Western Civilization and the
   Division of Europe   *Peter van den Dungen*   1
   - Europe: Unity Versus Fragmentation   *Panos D. Bardis*   15
   - Discussion   23

2. The Greek & Christian Heritage of Europe: Looking
   Back While Looking Forward   *David Gruender*   31
   - The Heritage and Values of Greek Cultural
     Models in Europe   *Evanghelos A. Moutsopoulos*   51
   - Comments   *Maria Golaszewska*   57
   - Discussion   63

3. The Rise and Decline of Europe from Limited Government
   to Unlimited Democracy   *Gerard Radnitzky*   69
   - "The European Miracle": Europe as the Exception Among
     the Advanced Civilization in History   *Ljubisa Rakic*   107
   - Comments   *Alexander Shtromas*   117
   - Discussion   121

4. Man, Society and the State: Christian and
   Marxist Perspectives   *Milan Damnjanović*   127
   - Comments   *Gordon Anderson*   145
   - Discussion   155

5. The Quality of Life in Capitalist and Socialist Economies
       Anthony de Jasay   163

- Elements in the Quality of Life   *José M.R. Delgado*   177
- Comments   *Károly Ákos*   181

6. Economic Cooperation and Integration of Europe
    Andrzej Werner   187
   - Comments   *Anthony de Jasay*   207
   - Prospects of European Integration Blocks
    Ivan Maksimović   211

7. The Ecology Factor: Common Concern for a Shared Environment   *Nansen A. Behar*   217
   - Comments   *S. Andreski*   227
   - Comments   *Vassilis Karasmanis*   231

8. Education for a Common Future: Cultivating a Pan-European Identity   *Adelheid Babing*   235
   - Pan-European Education for Peace and the Future   *Jean-Marc Gabaude*   247
   - Which Heart of Europe   *Tamás Kozma*   251
   - Discussion   255

9. The Emergence of a World Culture and Europe's Future   *Raymond Tschumi*   263
   - Discussion   281

10. The Role of Europe in Creating a Peaceful World Order   *Alexander Shtromas*   289
    - Comments   *Tadeusz Golaszewski*   303
    - Comments   *Stanislav Andreski*   309
    - Discussion   315

12. The Emergence of a World Culture and The Future of Europe   *Heinrich Beck*   327

PREFACE

The social, economic, political, and ideological transformations in Europe between 1985 and 1990 were staggering. The world witnessed the end of the cold war and the Berlin Wall, the end of communism in Eastern Europe, the breakup of the Soviet Empire, and the appeal of democracy throughout the world. The rise of a new Europe in the 1990s diverted, at least in part, the world focus on the rise of the "Pacific Era." The creation of a unified Germany has made possible that it will be the German Mark rather than the Japanese Yen which will become the leading world currency. A new Europe will play a major role in the world of the 21st century.

The idea of a "Common European Home," one of the themes of Mikhail Gorbachev's book *Perestroika,* did not only arise in Eastern Europe. Before his book was published in 1987, the Professors World Peace Academy was already organizing a conference on "The Common Heritage and Future of Europe." This volume is the proceedings of that conference, held in Dubrovnik, Yugoslavia, October 1–5, 1987.

In 1986, Chung Hwan Kwak, the Chairman of Professors World Peace Academy International (PWPA), emphasized the expansion of PWPA in Eastern Europe. This conference, organized by the Greek chapter of PWPA, was the first PWPA meeting in Eastern Europe. Since that time, the expansion of PWPA in Eastern Europe has been as rapid as the social changes themselves. By 1990, chapters were established in Poland, Czechoslovakia, Hungary, Yugoslavia, Bulgaria, Romania, and the Soviet Union.

This book reflects the common desire of Europeans, both East and West, to put aside ideological differences and work constructively together to create a new and peaceful Europe.

As a representative of the Board of Directors of PWPA International, I would like to take this opportunity to thank Professor Evanghelos Moutsopoulos and Mr. Thomas Cromwell of PWPA Greece for organizing the conference. With one foot in the East and one foot in the West, the Greeks have served as a bridge between the two parts of Europe. I would also like to thank Professor David Gruender of Florida State University for editing these proceedings, and Foundation Typography for producing this volume of PWPA. Finally, I would like to thank Professor Ljubisav M. Rakić, now President of PWPA Yugoslavia, for serving as a most generous host for the conference.

Gordon L. Anderson
Secretary General

WELCOME ADDRESS

Thomas Cromwell

It is my great pleasure to be able to welcome you to this conference on The Common Heritage and Future of Europe. The conference title is sweeping, embracing the past, present and future of our complex continent. But surely this is a good time for Europe to take stock of its development to date and to think about how best to move forward towards the fulfilment of its aspirations.

The most serious obstacle on the road to our continent's development is the division of Europe into two unreconciled camps. East-West tension and confrontation consume the creative energy and resources that should be mobilized to eliminate the problems that face Europe as a whole — economic under-development, social disintegration, pollution of the environment, political and military threats, economic competition from other regions of the globe, and so on. The unfortunate division of Europe we experience today is the result of ideological disputes that originated among scholars and ideologues, which were then translated into divergent socio-political systems. Through two great wars and many smaller conflicts in this century, Europe has paid with its blood for false ideologies and misguided ambitions. In the same way that poorly informed and ill-intentioned intellectual leaders of the past played an important part in plunging Europe into its many difficulties, surely well-informed and well-intentioned intellectuals today should pioneer the way to reconciliation, peace and prosperity for all of Europe. This is the challenge for Europe itself and for Europe in its global environment. If Europe is to regain a leading role in the world, it must mend its internal divisions and weed out from its midst those concepts and patterns of behaviour that have shown themselves to be inimical to the development of the continent. Our conference here is aimed at this dual objective. The topics cover a wide range of important issues, in this way exploring the potential for this type of dialogue to contribute to the betterment of Europe. I am sure we will hold subsequent meetings that will focus on specific areas of mutual concern to Europeans from East and West. Thank you for interrupting your busy schedules to come to this important gathering. Special thanks go to our convener and chairman, Professor Evanghelos Moutsopoulos, without whom this meeting could not have taken place.

I wish all of you a fruitful and enjoyable experience here.
Thank you.

COMMON EUROPEAN VALUES IN A CULTURAL SEARCH FOR PEACE

Evanghelos Moutsopoulos

Dear colleagues and friends:

I would like to welcome you to this picturesque and historic town of Dubrovnik, which is located almost at the mid-point of the European continent, and whose past and present represent a living example of European multiplicity within unity. "Europe, full of richness, refrain from displaying a purely singular visage," Gaston Berger, the prominent French scholar and thinker, wrote several decades ago.

The aim of our gathering here is to highlight the existence of a variety of cultural traditions within today's European reality, and to explore appropriate methods for taking advantage of the benefits that can be derived from improving mutual understanding among these traditions, beyond the confrontations that now divide Europe. This exchange may lead to further dialogue that ultimately will enable the diverse communities of Europe to share a common understanding of the nature of Europe's complexity itself. From such enlightened mutual comprehension will grow the inter-communal respect that is essential to the fulfillment of the highest aspirations we entertain for ourselves as Europeans.

Allow me to remind you of Heraclitus' wisdom when he said: "Hidden harmony is stronger by far than that which is openly displayed." This concept offers an excellent image of the situation in today's Europe. Our region of the world is witness to great ideological divergence and is divided into opposing politico-military camps, yet beneath the surface of these differences there is a certain cultural integrity that has made Europe the continent that leads the world. Religious, artistic, educational, social, economic, and political aspects of life in Europe have become models envied and imitated by the whole civilized world.

Our conference was conceived as an opportunity to emphasize what in Europe's common cultural heritage constitutes the core of our mentality, transcendant of the apparent incompatibilities that have grown up between various European groups over the centuries. One might even say that these differences underline the inherent richness of the respective value systems embodied in the cultural divergence, particularities that enable each community to acquire additional value through its own uniqueness. Augustine was right, I believe, in saying that "The beautiful is reducible to variety within unity."[3]

The urgent challenge that faces us is to locate accurately the points of divergence and to determine what is truly common among Europeans. This investigation is a necessary precondition to a discussion of areas conducive to cooperation in the future. If a unified Europe, that is a harmonious and peaceful Europe, is the common goal of all sensible Europeans, and I think all of us here hold that to be the case, then our endeavour at this gathering is of vital importance to the future of our continent and its continued leadership in the world.

Let me, at this point, express, on behalf of us all, our warmest thanks to the Professors World Peace Academy for its sponsorship of this conference. Peace has always been one of the main concerns of humankind. I hardly need to remind you that despite the prevalence of conflict in history and today, peace remains the principle objective of all religious traditions, with their billions of adherents worldwide.

It is my conviction that, by comparison, political ideas, on all sides, are on totally uncertain ground. In fact, political ideologues and leaders speak of peace while they are obviously preparing for war. Their unspoken motto would seem to be: *si vis bellum lauda pacem* [if one plans war, praise peace]. This may seem very clever but in the end it spawns hypocritical and misleading activity that conveys a hubris against human dignity. Therefore, I believe that intellectuals of all countries should cooperate to propose new models of peaceful life, thus promoting peace "from below". It is in this context that I consider our gathering here in Dubrovnik to be a significant event. Once again I welcome you all, wishing each of you an agreeable and productive stay here, and all of us the realization of our expectations through our joint efforts over the coming days.

Thank you.

THE COMMON HERITAGE AND FUTURE OF EUROPE
LIST OF PARTICIPANTS

Professor Károly Ákos, M.D.; Head, Research Group on Psychochronography, National Institute of Medical Experts, Department of Aviation Medicine, Budapest, HUNGARY

Dr. Gordon Anderson; Secretary General, PWPA International, New York, USA

Professor Stanislaw Andreski; Professor Emeritus, Faculty of Letters, Reading University, UK

Professor Adelheid Babing; Pedagogy Department, Humbolt University, Berlin, DDR (then)

Professor Panos D. Bardis; Department of Sociology, University of Toledo, Toledo, Ohio, USA

Professor Heinrich Beck; Philosophishche Fakultat, University of Bamberg, Bamberg, WEST GERMANY (then)

Professor Nansen A. Behar; Head, Economics Department, Institute for Contemporary Social Studies, Bulgarian Academy of Sciences, Sofia, BULGARIA

Mr. Thomas Cromwell; Secretary General, Professors World Peace Academy of Greece, Athens, GREECE

Professor Milan Damnjanović; University of Arts, Belgrade, YUGOSLAVIA

Professor José M. R. Delgado, M.D.; Centro De Estudios Neurobiologicos, Madrid, SPAIN

Professor Jean-Marc Gabaude; Philosopher, Cugnaux, FRANCE

Professor Maria Golaszewska; Head, Aesthetics Department, Institute of Philosophy, Jagiellonian University, Krakow, POLAND

Professor Tadeusz Golaszewski; Department of Pedagogy, Jagiellonian University, Krakow, POLAND

Professor David Gruender; Department of Philosophy, Florida State University, Tallahassee, Florida, USA

Dr. Anthony de Jasay: Economist, Cany, FRANCE

Dr. Vassilis Karasmanis; Philosopher, Athens, GREECE

Professor Tamás Kozma; Head, Department of Policy and Research Planning, Hungarian Institute for Educational Research Budapest, HUNGARY

Professor Evanghelos Moutsopoulos; Philosophy Department, Athens University, Member, Athens Academy of Sciences, Athens, GREECE

Professor Ljubisav M. Rakic M.D.; Institute of Biochemistry, Medical School, University of Belgrade, Belgrade, YUGOSLAVIA

Professor Gerard Radnitzky; Department of Philosophy, University of Trier, Trier, WEST GERMANY (then)

Professor Alexander Shtromas; Department of Politics and Contemporary History, University of Salford, Salford, ENGLAND

Professor Raymond Tschumi; Head, Department of English, University of Saint-Gall, St-Gallen, SWITZERLAND

Dr. Peter Van den Dungen; Lecturer in Peace Studies, University of Bradford, Bradford, West Yorkshire, UK

Professor Andrzej Werner; Author, Independent Peace Researcher, Warsaw, POLAND

Professor Jindřich Zelený; Vice President, Czechoslovak Philosophical Society, Prague, CZECHOSLOVAKIA

Professor Ivan Maksimović; Law Faculty, University of Belgrade, YUGOSLAVIA

NOTES ON CONTRIBUTORS

Dr. Károly Ákos, M.D., Ph.D. Head, Research group on psychochronography, Budapest

Dr. Gordon L. Anderson is Secretary-General of the Professors World Peace Academy; Adjunct Professor at the Unification Theological Seminary, Barrytown, N.Y.; Associate Editor of the International Journal on World Peace. He holds a Ph.D in Philosophy of Religion and an M.Div. in Christian Ethics. Most publications are related to peace and religion.

Professor S.L. Andreski, Professor Emeritus, University of reading, England; Honorary Professor, Polish University of London.

Professor Adelheid Babing, Doctor of Sciences; Director for research activities in Department of Pedagogic Sciences, Humboldt University, Berlin; some years editor of several journals. Subjects of own research activities and publications: connections of lifestyles of pupils and situations of learning in the schools, consequences for certain aspects of concepts of education; individual differences between pupils and their meaning for methods of teaching; promotion of special gifted children in the schools of GDR.

Professor D. Bardis, Professor of Sociology, Toledo University. Editor-in-Chief and Book Review Editor, *International Journal on World Peace* and *International Social Science Review*. Author of 16 books, including a novel (*Ivan and Artemis*) and an anthology of poetry (*A Cosmic World of Melodies*), as well as over 400 essays and scientific articles. Made first English translation of Archimedes' lost book *On Balances*. Composer of over 20 songs for the mandolin.

Professor Heinrich Beck, Dr. Phil. Member of national and international philosophical Institutes and Societies. Member of honour in Argentina, Brazil, Mexico. Professional functions: Ordinary Professor for Philosophy at the University of Bamberg, Germany; Extra-ordinary Professor for Philosophy at University of Salzburg, Austria; Honorary Professor for Philosophy at Universidad del Salvador, Buenos Aires. Studies: philosophy, psychology, theology, pedagogics, sociology, biology, physics. Lectures at universities and congr. in several countries of Europe and esp. Latin America (Argentine, Chile, Brazil, Ecuador, Mexico). Philos. investigations and publications esp. in metaphysics and philosophy of culture (15 books and 130 articles), p.e.: *Kulturphilosophie der Technik*, Trier 1979; *Entwicklung zur Menschlichkeit Durch Begegnung Westlicherund Ostlicher Kultur*, Bern-Frankfurt-New York, 1988.

Nansen Behar, Professor, Head of Department "Economics" of the Institute for Contemporary Social Studies with the Bulgarian Academy of Sciences. Doctor of Economic Sciences at Higher School of Economics, Sofia. Member of the Governing Board of the "Ecoforum for Peace". Member of the Executive Council of the world Federation of Scientific Workers. Author of seven books (*Factors and contradiction of Economic Growth, Global Progress and Social Structures, Comparative Analysis of Economic Systems* and others) and more than 140 scientific articles in seven languages.

Thomas Cromwell, Publisher of *The Middle East Times*, organizer of numerous conferences in the Middle East.

Milan Damnjanović. Born 1924. Ph.D. at Vienna. Ord. Professor at Univ. Belgrade, President of the Society for Aesthetics and Vice President of the International Association of Societies for Aesthetics. Areas of teaching and research: Aesthetics *viz*. Philosophy of Art and Unity of Modern Philosophy. Publications: 10 books in Aesthetics, and Unity of Modern Philosophy. Editor in chief: Journal for Aesthetics .

José Delgado, M.D. Professor of Neurobiology, Centro Estudios Neurobiologicos, Madrid, Spain.

Jean-Marc Gabaude. Professor of Philosophy at the University of Toulouse, director of doctoral studies. President of the Philosophy Society of Toulouse. Author of books and articles on philosophy and pedagogy.

Professor Maria Golaszewska. Head of Department of Aesthetics in the Institute of Philosophy at the Jagiellonian University in Cracow. Master's degree in philosophy at the Jagiellonian University in Cracow in 1950, doctor's degree at the Catholic University of Lublin 1956; professor in 1984; research work and teaching at the Jagiellonian University since 1957. Field of interests: aesthetics related to philosophy, philosophical anthropology, axiology (theory of values). The main books: *Creation and the Creator's Personality* Lublin 1958; *Philosophic Foundations of Literary Criticism*, Warsaw 1963; *Awareness of Beauty. Problems of the Genesis, Functions, Structure and Values in Aesthetics*, Warsaw, 1970; *An Outline of Aesthetics. Problems, Methods, Theories*, Cracow 1973, (2nd ed 1984, 3rd ed 1986); *Man in the Mirror of Art. A Study from the borderline of aesthetic and philosophic anthropology*, Warsaw 1977; *Aesthetic of Reality*, Warsaw 1984; *Aesthetics and Anti-aesthetics*, Warsaw 1984; *On the nature of aesthetic values*, Cracow 1986; *Who is an Artist?*, Warsaw 1986. The bibliography of Golaszewska's works consists of some 180 items, 30 of them in English and French.

Professor Tadeusz Golaszewski. Head of Department of Adult Education in the Institute of Pedagogy at the Jagiellonian University. Masters degree in polish philology at the Jagiellonian University in Cracow in 1951 and in sociology in 1960; doctor's degree at the Jagiellonian University in 1964; professor in 1970. Field of interests: adult education, theory of propagation of culture, social sociology, aesthetic education, theory of culture, social psychology. As participant in the polish resistance against Nazis during the 2nd World War, I am interested directly in the movement for World Peace. Published 7 books (sociology, problems of childrens aesthetic education, an analysis of school system, and so on) and about 120 articles.

Professor David Gruender. As a philosopher and historian of science and student of epistemology, ethics, and social and political philosophy, he taught at Kansas State University, Case Institute of Technology, and since 1967, at Florida State University.

de Jasay, Anthony. Mr de Jasay is a graduate of Budapest and Perth, and a former Research Fellow of Nuffield College, Oxford. He published a number of papers in the *Journal of Political Economy, Oxford Economic Paper, The Economic Journal* and *Review of Economic Studies*. In 1962, he left academic life and was a private banker in Paris till 1979. He published *The State* (Basil Blackwell, Oxford, 1985); *Social Contract, Free Ride* is forthcoming from The Clarendon Press, Oxford.

Vassilis Karasmanis, D. Phil (Oxford). Lecturer of Philosophy, National Technical University of Athens.

Tamás Kozma, Research Professor, Head of Department, Hungarian Institute for Educational Research. Born 1939, Budapest, Hungary. Field of Interest: Sociology of Education. Field of action: Educational planning and policy analysis.

Ivan Maksimović. Professor Ivan Maksimović is Full Professor at the Law Faculty at the University of Belgrade, Yugoslavia. He is also a member of Serbian Academy of Science and Arts. Professor Maksimović is an author of many books and hundreds of other works (essays, articles, *etc.*) in the field of economic theory, political economy and comparative systems. During his university career up to now Prof. Maksimović has been lecturing at various university centers inside the country and abroad — in U.S.A., China, U.S.S.R., England, France, *etc.* For many decades Prof. Maksimović has taken an active part in the organization of scientific and economic life and institutions in Yugoslavia.

Ljubisav Rakić, M.D., Ph.D. Born 4/11/1931 Sarajevo, Yugoslavia. Professor of Bio-chemistry and Neurobiology, Faculty of Medicine, University of Belgrade, Yugoslavia. Research interest: Neurobiology of Behavior. Postdoctoral training at Brain Research Institute, UCLA, Los Angeles, California (1960–1962). Member National Academy of Sciences in Yugoslavia. Professional position: Head, department of Research, University Clinical Center, Belgrade. Published more than 250 papers in scientific journals. Member many international scientific and professional societies. Member Advisory Committee on Health Research of World Health Organization, Geneva.

Dr. Gerard Radnitzky, Professor of Philosophy of Science, University of Trier, West Germany. Author of *Economic Imperialism, Centripetal Forces in the Sciences,* and many other books.

Dr. Alexander Shtromas, Professor of Political Science, Hillsdale College, Hillsdale, Michigan. Born in the Baltics and educated in the USSR, he is a recognized authority on Soviet studies. He is editor of the 4-volume reference work *The Soviet Union and the Challenge of the Future.*

Professor Dr. Raymond Tschumi. Poet, essayist, Professor of English Literature at Saint-Gall University (Switzerland), Raymond Tschumi has issued a trilogy on long term historical perspectives. The three books, *Théorie de la Culture, La Crise Culturelle* and *A la Recherche du Sens* were published in Lausanne (L'Age d'Homme), and the first was translated into English (*Theory of Culture*, NOK, New York).

Evanghelos A. Moutsopoulos, Professor of Philosophy, Univ. of Athens. Member Athens' Academy of Sciences. President of several philosophical societies, national and international. Corresponding Member of several Academies national and international. Author of about 40 volumes on philosophy and of about 400 articles and papers presented to international philosophical conferences. Holder of several philosophical prizes. Former Rector of the Univ. of Athens. Has taught at several Universities in Europe and in North America.

The present paper takes its place within a research project entitled "The Genesis of Expression", which investigates long term artistic, especially literary processes, in so far as they express changes in consciousness. These changes consist in crossing the thresholds which separate the five main phases: magic, mythic, mystical, artistic-scientific and critical post-post-modern.

Dr. Peter van den Dungen, Lecturer in Peace Studies, University of Bradford, U.K. Research on history of peace thought and international organisation. His publications include *Foundations of Peace Research, The Making of Peace,* and *West European Pacifism & the Strategy for Peace.*

Dr. Andrzej Werner, author, independent peace researcher. He received his LL.B and LL.M degrees at University of Warsaw. In 1956 Dr. Werner joined the Faculty of Law there and has held academic posts till 1962. His Ph.D. he earned in political science from Polish Institute of Foreign Affairs, 1975. His principal area of work has been East-West trade and international relations. This experience he wants to use toward undoing the present divisions of Europe. Among his publications are two books on European unity and economic integration.

Professor Jindřich Zelený, Vice President of the Czechoslovak Philosophical Society, corresponding member of the Czechoslovak Academy of Sciences, member of the Steering Committee of FISP (*Fédération Internationale des Sociétés de Philosophie*), member of the presidium of Internationale Gesellschaft für Dialektische Philosophie—Societas Hegeliana. Professor for philosophy at the Philosophical Faculty of the Charles University, Prague.

THE EVOLUTION OF WESTERN CIVILIZATION AND THE DIVISION OF EUROPE

Peter van den Dungen

More than the name of any other continent, 'Europe' denotes not only a geographical concept but also a cultural one, an idea. Those who play down the latter, or deny it altogether as Bismarck did in 1876 when he wrote, "Anyone who talks of Europe is wrong — [It is merely] a geographical notion", does not make it any easier for himself, since the notion of Europe as a geographical entity is not devoid of serious difficulties. One view, identified with President de Gaulle and recently taken up again by the popular peace movements in the West, envisages a Europe stretching "from the Atlantic to the Urals". Neither the Atlantic coast, nor the Ural mountain range constitute, however, the natural or historical boundary of Europe.[1] The spread of European ideas and institutions, and of her own peoples, to North and South America since the 16th century has created, on the other side of the Atlantic, if not a duplicate European civilization, at least an extension of it, reflecting in its variety, North and South, the different cultures of the respective settlers and thus the variety of Europe herself. With respect to, particularly, North America, this commonality of historical background, and shared values, interests and aspirations, had led to the notion of a trans Atlantic relationship and history — rather than a merely European one — which encompasses both the old and the new worlds. Already in its topography, this new world, from New York in the east to New Westminster in the west, expresses its affiliation with, and even affection for, the old.

Hence, not the eastern Atlantic but the western Pacific can be regarded as the westernmost natural boundary of Europe.

The recent development of modern telecommunications and the ease and speed with which the Atlantic can be crossed, have reduced it to a lake comparable to the Mediterranean in size and in terms of its importance as a crossroads for the exchange of goods and ideas, linking the two worlds together. It is true, of course, that the Mediterranean civilization, about which Braudel has given us such detailed accounts, linked together more heterogeneous cultures, allowing for a fruitful interchange between the peoples of Europe, the Middle East, and North Africa. If Europe has expanded across the Atlantic in the last half millennium, in the half millennium or so preceding this, it was the world of the Mediterranean which played a vital role in the making of Europe. The year 1492 is symbolic both for inaugurating the age of discovery *and* for closing the Moorish reign in Spain (with the fall of Granada). Just as since 1492, the history of Europe has increasingly acquired a trans Atlantic dimension, so that same year saw the removal of the last political center of the Islamic presence in Europe, in which the Mediterranean world had played such an important role.

Islam's contribution to Europe is at least twofold: for much of Europe's early existence, the only other civilization it knew was that of Islam and it was the threat posed by it that forged, out of the chaos following the collapse of Rome, Europe's consciousness of itself as a distinct geographical and cultural region.[2] Historians of Europe have frequently observed that the drive for unity seems directly related to the presence of an outside threat, and that therefore the impetus for creating unity is often a negative one. (According to some, the successful unification of Western Europe since the Second World War is similarly inspired by the existence of an outside threat.) But a more precise and positive legacy of Islam in Europe was its transmission, in part through Spain, of the teachings of Hellenistic science and philosophy as well as those of Arab mathematicians, cartographers, and philosophers. In addition to learning and scholarship, the Islamic legacy also includes various artefacts, including important technological inventions, such as the waterwheel. This was, after all, an age when Islamic civilization far exceeded anything which Europe had to offer. During its occupation of the Iberian peninsula, Islam provided the bridgehead between classical antiquity and Renaissance Europe and played a vital role in putting Europe on the road to its own unique development.³

The definition of 'Europe' is problematical, as is that of 'Western Civilization'. If at times the two are held to be virtually identical, it is considerations such as the above, concerning the debt which the European world owes to Islam, which made the Polish historian Oscar Halecki observe: "Those who call European civilization western are inclined to decide in advance one of the most difficult and controversial questions of European history".⁴ Instead of elaborating this question, let us briefly return to the notion of Europe "from the Atlantic to the Urals" to draw attention to the well-known difficulty presented by the second part of this description. Any discussion of Europe, and sooner rather than later, confronts the question whether Russia is "in or out", and concludes that the situation is ambiguous; depending on the aspect or the historical period under consideration, the answer will be different. When the basis of European unity was seen as residing in Catholicism, Russia was excluded since the inclusion of an Orthodox member would destroy the very basis of unity. But in the 19th century, European conservatism regarded Russia as an essential part of Europe since this country contributed her share to suppress revolutions and defend the *status quo* against subversion and dissension.⁵ Some, stressing the despotic nature of Muscovite autocracy, have seen in this Russia's Asiatic streak, and on that basis have excluded her from Europe. Others, on the contrary, have regarded Russia as Europe's necessary bulwark against the "yellow peril". Russia's steady advance in the 19th century towards the Pacific Ocean has made her an Asiatic as well as a European power, thereby further complicating her status *vis à vis* Europe. The discussions in the West regarding Russia's "European" character are paralleled, of course, in the divisions in Russia herself between westerners and slavophiles: between those who have been attracted to the west and those who have been repelled by it, seeing it as hostile and detrimental to Russia's own essential nature and mission.

The contrasting of Europe with Asia was already used by the

first author who described Europe as an entity, Hippocrates. This he did in his treatise *Airs, Waters, Places,* which dates from the end of the 5th century B.C.[6] Jumping across millennia, Asia likewise featured in the striking observation of two French geographers, Mantelle and Brun, who in their *Géographie Universelle* (published in Paris in 1816), referred to Europe as "This narrow peninsula, which appears on the map as no more than an appendix of Asia", and who went on to emphasise the dramatic discrepancy between this morsel's size and its significance, since it had become "the metropolis of the human race",[7] a statement which was to become even more true in the course of the next century, and to the meaning of which we presently turn.

In attempts to define the European phenomenon, it is conventional to take as a starting point an historic analysis of the genesis of this idea, an enquiry, in other words, into the *causes* which produced the idea of 'Europe'. Typically, in order of their chronological appearance, these are the experience and legacy of the Roman Empire and, through it, the legacy of Hellas; of Christianity and the Latin world; and a set of beliefs stemming from the late seventeenth century scientific revolution and the eighteenth century enlightenment. A more unusual approach, namely through an analysis of Europe's *effects,* has been undertaken by Denis de Rougemont, in his spirited defence of the European idea. He has suggested that Europe be defined as "that part of the world which made 'The World'".[8] This seems a fruitful way of approaching the question we are concerned with in this paper.

De Rougemont writes of "the worldwide adventure of the Europeans" (the title of his first chapter) which was "of decisive significance for the whole of mankind". It seems reasonable to argue that this "adventure" constitutes an important, perhaps the most important, characteristic of the evolution of Western civilization. What distinguishes this civilization from all others is its historically "worldwide function".[9] It has acquired this function by virtue of its dynamism and restlessness, forever discovering and expanding. The history of the West is in essence, de Rougemont suggests, a multi-faceted Odyssey, and its heroes are so many Ulysseses.[10] They are represented not only by the latterday Ulysses *par excellence,* Columbus, and his fellow voyagers of the seas, but equally by those countless scientists and philosophers who, while staying at home, explored other aspects of reality with consequences no less far reaching.

The basic fact remains, however, that Europe forged links between continents which before her time had lived in the most complete ignorance of one another.

> Through her, the human race became conscious of its unity. The universalist idea, the very idea of a human race... are the creations first of Greco-Roman Europe, then of Christian Europe and finally of technological Europe. In this sense it may truly be said that "Europe made the world".[11]

This same idea also seems to be implied in Max Scheler's belief that "if there is at all the possibility of a history of humanity as a whole, it has begun only in our own day, perhaps in 1914". Scheler makes the important point that "humanity is *not* history's point of departure but that it is 'history's *task,* perhaps its result".[12] In this task Europe's "adventure" has played a seminal role.

A number of interesting paradoxes and ironies suggest themselves when we pursue the theme of Europe's expansionist adventure when we start with the period of the great discoveries of the late 15th and 16th centuries. While Christendom, *i.e.,* the Europe of the Middle Ages, was dissolving, a larger entity, namely the world itself, was being discovered, explored, and exploited (the latter, admittedly, in more ways than one). The decline of continental unity (or at least of a large part of it), as a result of the Reformation and the emergence of the sovereign state and the gradual growth of nationalism, coincided with the discovery of other continents, a first, necessary, step in any process of creating global unity. Let us now briefly consider the process of European expansionism over the globe not from its starting point but at its conclusion. When the European colonial period came to an end, a long process which started with the emancipation of the thirteen colonies to form the United States of America in the last quarter of the eighteenth century, followed in the first half of the nineteenth century by the liberation of Latin America, and virtually completed in the aftermath of the Second World War with the independence of the colonies in Africa and Asia, and when a world-wide civilization had, if only embryonically, come into existence — at this point Europe, the creator of this new world, had itself become the victim of a new imperialism, which tragically divided it.

But this is only half the story, for the period in which the individual European states lost their empires was also that in which they began to unite — a remarkable coincidence which can be explained by the dialectical evolution of the same phenomenon of nationalism.[13] Already in the eighteenth century the disciples of Rousseau, followed by Herder, Bentham, and Fichte, had denounced colonial expansion as a mortal sin on the part of Europe, since it was held to aggravate the division of Europe into rival nations. Certainly, imperial rivalry proved to be an important factor in that complex of causes which resulted in the First World War. Both World Wars, however, led to two opposite reactions: on the one hand, the World War I settlement articulated the idea of the right of nations to self-determination — which was to prove a spur behind the drive for decolonisation, even though this principle was inadequately implemented in the European arena (which is not surprising given the difficulties involved). On the other hand, following World War II, plans for European unification were being pursued in earnest and with some degree of success, even if this involved a truncated Europe. The mania of European nationalism had apparently run its course, had dethroned Europe from its world-wide pre-eminence in the process, and had resulted in the painful division of which we are all aware. That part of Europe which was free to do so at long last started the process of peaceful unification. For these countries it is true what Denis de Rougemont has said: "They lost the world and found Europe again".[14] A second feature of our situation to which he draws attention, just as paradoxical, is that Europe's political retreat coincided with the accelerated adoption of her civilization by the decolonised world — not, it is true, in its entirety, and all at once, and not some of those values which we prize above all (and which cannot be created overnight, such as the ideals of freedom, liberty and justice, and attitudes of humaneness and compassion — all rooted in a fundamental belief in the uniqueness and worth of the individual human person).

In this connection it is interesting to point out that even when the non-western world is reacting most violently and vigorously against Europe, it does so frequently by invoking concepts and in the name of creeds which it has borrowed from her: nationalism, materialism (economic progress), marxism. Perhaps an exception should be made for the current upsurge of Islamic fundamentalism which is equally hostile to the "capitalist" world and its atheistic communist offshoot. But this is likely to be a temporary phenomenon, the result of excesses of fervour and fanaticism to which revolutions are notoriously prone and which they have never sustained for long. Even so, it is clear that the Iranian regime which is spearheading this revolt is unable to reject many features of the world it is rebelling against, ranging from membership in the U.N. to economic cooperation with its declared enemies. It seems that the exigencies of survival today increasingly impose, even at the height of division and discord, elements of unity and accord. This conclusion can only be reinforced when we introduce yet another consideration with paradoxical overtones in the evolution of western civilization. It is this: No sooner had the basis been laid for the construction of a global civilization, than that other embodiment of Ulysses, Faustian man, discovered a power which enabled him to destroy, for the first (and perhaps last) time, the entire terrestrial creation. The threat of war has suddenly become global and total in ways which it has never been before — "omnicide", "ecocide", "exterminism" — these are the alarming yet accurate descriptions of the potential outcome, henceforth, of any major conflict. In this unexpected and uncomfortable way, too, the west has unified the world. Ecological considerations as a result of world-wide industrialisation are leading to similar conclusions and reinforce the view of a very fragile "spaceship earth". We can only hope that such a perilous prospect will stimulate the search for greater cooperation and unity so that eventually, in dialectical fashion, nuclear (or even post-nuclear) weapons will make themselves as well as all other weapons of mass destruction obsolete and redundant as a result of the positive processes which they set in motion or accelerated.

Meanwhile, the division of even a small part of that same world is real and seemingly intractable. It is ironic that the eastern part of Europe is in the grip of an ideology whose founding fathers claimed for it a unique capacity for unifying mankind. Communism was destined to overcome "the vicious traditional divisions between classes, nations, and races (it would overcome the divisions between religions by extinguishing the religions themselves)".[15] But this *parvenu* ideology, itself, of course, the product of the West — but for which it had no need — proved no match for traditional nationalism, racialism, or, least of all, religion. Increasingly, communism in Russia has come to be interpreted as Russia's device for catching up, technologically, economically, and socially, with her western neighbours — and thus may be seen as a variation of a traditional concern of Russian history. In this interpretation, also put forward by Toynbee, the Bolshevik Revolution of 1917 was a resumption of the revolution that had been started by Peter the Great two centuries before. Toynbee writes:

> The constant disturbing factor in Russian history has been the accelerating progress of technology in the West since the 17th century. This dynamic development...has been a challenge to the non-western majority of mankind. It has confronted all non-western peoples with a choice between mastering western technology and falling into subjection to technologically more efficient western Powers.[16]

Michael Howard, likewise, has noted that, since the eighteenth century, Russia became increasingly aware of the relationship between state power and economic development, and realised that she could only compete with the West, and be an actor in history rather than a victim of it, if she copied the West. The same lesson was later learned by the Turks, the Chinese, the Japanese, and — gradually and reluctantly — by the entire world.[17] In this way, as well as in the conflict Russia experienced between the need to

"Europeanise" and the desire to keep her own identity ("We want your technology but not your culture"), Russia was to be a prototype for the developing world.

In Russia, China, and elsewhere, marxism has been seen as the ideal instrument for bringing about this transformation. Toynbee's view that psychology rather than economics is decisive in the adoption or rejection of a new ideology or religion is aptly illustrated in the present case:

> Marxism attracts non-western peoples by the qualities that repel westerners. [Through] its violence and radicalism... Marxism fitted the mood of the non-western peoples when these were ripe for revolting against western dominance. It is a creed of western origin that indicts the western "establishment".[18]

Division, of course, is nothing new in Europe — rather the contrary as her history has alternated between periods of unity and division, the latter as a result of religious schisms or dynastic and national rivalries. Napoleon's and Germany's bids for power forged, however temporarily and expediently, unity among the other European states. We have already mentioned how, for some, the expansion of Russian power since 1917, and especially since 1945, has similarly been the main stimulus for the creation of the European Community. What distinguishes the present division from those divisions in Europe of the past is the wholly artificial and unwilled nature of the divide: it has been imposed from outside and is not the result of any organically grown developments. Left to their own, most countries of Eastern Europe, especially the largely Catholic ones of Poland, Hungary, and Czechoslovakia, and, within the Soviet Union, the Baltic States (as well as, of course, East Germany), would not have found themselves so artificially cut off from the rest of Europe as is presently the case. As James Joll has said,

> it is the Iron Curtain alone that makes us content with thinking of the Europe of the Six [as it then was] as "Europe". If the Iron Curtain were to be torn down, then we would begin to

realize how much of Eastern Europe and even Russia itself shared a common European tradition and how it does not really make sense, historically at least, to talk of a Europe which does not include Königsberg and Cracow, Breslau and Budapest, or even for that matter Goethe's Weimar.[19]

When he delivered his lecture, almost two decades ago, Joll spoke of the Europe of the Treaty of Rome as a "rather provincial affair", and expressed doubts "whether it will remain an inward-looking small grouping...or whether it is capable of expansion and growth".[20] Ten years earlier, Pieter Geyl, in a somewhat similar *tour d'horizon* of Europe, had likewise expressed his astonishment that the creators of "the Six" had presumed to claim for it the name 'Europe', and that the Europe enthusiasts, moreover, were apparently blind to the dangers inherent in their creation. Refusing to believe that the association of 'the Six' was only a beginning, Geyl wrote: "I am afraid that, under cover of a devout use of the name 'Europe', a dangerous division of Europe is being prepared".[21] It seems that these apprehensions and doubts have been fully disproven by the dynamic development and expansion of the Community which, after having reached a doubling of the original membership in the meantime, is still faced with a queue of further applicants. There is nothing necessarily divisive in this grouping: on the contrary, together with those northern and neutral European countries who are not members of the Community, it is able to bring its combined weight to bear on European wide issues, and for the development of pan European instruments of international relations such as the Helsinki Final Act.

The present Community closely resembles, in its membership (but also in other respects) the "European Parliament" which William Penn advocated three centuries ago as a necessity to prevent Europe's "incomparable Miseries".[22] He predicted that it would be "A Great Presence", representing as it would the "Best and wealthiest part of the known World; where Religion and Learning, Civility and Arts have their Seat and Empire".[23] Some believe that this is still the case and that, now that a large part of Europe has come together for the first time, the "Great Presence" has become a reality — one which has an important role to play in the further evolution of western civilization. But the history of Europe since Penn's days (and before!) has filled more recent commentators with apprehension of the possible impact of this new "superpower in the making" (Johann Galtung). Galtung speaks of an occident exporting "its self-destructive inclination", and believes that it is, together with the Nipponic civilization, the most dangerous of all existing civilizations — "belligerency is rooted in the civilization itself".[24] Michael Howard appears to provide a striking illustration of this thesis in his analysis of the role played by war in the making and unmaking of Europe. In his view, the old Europe, "the Europe made and unmade by military conflict and military power, belongs to the past", and he is unable to contemplate a new Europe "with either conviction or relish.... There is not really very much in the history of Europe that merits our regrets".[25] The "miracle" of a free Eastern Europe would, in his opinion, lead to the re-emergence of a pattern "that two world wars were fought to avoid: a Europe entirely dominated by a reunited Germany" a prospect which does not appeal either to many Europeans or, not least important, Russians. As regards the Europe of the Community, Howard's use of language is evocative of his lack of enthusiasm for it, since he sees it as "a useful piece of mechanism so long as it is not taken too seriously or required to support a political burden beyond its very limited capabilities".[26]

Whether one takes one's stance with convinced Europeans (such as Denis de Rougemont or Pieter Geyl), or with sober-minded or passionate critics, let us hope that the excesses of Europe's history will not be repeated in the future, and that, looking back on her own history, Europe will be able to say, in the words with which Victor Hugo inscribed a book of juvenile verses: *"Bêtises que je faisais avant ma naissance"* [silly things I did before my birth]. As regards the question of its division (a division which goes beyond the geographical and which deeply affects Russia itself), it is impossible to predict when and in what way it will be overcome. But, with that great European of our time, Salvador de Madariaga, we may be tempted to say *"Eppur Europa si muove"* [But Europe moves].[27]

NOTES

1. For a summary of the fascinating debate on the Urals as constituting the boundary of Europe and Asia see Denys HAY, *Europe: The Emergence of an Idea* (Edinburgh: Edinburgh University Press, 1968 2nd ed. 123–127.
2. Michael DYNES, 'The age-old debt we owe to Islam', *The Times*, 15 August 1987.
3. *Ibid.*
4. Quoted in Geoffrey BARRACLOUGH, *European Unity in Thought and Action* (Oxford, Basil Blackwell, 1963) 5.
5. *Ibid.*, 39–40.
6. Denis de ROUGEMONT, *The Meaning of Europe* (London, Sidgwick and Jackson, 1965) 29.
7. *Ibid.*, 14.
8. *Ibid.*, 11. It will be noted that this definition allows for an interesting continuation of the debate concerning Russia's European belonging. Much of the 20th century world has been made by communist Russia, and, from this point of view, Russia (in the shape of the Soviet Union) has been very European. The nature and manner of what has been made — at home as well as abroad in Eastern Europe and further afield — is such, however, that for many Europeans (including many Russians!) Russia has put itself, once more, firmly outside the European tradition.
9. *Ibid.*, 11, 16.
10. *Ibid.*, 24.
11. *Ibid.*, 23-24.
12. Max SCHELER, "The Idea of Peace and Pacifism", *Journal of the British Society for Phenomenology*, 7 (October 1976) 161.
13. de ROUGEMONT 94.
14. *Ibid.*, 96.
15. Arnold J. TOYNBEE, "Looking Back Fifty Years", in *The Impact of the Russian Revolution 1917–1967: The Influence of*

Bolshevism on the World outside Russia (London: Oxford University Press, 1967,) 3.
16. *Ibid.*, 8.
17. Michael HOWARD, "War in the Making and Unmaking of Europe", in his *The Causes of Wars and other Essays* (London: Temple Smith, 1983) 157–158.
18. TOYNBEE, 11.
19. James JOLL, *Europe: A Historian's View* (Leeds: University Press, 1969) 21.
20. *Ibid.*, 19.
21. Pieter GEYL, "The Historical Background of the Idea of European Unity", in his *Encounters in History,* (Gloucester, Mass.: Peter Smith, 1977) 315–316.
22. William PENN, *An Essay Towards the Present and Future Peace of Europe,* (London 1693) 67.
23. *Ibid.*, 29.
24. Johann GALTUNG, "Peace and the World as Inter-civilizational interaction", in Raimo Vayrynen, ed., *The Quest for Peace* (London: Sage, 1987) 343–345.
25. HOWARD, 168. Howard's view must, at any rate, be qualified, since the role of military power is obviously not confined to Europe's past but is still very much in evidence today.
26. *Ibid.*, 167.
27. Salvador de MADARIAGA, Portrait of Europe (London: Hollis and Carter, 1952) 6. The reference to Hugo is taken from the same book, 3.

EUROPE: UNITY VERSUS FRAGMENTATION

Panos D. Bardis

"In Europe there are also tribes that differ from one another in stature, in shape, and in bravery."
HIPPOCRATES, *Airs, Waters, Places,* XXIV, 2–4.

I. INTRODUCTION: THE DREAM OF UNITY.

Dr. Peter van den Dungen's "The Evolution of Western Civilization and the Division of Europe"[1] is a brilliant essay that contains four main features: first, an excellent analysis of Europe both as a geographical concept and an idea; second, an expert history of European unity and division; third, a somewhat optimistic statement about continental cooperation in the future; and fourth, some emphasis on global unity.

II. THE GREAT PHYSICIAN'S BELLICOSE PATIENTS.

Etymologically and mythologically, the name of the continent signifies unity beyond its own geographical boundaries.[2] Indeed, Europa was the daughter of Agenor, a Phoenician king. In other myths, she was the Full Moon, the Great Goddess as mother of the continent, and the Moon-cow identified with Io, Hera, Hathor, and Kali. More importantly, the Moon-cow rode Nandi, who was Shiva disguised as a white bull, before Europa rode Zeus, also as a white bull. The name itself, which was the surname of the Mycenaean Demeter, and which is related to the Vedic Uruasi, "the wide-spreading dawn," may derive from the Greek *erebus,* which, like the related Gothic *riqis,* means darkness. Thus, Europe is the land of the setting sun, as opposed to Asia, the land of the east. Two more theories refer to the Greek *eurys* (wide) and *ophrys* (brow) or *ops* (eye or face), as well as *eu* (good) and *rheo* (flow). Accordingly, Europe, would mean broad-browed broad-eyed, broad-faced, or fair-flowing. Yes, Europe is both an idea and a geographical concept with protean boundaries. Depending on the criterion that one employs (linguistic, religious, economic, *etc.*), these boundaries shift in various directions. Besides, modern transportation and communication have changed the Atlantic into a lake and the world into a global village, which makes it parochial to speak of Europe as a self-contained unit. Even much smaller units are often defined by protean boundaries. Chicago's metropolitan area, for instance, has become one economic unit, but it consists of 1,642 independent governments![3] A long time ago, Hippocrates (460–377 B.C.), in his Airs, Waters, Places, attributed European unrest and division to the continent's heterogeneity. Let me translate a relevant passage:

> Therefore, I believe that the inhabitants of Europe are more courageous than those of Asia. For where there is uniformity there is slackness, while heterogeneity generates endurance in body and soul. Rest and slackness reinforce cowardice, but endurance and exertion engender manliness. For this reason, the inhabitants of Europe are more bellicose, and also because of their laws, since they are not under kings as are Asians (XXIV, 23–33).

Geographical size has practically nothing to do with cultural attainments. What is the smallest geographical unit that has given us the largest number of great culture centers? Perhaps the Peloponnesus. Just think of Corinth, Elis, Mycenae, Olympia, Pylos, Sicyon, Sparta, *etc.* Professor van den Dungen is right again: artificial political divisions may be imposed even on homogeneous units, and artificial bonds on heterogeneous entities. In ancient times, the history of the Achaean League illustrated these points admirably, especially under Aratus in 228 B.C., and later under the Roman Titus Quinctius Flamininus. Europe's unity and division cannot be studied without considering the Near East and

North Africa. After all, extra-European civilizations were also important, and Europe borrowed much from them. Let me only mention the Pythagorean theorem, one of whose many nicknames is *hecatomb,* namely, a sacrifice of 100 oxen. Why? Because the Pythagoreans considered its proof exceedingly important. Egypt's geometers, however, had discovered this principle long before Pythagoras (530 B.C.). In any event, unity within this entire area seems to have followed a U-shaped curve throughout history, its lowest arc covering mainly medieval and early modern times.

III. THE FIRST UNITED NATIONS AND THE CYNICAL FARMER.

Nowadays, although it is probably too late, we must always speak of international, not only European, unity and cooperation. Such a dialogue must further be based on genuine moral responsibility which, as David Hume (1711–1766) would explain, makes sense only if the world, which is *descriptive,* includes the *proscriptive* (what ought not to be) and the *prescriptive* (what ought to be). But is European, and international, unity gradually intensifying? Perhaps. Despite the countless ups and downs, it seems that, both theoretically and practically, both voluntarily and forcibly, we have moved from international anarchy to relative order and cooperation The first UN-like organization was the Greek *Ampictiony,* which was introduced about 900 B.C.[4] Some of its goals were interstate *eunomia,* or good order, economic cooperation, solution of social problems, formation of international law, *etc.* Later developments include Dante's *De Monarchia* (1310–1312), Francisco Suarez' *Tractatus de Legibus ac Deo Legislatore* (1613), Hugo Grotius' *De Jure Belli et Pacis* (1625), the League of Nations, and the United Nations. Let us hope that this trend will continue more fruitfully. Such cooperation, some authors believe, must include free migration, as if national boundaries did not exist. Joseph Carens, for instance, writes:

> Many poor and oppressed people wish to leave their countries of origin in the third world to come to affluent Western societies... there is little justification for keeping them out... [we must] respect all human beings as free and equally moral persons.[5]

At least three political theories would support this philosophy:
1. Utilitarianism, with its emphasis on "maximizing utility," asserts that, when utility is calculated, everyone counts for one, which implies moral equality.[6] Of course, the problem of defining utility remains;
2. John Rawls stresses social welfare and an activist state;[7]
3. Robert Nozick, a property rights advocate, believes in moral equality and that everyone has the same natural rights, albeit in practice these rights generate material inequality.[8]

Another avenue leading to social justice and cooperation is universal modernization, as there is no excuse for hunger, primitive agricultural techniques, medieval public health, infanticide, clitoridotomy, and the like. Unfortunately, modernization is still a confusing and controversial concept, often identified with Europeanization, Americanization, Westernization, and industrialization. But, first of all, must we speak of the "Western Industrial Revolution" as if English, Dutch, and French history were the same? Then, is it not offensive to expect Japanese, South Korean, and Taiwanese technology to be accompanied by nontraditional family systems? Technology itself does not constitute a panacea, despite Western enthusiasm about it. In Ouagadougou, Burkina Faso, an American industrialist bragged ecstatically, as he showed appropriate slides, that his factory could take a cow and change it into cans of meat. An unimpressed African farmer interrupted: "Now, can your factory change those cans into a cow?"

IV. From Homeric Fate to Elementary Particles.

European unity, on the other hand, should be easier than international unity. Heterogeneity, however, has been an obstacle to such cooperation for thousands of years. According to Hippocrates,

> The people of Europe differ from one another in both stature and shape, because of seasonal changes, which are great and frequent.... For this reason, I believe, the physique of Europeans varies more than that of Asians and their stature differs very much in each city"
> *(Airs, Waters, Places,* XXIII, 2–15).

Legends have also been a major impediment. For, unlike

myths, which employ divinities to explain nature, legends use heroes and heroines to interpret national history. Chauvinism thus becomes a dominant sociopolitical force. Absolute unity, of course, is not desirable, for some degree of fragmentation is creative. But is the fragmentation of the United States and Protestantism an unmixed blessing? Is the unity of the Union Soviet Socialist Republics and Catholicism an evil? Was Nikita Khrushchev entirely wrong when he asserted that the Soviets, not the West, enjoy true freedom — freedom from decision making? How have Americans used their freedom? In 1980, only 52 percent of all eligible citizens voted; in November 1986, only 37 percent. And who are the most apathetic Americans? Young people, many of whom march and howl in the streets in an effort to solve the problems of the world. In 1976, of those aged 18–20, only 38 percent voted. But, as Dr. van den Dungen has suggested, there is some progress. The European Community of the original Six, the Nine in 1973, and the Ten in 1981 has accomplished much. The Council of Ministers, the Commission, the European Parliament, the Court of Justice, and the Court of Auditors would be envied by the ancient Amphictionic Leagues. The community's Economic and Social Committee, and the Consultative Committee, are particularly important. Rising standards of living, increased education among the masses, and the like, will undoubtedly reinforce such cooperation in the future. Once more, however, international unity must be stressed at the same time. After all, there is only one race — the human race. And the things that unite us are more important than those that divide us. Even philosophical systems that appear to differ substantially actually converge in many respects.[9] India's *Upanishads* include philosophical dialogues similar to Plato's (427–347 B.C.). The Jains of Mahavira (619–546 B.C.) and Leucippus (450 B.C.) developed the first atomic theory. Confucius (551–479 B.C.) gave us *Chung Yung (The Doctrine of the Mean),* while Solon (639–559 B.C.), one of the Seven Sages, said, *"Meden agan"* ("Nothing in excess"). Both Buddha (563–483 B.C) and Aristotle (384–322 B.C.) wisely preached the Middle Way. And so forth and so on.

    My final illustration is European science.[10] Unfortunately,

European scientists are divided by a common history as the British and Americans are divided by a common language. Some of the specific obstacles are cultural, linguistic, and regional heterogeneity; economic and political rivalries; the difficulty of transferring between social security systems; lack of equivalence in professional qualifications; the high cost of airfares; *etc.* But cooperation presents advantages. For instance, bringing together former belligerents has been one of the original arguments since the 1950's. Moreover, it is more efficient to pool national resources and skills than to fragment them. Similarly, networking, or linking researchers in existing laboratories, is more economical than creating major new ones. And cooperation in technological research with commercial applications diminishes economic competitiveness among European industries, which explains the rise of such cooperation in the early 1980's. These advantages have recently promoted cooperation among European physicists, who now lead the world in the study of elementary particles. In fact, in some respects, European physics is more advanced than American physics. It is also revealing, that European scientists were able to send a spacecraft to study Halley's Comet while their American counterparts were doing nothing in this area. Unfortunately, European science still means Western European science — as Dr. van den Dungen's political argument would lead us to expect — since there is no cooperation with the nations behind the Iron Curtain. The only exceptions are Yugoslavia's membership in the European Science Foundation and the European Physical Society's inclusion of East Europe.

Finally, one of the most encouraging signs is a development that is not widely known even among scientists, although it involves cooperation between European and other nations. This is a North Atlantic Treaty Organization program which began in 1958, and which supports nonmilitary scientific exchanges. No other similar program has ever included more scientists than NATO's has namely, 250,000 between 1958 and 1987. It seems, then, that human beings pursue noble goals and ideals slowly, gradually, and in stages. Influenced by Herodotus (484–424 B.C.), Gianbattista Vico (1668–1744) speculated about three types of general organization the divine, the heroic, and the human. In a new book,[11] I refer to another kind of triad which are involved in the development of cooperation, democracy, freedom, and the like. Among the Hebrews, for instance, Jehovah was a tribal god, then national, and finally universal. In poetry, Homer's (800 B.C.) *epos* stressed mythology and fate, while Hesiod's (750 B.C.) epic work did the same in *Theogony* but emphasized the beginning of individual emotions and social interaction, which Sappho's (580 B.C.) lyrics cultivated much more extensively and intensively. In politics, the tyrant was absolute, then came Draco (621 B.C.), whose harsh code limited even the tyrant, until Solon introduced democracy. Genghis Khan (1162–1227) butchered and bragged about it, today we butcher and use euphemisms about it, but in the future (I hope!) we will both preach and practice love. In the United States, we used to speak of racial inequality openly and practiced discrimination equally openly, now we advocate equality and practice discrimination, but in the future (I hope!) we will both preach and practice equality. In international relations, we used to be apathetic and uninformed *noncritics,* now we are half-informed *monocritics* who attack only one side of each issue, but in the future (I hope!) we will be informed *amphicritics* who will study both sides and then decide wisely. My dream is the same concerning European and global unity. After all, as Plato says the organisms prefer gradualism, since they are unable to adjust to cataclysmic changes.[12] Count Richard Coudenhove-Kalergi's 1926 dream in Vienna cannot come true overnight.

V. Conclusion: The Birth of Prometlas

In 1838, in his *Prolegomena zur Historiosophie,* A. Cieszkowski was one of the earliest philosophers to speak of *praxis*. Epistemology and critical sociology, however, have not achieved much in this area since then. In fact, throughout history, two types of leaders have been prevalent. One is the Prometheus type, who thinks but does not act. The other is the Atlas type, who acts but does not think. Perhaps the problem of unity will be solved when a new kind of leader appears, the kind that both thinks and acts. Let us call him *Prometlas!*[13]

NOTES

1. Preceding.
2. Panos D. BARDIS, "Heavenly Hera Heralds Heroines" (in press).
3. William OGBURN and Meyer NIMKOFF, *Sociology* (New York: Houghton Mifflin, 1940), 892.
4. Panos D. BARDIS, "Amphictyony: The First United Nations," *The International Journal of Legal Research* 2 (1967): 11–16.
5. "Aliens and Citizens: The Case for Open Borders," *The Review of Politics* 49 (1987): 251.
6. Amartya SEN and Bernard WILLIAMS, eds., *Utilitarianism and Beyond* (Cambridge: Cambridge University Press, 1982); Peter Singer, *Practical Ethics* (Cambridge: Cambridge University Press, 1979).
7. *A Theory of Justice* (Cambridge, Massachusetts: Harvard University Press, 1971), especially 136–142
8. *Anarchy, State, and Utopia* (New York: Basic Books, 1974), 12–23, 89–118.
9. Panos D. BARDIS, "The Family, Education, and Absolute Values," in press.
10. David DICKSON and Colin NORMAN, "Science and Mutual Self-Interest," *Science* 237 (September 4, 1987): 1101–1102; David DICKSON, "Networking," *ibid.:* 1106–1107; Colin Norman, "Unsung Force in Science Exchanges," *ibid.:* 1113; David DICKSON, "Europe Ends at the Iron Curtain," *ibid.:* 1114.
11. Panos D. BARDIS, *South Africa and the World Marxist Movement* (in press)
12. *Statesman,* 170.
13. Panos D. BARDIS, "Power: Entropic and Syntropic," *Alternatives* 9 (1983): 483–488.

COMMENTS ON "THE EVOLUTION OF WESTERN CIVILIZATION AND THE DIVISION OF EUROPE",

Professor Jindřich Zelený

In my view, there are many interesting ideas in the paper "The Evolution of Western Civilization and the Division of Europe" presented by Dr. Peter van den Dungen. I appreciate very much his description of what he calls "a number of interesting paradoxes and ironies" in Europe's history, *i.e.,* his description of interrelations between the processes of disintegration and new forms of integration in Europe, especially in the period which starts with the great discoveries of the late 15th and 16th centuries. As I am no expert in historiography, I can only say that these parts of the paper under discussion seem to me to present very interesting and penetrating ideas, often expressed in a brilliant style. My criticism will only concern some aspects of the author's assessment of the recent period of Europe's history, namely the assessments of the Marxist-Leninist revolutionary movement and of the theoretical nature of Marxism. Luckily enough, even here I can start with acknowledging that I fully agree with Dr. van den Dungen's decisive statements regarding our peril. Indeed, we find ourselves today in Europe and elsewhere in an unprecedented situation. Mankind has discovered a power that enables us to destroy, for the first time, the entire terrestrial biosphere. The threat of war has become global and total in ways in which it has never been before. No doubt, 'omnicide', 'ecocide' — these are the alarming yet accurate descriptions of the potential outcome, henceforth, of any major conflict. Ecological considerations are leading to similar conclusions, and re-inforce the view of a very fragile 'spaceship earth'. And I wholeheartedly agree with his words.

> We can only hope that such a perilous prospect will stimulate the search for greater cooperation and unity so that eventually, in dialectical fashion, nuclear (or even post-nuclear) weapons will make themselves as well as all other weapons of mass destruction obsolete and redundant as a result of the positive processes which they set in motion or accelerated."

While we agree on what the present situation is like and what it requires, we may disagree in answering the question of how the present situation came about. I perfectly understand that it would not be desirable to accentuate differences in viewing the genesis of the present situation if there is a fundamental consensus on where we are now, and what to do about it. The most important thing now is to do what we think is in our common interest. However, a friendly discussion of some differences in explaining the genesis may prove stimulating and useful even for deepening our future cooperation and finding new realistic ways of it. Well, in this spirit I should like to say that I find the stated evaluations of the October Revolution of 1917 and of the socialist revolutions in some East- and Central European countries false. The author believes that the present division of Europe has been imposed from outside and is not the result of any organically grown developments. It seems to me that the author sees no creative cultural initiative in the socialist revolutionary movement. All human values worth fighting for come from Christianity and from the capitalist Western civilization. On the other side of the divided Europe, allegedly only derivations can be found.

I have my own personal experience as far as the development of Czechoslovakia after 1945 is concerned. As one of the young socialists, I participated in the fight against the fascist occupation of our country, in our national and democratic revolution which brought about step by step revolutionary socialist changes and led to Czechoslovakia's unity and cooperation with the Soviet Union and other socialist countries. I know from my own experience that this was a deeply democratic process, an act of self-determination of the great majority of our people, an outcome of an organically grown social development. It was not a *coup d'état* imposed from outside. By the way, even many Western friends of mine with whom I talk about these historical events usually forget that for the Czechoslovak people, after 1945, a Western type *bourgeois* democracy could not be a desirable form of state, because of our own bitter political experience. We lived for twenty years, before the second world war, in a state which was one of the best examples of the *bourgeois* democratic form of government. Our national freedom and state independence were based on the alliance with the Western democracies, first of all with France and Great Britain. When Hitler came, this form of political organisation and these alliances proved unable to ensure our national freedom and even existence. Naturally, after the war, the great majority of our people looked for better ways and alliances to ensure that such a threat to our national existence would not happen any more. Excuse me for being personal. But I think it may help the reader to understand what is not easily understandable from secondhand information only. As to the question of the cultural creativity of Marxism, just one small point. I think that the philosophical, logico-ontological part of Marxism, *i.e.*, materialist dialectics, can properly be conceived of as a kernel of a new historical type of scientific rationality. Compared with the Aristotelian or the Cartesian (or, if you will, Newtonian) type of rationality, materialist dialectics exhibits some new important characteristics which enables it to serve as a methodological basis of a co-evolutive conception of man acting in Nature, and their interrelation. There is no room here to go into detail.[1] I mention this point here only to counter the tenet that there was no need for Marxism in Western civilization.

In conclusion, I fully agree with the author's statement that the exigencies of survival today increasingly impose, even at the height of division and discord, elements of unity and accord. The division of Europe is only *seemingly* intractable. It has been for some time intractable, but it becomes tractable now and in the future because of some important new circumstances. Let us support taking all possible practical steps towards cooperation in our common European home.

NOTES

1. A more detailed discussion of these problems can be found in J. ZELENY: *The Logic of Marx,* (Oxford: Basil Blackwell, 1980) and in IDEM: *Dialektik der Rationalität* (Berlin: Akademie Verlag, 1986), (also Köln: Pahl Rugenstein, 1986).

DISCUSSION ON VAN DEN DUNGEN

José Delgado

What our present world needs from all of us is new ideas. Naturally it would be pretentious for me to tell you what these new ideas are, but as the matters of a possible discussion I would mention technology, biology, the purpose of human life, be it material or mental/spiritual.

Panos Bardis

I think that Dr. Delgado is quite right. Futurology is important, although much of it is voodooism. Now, talking about scientific cooperation in Europe, I would mention only one sphere — Eureka, which is quite important.

Tamás Kozma

I have two questions directed to Dr. van den Dungen. First, you seem in your paper not to consider enough the Eastern Christianity and its influence to the European culture. Second, if we are thinking in Marxist terms or in the history of Marxism, do you think that the spread of Marxism into Latin-America and into some of the Asian countries is a special type of European influence? If Marxism is a part of the European heritage should we define that kind of spread of Marxism, especially into Latin-America, as a special new form of how European tradition, heritage and civilization influence the third world countries? What is your opinion about this?

Nansen Behar

I have two questions to Prof. Peter van den Dungen. First it seems to me that the excellent paper which was presented here would be even more interesting if some notions were defined in it in a more detailed way. I would prefer to say: Euro-American civilization, because if we speak of European civilization as the western civilization, we have to take into consideration some variations between west and east European civilization, which is not very acceptable if we have the notion of civilization in a very large historical content. In this case, the description of the western civilization as effective for the future of Europe will become more clear. Second, what is the role of the Soviet Union in the European scene? Is the Soviet Union part of Europe or not?

Alexander Shtromas

First, I would like to ask Peter van den Dungen to specify maybe what his own view is. I think, of course, that the Soviet Union is a part of Europe, but how we live in that context is a quite different question. Muscovite autocracy died in the 18th century, and Russia entered into a sort of Europeanising stage of its development.

Second, quoting Toynbee interpreting the Russian revolution is a preposterous point of view. Russia was the fastest developing country in the turn of the century. It attracted more immigrants and capital than the United States of America in that time. To Prof. Zeleny, I would also like to direct two questions. First when you say that the great majority of the Czech people was really inclined to change the prewar ways of governing the country, do you refer to the 38.5% of the people who voted for the Communist party in the 1946 election? It, no doubt, was a free election, with no foreign interference. However would you say that no foreign assisted coups have imposed socialism upon Czechoslovakia? Could you make those points clearer? Second, the paper which we have discussed, and the commentaries on it, didn't give us enough implications for the future. What kind of evolution do you refer to? Where is it going to lead us in the next few decades? I would like all three members of the panel to refer to this question in their final remarks.

Discussion on Van Den Dungen

Ljubisav Rakic

I would like first to question Prof. van den Dungen on the consolidation of future development not only of European, but also of worldwide civilization. There will be in the future intense interactions between different civilizations. My second question is addressed to Prof. Bardis and it is related to the future of political structuresof different societies. All existing political structures do not operate, either in totalitarian or less totalitarian or democratic societies, *etc*. We have a loss of interest of the majority of populations, even in the society organized on the classical western type of democracy, for participation in political life. Policy and politics become a profession. For me, this is the beginning of the end of democracy.

Stanislaw Andreski

One cannot really dwell too much upon the past because the present is very different. There is a general bulldozing of ethnic differences throughout the world and especially in Europe. Hippocrates would say that national differences have lost their character of endurance. We must not necessarily imagine that former historical divisions will go on playing such a fundamental role as in the past.

Peter Van den Dungen

I think the topic is very large. There has been indeed a lack of definition. I had to make a choice. To Prof. Shtromas, I must say that Arnold Toynbee is a historian whom I admire and enjoy reading and who has the kind of background requisite for an ambitious analysis, although it is quite possible that he is wrong on some matters of detail. On the two general points raised by Prof. Delgado and Prof. Rakic, I agree that my paper was indeed somewhat oriented towards the past. This, again, I think was a choice.

I also certainly very much agree with Prof. Andreski that things are changing, and changing rapidly. *En passant*, I mentioned one or two of points connected to the one rightly highlighted by Prof Zeleny. I conclude by saying I am very grateful for the comments made. Without exception I accept them. But it was not in my power for one reason or another to incorporate them beforehand in my presentation.

Panos Bardis

These incisive questions are complex. Let me be laconic. I do emphasize four things: first there is increasing unity, and there will certainly be a cooperation in the future; second. I do present some obstacles which generate ups and downs which will continue, but I am optimistic; third, I have spoken from the very beginning about a combination of European and global unity and cooperation which I think must and will take place; and, fourth, helping in this direction. As far as the future of political structures is concerned, let me be laconic again: first we all know the weaknesses of capitalism, communism, socialism and so on; second as Churchill said, democracy is the worst form of government except for the rest of them; third, there is certainly a professionalization of politics and we all know what this means; fourth, I think that as information, knowledge and education increase among the masses, and as technology, transportation and communication become more intense, we will be able to have contacts with all of the peoples of the world. This is going to generate love, admiration for those people, sympathy for their problems, mutual respect for the dignity of man, and so on.

Jindřich Zelený

There have been two questions addressed directly to me. Prof. Shtromas was right in assuming that I am referring to the development after '45 to '48 in my country. The question is not only that of the results of the elections of '46. It is correct that in these elections the Communist party received 41 or 42 per cent, and the Social Democratic Party 10 per cent, which means 51, and this is not a great majority. however, I cannot agree with the view that in '48 there was a coup of the communist party, because everything took place according to the constitution.

I think that the acceptance of the new politics of disarmament and cooperation, as advanced by Gorbachev, is the more likely way of approaching the future cooperation and unity of Europe.

THE GREEK AND CHRISTIAN HERITAGE OF EUROPE: LOOKING BACK WHILE LOOKING FORWARD

David Gruender

In times of trouble, we are often moved to look back at our earlier experiences and those of our common culture to see whether they might shed some light on our present predicament. Human beings have little to go on in a confusing world beyond their own past experiences and whatever they may have preserved from their ancestors, along with the understandings and crystalized values they may have gleaned from this. As we all know, however, human history, while it has its triumphs, is also replete with tragedies and catastrophes, some of which mankind has, inadvertently, fashioned for itself. Much that has passed for understanding we can see later to have been seriously flawed. And only some of the ideals and values seem later to deserve the worth placed on them, while those appropriate to our new problems may have been only dimly sensed.

Nevertheless, the purpose of the "humanities", among which my field of philosophy is normally included, is often described as being to "transmit" this "heritage" of civilization to the young. It is almost always put this way when administrative authorities are asked to justify expenditures in the area, or, while contemplating dubious developments in contemporary civilization, urge us to redouble our efforts. So put, however, the execution of this noble duty holds several traps for the unwary. One is the genuine problem of understanding both our own past experiences and those of our forebears preserved in history. For one thing, human memory is selective, commonly screening out unpleasant aspects of past life, thereby giving us an erroneous understanding of it. Recorded history is subject to this and other biases, of which, perhaps, the most important is that, forced to select from a vast amount of data, the historian must make some judgements of value and importance, and, thus, may leave out parts of the complex picture whose importance does not come to be recognized until later when, perhaps, the data is no longer available. Worst of all, of course, the facts may never have been recorded, or the historical accounts may have been lost by a careless posterity.

Another trap we may fall victim to is that contained in the ambiguities of the advice to humanists to preserve the heritage of civilization. A heritage is something worth passing on. Knowledge has this worth, but its counterfeits — ignorance, dogma, and misunderstandings — do not. Similarly, mankind has, from time to time, aspired to noble objectives, and striven against great odds towards their achievement. And sometimes, as we all know, it has pursued goals that were petty, mean, selfish, and narrow, and, plastering over all this with rhetoric, has striven mightily, and often successfully, to achieve these also! Our heritage includes them all indiscriminately, and there is no easy way to tell one from the other.

On top of these difficulties, as though they were not enough, is another of equal seriousness: the world, as Plato lamented, and Galileo rejoiced, is always changing. The circumstances we find ourselves in are often new ones, bearing no obvious analogies to those of the past. If we are to seek to rearrange our lives to meet the challenges they offer, looking back at our heritage — even if we surmounted the difficulties in understanding it I have just described — would be likely to offer little detailed knowledge to assist us. But the world of nature in which we find ourselves is not the only thing that changes. Human civilizations are dynamic, not static things, and the restlessness of human genius is continually creating new patterns of human expression, and exploiting for the first time human possibilities only implicit in earlier forms, or never before imagined. The consequences of these new patterns may, occasionally, be anticipated, but they are commonly dimly perceived at best, and often are left to later generations to cope with. For all of these reasons, I am conscious that our Greek, Roman, Judeo-Christian, and, for that matter, Islamic heritage, for they are all woven together, while it can provide us with material that would be invaluable as we face the choices that will affect the future of the human race, must be examined with all the care and honesty we can summon, making our evaluations as explicitly as possible, so that they can be weighed and appraised by others. It is in this spirit that, with a sense of deep humility, I offer the following appreciation and evaluation of that heritage for your consideration in the present context, fully aware that a science of civilization, summoned by Comte, does not yet exist, (although the social sciences have made a beginning), and that, in its absence, care for the future of civilization does not permit us to wait passively. First we must recognize the historic fact that, whatever we may think of it, ours is a heritage shared by Eastern and Western Europe, regardless of other differences that have arisen. The existence of that common heritage, therefore, constitutes one of the resources we have in seeking to move beyond the present differences. For lasting human agreements are best founded on shared perceptions, understandings, and values. At the same time, our civilizations have diverged, emphasizing different elements of the old cultural synthesis, as well as creating new elements leading in different directions.

Let us begin by looking at those Greek and Judeo-Christian elements which may yet yield positive results, if only we can recognize their value. We must do so together with their contraries and contradictories, however, for we do not have the luxury of assuming that cultures are consistent through time. Indeed, they are often far less consistent than individual people, since they embody the views of many, and human beings at large do not hold consistency at high value. It is impossible to reflect on the attributes of this culture without noticing the importance it places on rationality. Whether we think of Greek philosophers and scientists; the social institutions of Greek and Roman civil government; Hebrew, Christian, and Islamic scholars seeking better understandings of the meaning of their sacred books and doctrines, or trying to persuade the multitudes — a common element of rationality stands out. It shows itself in a recognition of a responsibility to give reasons for the acceptance of the views that are offered, and a corresponding duty to consider the reasons of others. Where social decisions and actions are required, another aspect of rationality shows itself: the recognition that the actions taken will affect the common weal and need to be justified in those terms, and that those who act in the name of this common good are ultimately responsible for the outcomes of their actions. Knowledge of the nature of the world in which one is to act is taken as a good thing, and where methods for acquiring more such knowledge become known, their use is taught. Under the influence of this ideal, we have seen periods of remarkable growth of human knowledge of the universe man inhabits, as well as a modicum of understanding of human phenomena. One of these began with the rejection by ancient Greek philosophers of mythic explanations of both the natural and social worlds. The result of their persistent questioning and rational criticism of plausible answers led to Plato's vision that humankind could understand the natural world in which it lived, and organize its social life to provide the greatest benefits for all. Aristotle deepened this vision by greatly enlarging the base of knowledge, from biology to physics, astronomy, and politics, and by hammering out the elementary principles of logic in accordance with which standards of rationality in knowledge and action could themselves be recognized, understood, and applied to life at large. An important part of this work was Aristotle's careful analysis of the responsibility each of us has, as persons, for our own actions, as well as the explicit recognition that the function of the state is to benefit all of its citizens by enabling them to work together in a society in which their just goals and aspirations may be balanced against one another for optimal individual and mutual benefit and happiness. This can only be achieved, he asserts, if governmental forms provide some voice and participation for all classes of citizens, despite his distaste for that form he called 'democracy'. After Aristotle, the growth of knowledge of nature accelerated, with Euclid synthesizing the knowledge of geometry into the first surviving explicit axiom system, in which those things to be taken for granted were stated first, and then each item of knowledge — a theorem — was fit into a place in the scheme such that it could either be proven from these alone, or with the additional help of others already proven, thereby serving as the first example of the kind of logically organized body of knowledge Aristotle had envisioned. Euclid's scheme stands to this day as the very ideal of what knowledge can be.

The development of mathematics and mechanics went hand in hand, as algebra, conic sections, the analysis of simple and complex machines all began to be worked out, with Archimedes, building on the achievments of Eudoxus, even laying the foundations of the calculus, while using advanced technology to help hold off the Roman siege of Syracuse for ten years. Ptolemy worked out a prodigious theory of astronomy, synthesizing all existing knowledge of the stars and planets, and Hero discovered the law of virtual work while studying the performance of complex machines, inventing a steam engine along the way. This tremendous explosion of knowledge of nature all occurred within a period of about eight hundred years. Parallel to this astonishing development, the Greek city-states, beginning as monarchies, evolved into sophisticated political entities using a wide variety of social, political, and economic mechanisms as they moved from an agrarian life to that of manufacture and trading, establishing colonies of Greeks sent out from home to found new cities throughout the Mediterranean world. This led, naturally, to an unusually broad cosmopolitan outlook, as well as to serious attempts to understand why some social systems seemed to work better than others. Plato's *Republic* and Aristotle's *Politics,* which have already been mentioned, are examples of such studies, but it is important also to recognize the wide practical reasoning and actual experimentation with various forms that characterized the vigorous political life of the Greek city-states, from the dual kingship of Sparta to the direct democracy of Athens. Of course, we would be neglecting much of great value if we looked at only these two dimensions of Greek civilization. In the same period they produced poetry and drama that expressed and reflected on the values of their lived experiences and the meaning of these for individual human beings: sometimes with laughter, sometimes with tears, and sometimes with rejoicing. The portion of these works that has survived still speaks to us across the ages with unabated and moving eloquence. What remains of their architecture and sculpture has a similar effect on us, and although much of the ceramics proved durable, we can only imagine the magnitude of their achievements in music and painting. But the ancient Greeks were a proud people in which the code of the warrior stood highest. They looked down on others, calling them barbarians, for, not knowing the beauties of Greek, barbarians could only say "bar bar bar" to each other. And while Greek eagerness to fight, and their courage and brilliance in battle, whether on land or sea, accounts for the survival of their culture in a hostile world, their desire to dominate one another, and the ruthlessness with which they finally pursued this goal, resulted in the destruction of Greek civilization as such, which soon collapsed after the brief folly of Alexander's attempt to conquer the "world", and Hellenistic culture found itself gradually swept into that of Rome. The growth and development of knowledge did not long survive the civilization which had, however grudgingly, sustained and nourished it. This love of domination, which begins as a means of self-defense but quickly becomes appreciated for its own sake, converting a defensible means to an indefensible end, became another striking feature of our civilization. Remnants of Greek culture were, however, preserved in the Roman civilization which swallowed it up. And if the Athenians showed a penchant for domination of others late in their independent life, Romans built an empire on it. This empire started from the independent city-state of Rome, which, in a series of developments not wholly unlike those of the Greek cities, had devised representative and republican forms of government, as well as a tradition of respect for the laws they produced. While Rome did not contribute much to expand human knowledge of nature, it tolerated the Greek institutions of learning at first. It had already developed social, political, and economic systems of its own, but Cicero, Seneca, Marcus Aurelius, and others studied Greek theories of these matters, to which they added new elements, couched in terms of Roman experiences. Among those most important for our purposes was the extension of Greek and Roman cosmopolitanism to a sympathy for the entire human race, as embodied, for example, in Terence's famous words, repeated by Cicero: *"Homo sum: humani nil a me alienum puto"*—"I am a man: I regard nothing human as alien to me". With this ideal there are, no longer, any barbarians: only fellow human beings. And, as a kind of corollary to that recognition of our common humanity, we must mark the introduction of the Stoic concept of "natural law": that "above the laws of nations stands the law of all mankind" — a law to serve as an ideal for nations, and which regards each human being, however humble, as bearing the dignity of his Creator, and thereby deserving at least those rights that our common creation entails.

Let me emphasize that what I am talking about here is the discovery of knowledge and the exploration of ideals and values. I am very far indeed from asserting that Greek society was, through and through, permeated with a love for the seeking of new knowledge, or a total abhorrence of rulers not responsible to their subjects. The decision made by an Athenian jury to execute Socrates should sufficiently remind us of the contrary, nor was he alone among philosophers in arousing Greek ire. Similarly, knowledge of the evils of tyranny in Athens and other Greek cities arose from their intimate acquaintance with it, as well as their occasional inability to provide stability for its alternatives. In Rome, in this connection, we should remind ourselves of Cicero's assassination. But what is important is that they had a Socrates and a Cicero to kill, and that, thousands of years later, ideals of these courageous men can still inspire us, while the buildings of their ancient cities lie in ruins, and the "grandeur that was Greece and the glory that was Rome" are but schoolbook memories. In fact their ideals have been transmitted to contemporary European civilization, where they have been, perhaps, only a little better received and assimilated than in ancient times. But we do have them, and to them we have added important elements from our own experiences, and European civilization is vigorously alive. While it faces serious problems, and even possible disasters, some of its own making, it has far more knowledge than its ancient predecessors to help it understand the future consequences of its actions, and it has means of communication and international institutions that could be harnessed to the search for effective solutions. But, of that more later. Now we must return to our historical task. This brief look at Roman civilization, however, brings us to the next topic: Christianity, for their history is intermingled. Christianity began as an outgrowth of the ancient Hebrew religion, whose adherents occupied a small area of what had, by then, become the vast Roman Empire. Early Christians moved throughout that empire and sought converts from other sects, preaching the importance of personal humility, selfless love of others, efforts for the common good as opposed to mere personal self-service, and care for each human soul. It was an other-worldly religion, emphasizing the mystery of life in the world, but promising its members — and those alone — a chance at a happy life after death. I hope I may be forgiven for speaking detachedly or profanely of matters that are sacred to some, but our task requires it. This sect was often repressed in the Roman Empire as threatening to the official religion, but it persisted through centuries of persecution. In the meantime, the Empire experienced increasing pressure on its boundaries by new peoples arriving in Europe from Asia. Its response to this pressure was complex, but included an increasing militarization of the mechanisms and offices of government, along with a reduction in the role of the Senate and the other elements of traditional Roman civil government, which, while less important after Julius Caesar's ending of the Republic, had, in spite of that, remained part of the very warp and woof of Roman society. Another adjustment adopted was to welcome some of the newcomers into the Roman armies. They needed only to learn the language, the discipline, and Roman tactics, and were happy to fight for the glories of civilization and a regular pay day. That they were not asked to learn anything else about Roman life was, perhaps, not their fault. And, since winning battles was something done with armies, and better done with happy armies, it soon became apparent that the government needed to be more responsive to the views of its soldiers than to its citizens. In rather a short time, few of these soldiers were of original Roman stock; likewise for their commanders, who, after all, were chosen for their ability to win battles. In this fashion, the Empire both abandoned its civil traditions, and acquired emperors who were born and raised far from Rome. One of these was Constantine, a native of the land on which we meet today, who, when he retired from fighting, decided to settle down in a more defensible location in a wealthier part of the Empire, so abandoned Rome for the old town of Byzantium, in the East, which he rebuilt into Constantinople. He also adopted Christianity as the new state religion. But, in its wisdom, Christianity had prepared for this. As long as, following Julius Caesar, the emperor was proclaimed as divine, Christian theology was forced to be hostile to the Empire, for it worshipped another God. However, after Diocletian, with his multiple little caesars and little augustus's, that view was less plausible. Hence the Emperor Constantine and the Bishop of Rome were perfectly content to adopt the suggestion of Clement of Alexandria, among others, that the emperor, although not himself divine, ruled by the will of God, and on His behalf. This gave the emperor the blessing of the Church to rule as he saw fit, and gave the Church the authority to advise the emperor as to God's will. After this, the old relic of republican days that the Senate consent to the appointment of the emperor, became pointless. The Senate continued for a while as an organ of the municipal government of Rome. The emperor became an absolute monarch who ruled by divine right; the cycle from representative government to tyranny, from rational self-rule to unbridled despotism was complete.

But it is too soon to stop and moralize. There are other events to recount before we can be ready to draw conclusions. The Church had, by and large, adopted the basic plan of Roman civil government for its own organization. That made the bishop of Rome its "first priest", for all practical purposes, for Christians thought of themselves as citizens of the Empire, and, hence, of the city of Rome itself as the capital. Constantine and subsequent emperors recognized this position of the bishop of Rome. Likewise the bishops of Rome recognized the authority of the emperors, and, after their election, politely notified them of this fact and awaited their confirmation. This arrangement was bound to produce tension, however, for Rome was no longer the capital. When, after Constantine, co-emperors for the West were appointed, they preferred to fortify themselves in Milan or the marshes of Ravenna, rather than the easily-taken city of Rome on the plains of Latium. So the bishops of Rome often found themselves the only figures of authority in the city. In addition to that, they early identified their primacy with the claim that the bishop of Rome had received his position from Peter, the acknowledged leader of the apostles, and, hence that their position of unchallenged leadership stemmed from this apostolic succession; the bishop of Rome occupied the "see" of the first of the apostles. The patriarchs of Constantinople could never claim that sort of precedence, as the bishops of Rome had doubtless foreseen; serving as the religious leader of the new capital just could not put one first. This tension was only increased when, in such important affairs as the protocol at councils of the Church, successive bishops of Rome listed the bishops of such older centers of Christianity as Alexandria and Antioch ahead of their colleague in Constantinople. Other forces moved to further separate the paths of East and West. In order to convert the Germanic peoples that surrounded it, the Western Church had to adapt to their customs; the Eastern Church, in the well-fortified capital of a prosperous empire, could follow its own bent. The Eastern kept to its Greek language; the West to its Latin. When subject to invasion, the bishop of Rome could seldom count on much help from the emperor in Ravenna, and not at all from the one in Constantinople. At the same time, to join the co-emperor in the relative safety of Ravenna would have been to forfeit the apostolic argument for the primacy of the see of St Peter. This led the holders of the office to develop considerable political agility and imagination. When one of these lent his moral support to a king of the Franks against his rival, it was only natural for him, later, to ask for the latter's help when Rome was faced with a Lombard invasion. That help was cheerfully granted, and when the Lombards lost the war, the victor donated what had become the Duchy of Rome to St Peter, suddenly making the occupant of his throne a temporal as well as a spiritual leader.

    The next logical step was taken when, having seen the results of conferring a papal blessing on one of a pair of rival kings, it was recognized that, as the emperor himself is chosen by God to rule in his Name on Earth, the best way to celebrate this is for the emperor-elect to come to Rome to be crowned by its bishop, the pope. Charlemagne in fact did this, coming to Rome in the year 800 to be crowned by Pope Leo III, who had refused to recognize the Empress Irene. But Charlemagne had no wish to stay in Rome, and, after the ceremony, promptly returned to Arles to rule what was then called the "Holy Roman Empire" from there, leaving the doughty bishop of Rome unchallenged in his own duchy. Thus, the Western Church embarked on its long odyssey as a major player on the political map of Western Europe. The Eastern Church, in contrast, devoted itself to religious works, and to the task of preserving and protecting the Greek literature that had come into its hands after several destructive periods. Even some time before this when disagreements arose between the pope and the Eastern emperor, who was always acknowledged as his superior, Constantinople did not always get its way. Differences were settled by envoys, occasionally, but sometimes they were not settled at all. In the year 692, for example, the Emperor Justinian II convened a council which condemned a number of Western religious practices, while ordaining Eastern ones in their place. When Pope Sergius II refused to sign the decree, the Emperor sent a symbolic troop of soldiers to Rome to bring the recalcitrant pope to Constantinople to face imperial justice, but the West was infuriated. The Co-Emperor in Ravenna bestirred himself, the militia of Rome was called out, and the Emperor's representative did well to escape with his life. In the next century, however, Pope Constantine travelled to Constantinople himself and succeeded in reaching a mutual agreement on another matter. But after Charlemagne, the pope was too well-situated to be practically subject to the East, and had already ceased asking the emperor to confirm his appointment to office. Indeed, things had gone so far that a couple of centuries later, in 1053, Pope Leo IX issued a bull excommunicating Oecumenical Patriarch Cerularius. As the Emperor would not receive the papal legates bearing such a message, they left it fastened to the altar at Hagia Sophia. The

Emperor continued to support the Patriarch, and the entire Eastern Church was strengthened in its alienation from Rome. Unfortunately, the enmity between the two branches of the Church did not decrease. Although occasional councils were held to seek to reconcile their differences, these continued to grow, and as their physical separation and conditions of life were markedly different, they lacked the common experience that might have been able to bridge their differences. Each came to regard itself as the one, true, "orthodox" inheritor and protector of the original Christian tradition, while it viewed the other as having imported foreign and unChristian elements, and to have succumbed to a perversion of the true faith. Thus Eastern Christians came to see Rome as a center of evil and a fit subject of hatred; Westerners saw Eastern unhappiness with the primacy of Rome and an insistence on preserving their own religious traditions as equally wicked.

In spite of these grave difficulties, the two halves of the old Empire cooperated to some extent in the crusades to free the Holy Land from the "infidel". Both faced serious pressures from well-organized and able opponents: Islam and the Turks, who, unlike the peoples who earlier invaded Europe from the north and east, were not likely subjects for conversion to Christianity. But, in spite of that pressure, these efforts at religious unity all fell short. On the very last attempt, with the help of Nicholas of Cusa, an agreement was actually reached between the two parties, and signed in 1439 by Pope Eugenius IV and the Emperor John VIII Paleologus, who had personally accompanied his religious leaders to the Council of Ferrara and Florence. However, when the Eastern leaders returned to Constantinople, the outrage of the Eastern population forced them to withdraw from the agreement. In the meantime, the metropolitan of Russia decided that henceforth his land would recognize no higher religious authorities than its own, who could be counted on to avoid the evils of the West. The Eastern Empire had been hoping for material help from the West against the threatened Turkish invasion. And Nicholas had been hoping to forge a similar agreement between the Western Church and Islam! But neither worked out. Islam was not interested, and Constantinople was taken by the Turks in 1453, leaving the

Russians as the last custodian of Eastern Christianity outside the new Turkish Empire. However you look at it, this is a long legacy of mistrust and mutual disappointment to leave to posterity. As it turned out, however, posterity did receive a vital side benefit from this failed attempt at harmony between the Eastern and Western churches, for the East had brought as a gift to the West at the start of their negotiations a large collection of manuscripts of major works of philosophy, science, and literature preserved from the ancient period in the original Greek. The translation, study, and wide dissemination of this material provided a large part of the fuel for the intellectual and artistic explosion called the Renaissance of Western Europe, from which the Europe of today was born.

There is one more part of the story we need to remind ourselves about before reflecting more fully. Being of Greek origin, all the major centers of higher learning were in the Eastern Empire. When, at the urging of the now-triumphant Christian Church, they were closed as a threat to piety by the Edict of Justinian, in the year 529, we see the beginning of another major transformation in European civilization. The schools did not actually close at once, and while there was a temporary resurgence of creative vitality as Justinian attempted to strengthen the Empire militarily, and began a major program of building in Constantinople, the schools did eventually close, and the long term result was a change in attitude toward the enterprise of seeking, preserving, and passing on knowledge. Scholars, having no longer a place to teach and study, were dispersed. Students, having no longer a place to learn, turned their attention to other pursuits. And the written record of what had so far been learned, having no social institution responsible for preserving it, vanished into darkness, leaving us with only those fragments that have accidentally survived. How the great library at Alexandria was lost is the subject of various tales, but the significant fact is that civilization had lost the means even to chronicle its own demise. The situation in the West was worse. Without institutions dedicated to learning, Western Europe, with the deaths of Boethius and Cassiodorus, also in the sixth century, lost all means of replacing scholars familiar with the full body of extant knowledge. From that time on, for example, those who wished to learn about geometry had to content themselves with handbooks which explained the Pythagorean theorem, along with others, but did not undertake to prove it. So much for the very model of what had counted for knowledge in antiquity. That the torch thus dropped was picked up, in part, by Islam, which, in succeeding centuries, came to gather Greek writings, translate them into Arabic, and then build a renaissance of philosophy, science, and civilization of their own — is another story that cannot be told here. We must be content with the skeletal knowledge that this material began to be known to the West through its contact with Islam, at first in a limited way through the crusades, for, after all, they were the despised "infidel", and, later, through the Christian conquest of the Iberian peninsula, which had become a jewel of Islamic high civilization, complete with universities, libraries, and scholars. Thus we have the irony that the Western lands of the old Roman Empire were able to recover from a rival civilization a part of the treasury of knowledge they had themselves lost hundreds of years before. That part was another source which helped to fuel the European Renaissance. But lost it was, both in the East and the West, and that loss is doubly tragic because it was a loss not only of a great portion of the contents of the body of knowledge so painfully accumulated over time, but, more importantly, it was an abandonment of the recognition of the human value of knowledge, in the sense in which this was conceived as the broad exercise of human intelligence in the search for better understanding both of nature and ourselves, so that we may, following the ideals of Plato and Aristotle, use the knowledge to seek to arrange our human lives for the best. This loss was the result of multiple causes, but we would be less than honest if we failed to notice that religious doctrines contained the elements of an opposing view which rejected these ideals. On this contrary view, which became widely influential for a while, the Earth was seen as but our temporary abode, and an interest in its details was not proper for our eternal souls, which ought to be focused on knowledge of God and what He wanted of us. Further, this Earth was created by God; to poke into its cracks and crevices with curiosity was vain, lacking in respect for His handiwork, and, thereby, impious. God, in his wisdom, has already provided us with whatever knowledge we need — in the Holy Bible. And Augustine, in spite of his own learning, tells us that is all a good Christian needs to know.

While this profound hostility to free inquiry never completely triumphed, it won many battles in its day, and has not yet taken its leave of contemporary civilization, although since Augustine's time there has been an increase both in the number of those claiming supreme authority, as well as in the number of canonical texts. Whatever one may think about that, the days of its victories mark the nadir of the ideal of rational inquiry. To the extent of its adoption of this view, we see European civilization turning its face against knowledge as a goal to be freely pursued — except insofar as the authorities allowed it — and against the testing of claims to knowledge by open, rational processes — in favor of their being settled by authority. This is a path to ignorance. If, as we must, we note what became the strong influence of Augustine's view that even Christians are not — without God's grace — capable of good actions, we see a parallel movement to abandon rationality in action as well. On the classical view, rationality in inquiry and rationality in action were closely linked. Just as mankind was thought capable both of achieving significant knowledge of nature and of himself by his own efforts, so it was held that through his own actions he could use this knowledge to plan and carry out a social life that would aim at optimal benefits to all members of the community, with those members having a say in the conduct of that life. A human community was, thus, conceived as the product of the actions of its earlier members, along with the reciprocal actions and interactions of its present citizens, all of whom could be taken to be responsible for those actions they chose. But when one brings together the doctrines that human beings are capable of but little knowledge, and that rests on authorities taken to be sacred, that they are incapable, by their own efforts, of actions aimed at an individual or common good; and that their rulers hold sway over these their subjects by sacred authority to whom alone a ruler is answerable, then, to all intents and purposes, rationality as an ideal of civilization has been abandoned. And as Christian leaders began organizing for the long battle of establishing the Church as the authoritative interpreter of the meaning of its canonical Scriptures, as well as the arbiter of its traditions and ceremonies, they found many difficulties. We have already mentioned disagreements between the Eastern and Western branches of the Church. In fact, many groups defended views and customs at some variance with those of Rome and Constantinople, and these arose from time to time since the earliest days of Christianity. Each group in these often long, bitter, and bloody battles between Christians, regarded itself as the right or "orthodox" view, and the other as wrong or "heretical". The way we use these labels today, of course, reflects the views of the winners of these battles, for that was one of the benefits of winning. In addition to disagreements between Christians, however, the Church also faced a large population that did not share its faith at all. These "pagans" (and it is well to remember that the word was a term of contempt) were an opportunity and challenge for conversion to the "true" faith — notice the implication that all others were false! This challenge became even more important after Christianity became the state religion, which led to further clashes as the Church began to demonstrate the same zeal for persecuting those of other faiths it had learned to expect from Roman governments when it was the victim.

Notable among the losers of these small wars, however, were the old Christian ideals that each human soul was a precious gift of creation, and that the highest ideals by which men could live on this Earth were those of forgiveness and unselfish love of all mankind. They were replaced with a far more parochial ideal: namely, that one owed significant duties only to one's coreligionists, and that those who insisted upon rejecting God's truth deserved whatever evil may befall them. This view, one must recognize, amounts to a dehumanization of one's opponents, the rejection of the Stoic ideal of our common humanity, and an excuse for any savagery, for its advocates often saw themselves, arrogantly, as the very agents of their avenging God. Hence the ideals of rationality in knowledge and action, representative government, and respect for all — largely disappeared from the successors to Greek civilization. The story of the slow and difficult process of their recovery, and the variety of ways in which later European civilizations, the inheritors of the traditions of the Eastern and Western Empires, have, haltingly, sought to revive and apply them to the very changed situations they found themselves in, belongs to other occasions. But it is fair to say, I think, that this process has been uneven, is far from complete, and, given our new recognition that we must all live with one another on this small and troubled planet, requires bold and imaginative extensions of ancient ideals. As we stand here today on the land bridge between the old Eastern and Western Empires and reflect on the situation facing European civilization now, it is hard to avoid the conclusion that we are getting ready to enter a new era. The restless turmoil of the movement of whole peoples about the continent that was the most noticeable demographic feature of Europe from ancient times to the present has ended. The last wars fought for "living space" reached beyond this continent to embroil the whole planet: World Wars I and II. They were so costly in human life, and so destructive to all parties and all human ideals, that efforts have been made to avoid both another war in Europe and what would be its inevitable corollary: another world war. Of course, our powers of killing one another are now so advanced that another world war would hold the promise of making any effort to chronicle its misery pointless: it does not seem likely there could be anyone left to read it. While we have succeeded, now, for more than forty years in preventing such a disaster, it has been by means that a visitor from another planet would find both astonishing and chancy. But although we have avoided a world war so far, we have had serious disputes in Europe which were resolved only by the application of extra-national armed force, and extended wars in the Middle East, Africa, and Asia, some of which are being bitterly fought at this moment. And, short of this, in many places we have seen national leaders posturing with their international adversaries like schoolboys on a playground, uttering threats and announcing their readiness for dire actions. Nor is this, by any means, the full catalog of our problems.

As we look back on the legacy of ancient Greece and Rome and the Judeo-Christian tradition, we can see unhappy precedents for all of this. One is bigotry and its hatred of other groups, whether designated by religious, national, class, or other differences, often extending to denial of their humanity. Another is zealotry, the conviction that since one's cause is right, it justifies whatever harm one may render the rest of humanity. It is also taken to justify denying a voice to a people over the manner of their government, on the grounds that, like Plato's guardians, only a small number in possession of the truth would know what is good for them, and their subjects would do better not to ask. Closely connected is the love of domination, often justified in terms of zealotry, as well as what is sometimes put as a need to protect the interests of one's country, often through a continuation of old geopolitical schemes that would be rendered unnecessary if other bases could be found for nations to deal with one another. It is especially dangerous because it feeds the egos of successful political leaders who practice it, often causing serious misjudgments. Even more important is the great value our ancient predecessors placed on war, and its relationship to the highest human virtues: courage, intelligence, tenacity, and the willingness to sacrifice oneself for the greater good. With the exception of portions of the Old Testament and the laments of the victims of war, I am not aware of any consideration of the possibility that there might be better ways of solving problems between nations until the work of Spinoza in the seventeenth century and Kant in the eighteenth. While we have taken the first stumbling steps to develop such better ways, our mores and our cultural "heritage" whisper to us that such ways must be, at their base, dishonorable.

Yet other parts of our heritage give us hope that this dismal outlook may be overcome, and by our own efforts. We have, since ancient times, recovered our interest in the search for knowledge of the universe around us and even, to some extent, of ourselves, and have made progress that would astonish our intellectual progenitors, in spite of the limitations we have, on some occasions, inflicted on ourselves. As a result of that knowledge, we can now understand the fragile balance of life on this planet, as well as that our common human welfare depends on how our future actions affect this balance. A measure of respect for rationality in thought and in action has returned, as well as a flickering recognition of our common humanity. We have made some grand statements about what this means in the *Universal Declaration of Human Rights,* but nations are far from agreement on how to apply these in practice, and there are not a few places on the globe where they are little recognized. But we have made a start, and while history teaches that civilizations can perish, it teaches too that the appeal of ideals can reach across boundaries and generations. Through the international organizations we have formed to enable governments to deal with the problems of conflicts between nations, as well as by separate agreements between nations, we have sometimes taken rational, if halting, steps to find solutions elsewhere than on the fields of Mars. In fact, the latter is now only a planet, not a god, and its exploration has been the object of ingenious international cooperation. Bigotry, while common, is no longer popular, and through widespread communications media, where they are freely allowed, public opinion on world issues forms from time to time and expresses itself, serving as an audience for world leaders to address themselves to beyond their national boundaries. That opinion is not friendly to zealotry, which seeks to respond by imposing controls on expression. We have yet to produce a significant number of national political leaders with the ability to envision the possible roles of their lands working with those of others with an interest in applying human knowledge, talents, skills, and ideals towards the solution of the world's problems; and international leadership is still in its infancy. Without this leadership, it is hard for the rest of us to work toward making these possibilities real. Yet our international achievements have not been negligible. Perhaps future historians can record that removing the scourge of smallpox forever from the face of the Earth was only the first step mankind took in choosing from among his ancient ideals those that would enable his posterity to work towards mutual human betterment, while learning to consign to the dead past those that lead only to destruction.

THE HERITAGE AND VALUES OF GREEK CULTURAL MODELS IN EUROPE

E. Moutsopoulis

Without overlooking what divides us, we should, above all, consider what may serve to unite us. Professor Gruender's text, "The Greek and Christian Heritage of Europe: Looking Back while Looking Forward", appears to derive from an effort to grasp and evaluate the profound meaning of the long process of historical development of our old continent, by establishing a dialectical relation between the intentionality of the European cultural consciousness, directed towards its own future, and the nostalgia of the glamour of its past. "History", Polybius claimed, "is the prophet of future events". By sustaining this, he was historiologically illustrating the Stoic conception of circular time, and announcing Vico's theory of recurrency and Nietzsche's vision of eternal return. Professor Gruender evidently understands the Polybian scheme as a manifestation of a direct connection of portions of time already experienced and to be experienced by human historical consciousness, a connection whose nature is related both to the notions of causality and finality. In other words, in order to better foresee and prepare the future, the human historical consciousness has to be simultaneously directed towards the past, thus creating the axiological links that unite these two portions of historicity, actualized at the level of the deeply experienced present.

Professor Gruender's attitude is deliberately almost exclusively, and strictly, historical. It is based not on assumptions, but on recorded and universally accepted facts. It, therefore, presents a highly strong profile of the succession of historical events and of their mutual causal links. The author starts with the most prominent and decisive event of antiquity, the rise of Greek civilization, which has imposed its seal upon the whole subsequent life of Europe, be it scientific, technological, or moral. I would just like to suggest that he present a slightly more detailed account of the growth of Greek civilization by mentioning what it seems to owe to the preHellenic and surrounding Eastern civilizations. This, I admit, would be only a complementary, though important view, necessary to an accurate history of events. In any case, the essential is there: the Greek civilization and culture mainly stems from the passage of consciousness from myth to reason, an attitude comparable, at the biological level, to the passage of man to the upright attitude, which liberated his movements, developed his brain, and increased his inventivity and creativity. Similarly, the dramatic liberation of man's mind (temporally reduced to the minimum of some decades) is an unrepeated, crucial moment in man's history.

Commenting on the Greek contribution to philosophical thought. Husserl stressed that, apparently, Greek philosophy is just one of the various systems of thought that have prevailed at various times and places; Mesopotamian, Hebrew, Chinese, and Indian thought seem to be as important expressions of common philosophical problems as Greek thought. However, Husserl estimates, compared to the former, Greek philosophy emerges from a completely new conception of the general problematic organized at all latitudes by human evaluation of the human consciousness concerning the explanation of cosmic reality and the integration of man into it. This uniqueness is due to the absolutely rational foundation of Greek thought. The same problems may relate to religious and biological concerns. But it is the first time they were understood in a totally scientific way within the Greek world. Professor Gruender makes this point very clear in his paper. Likewise, he insists upon some corollary effects of this mentality, entirely free from any kind of irrational factors, at the scientific, technological, moral, social, and political level. In effect, the notions of the "true', the 'efficient', the 'good', the 'equal', and the 'temperate', all of them related to the notion of 'measure', have never attained a higher degree of adequate expression. In this respect, one should never forget that even the idea of 'infinity' in the lists of the Pythagoreans, is conceived of as a negative idea, and that one has to wait until Plotinus to assist its conversion into a positive idea. Hence arose the conception of the world as cosmos, as harmony, as musical beauty dominated by numerical ratios — a conception which still prevails. Beauty, elegance, and perfection are subsequently applied as ideals to human conduct, and to that of politically organized societies. Even more than the Platonic ideal of the harmony of life, as expressed in the *Protagoras,* the Aristotelian ideal of the mean manifests the Stagirite's conviction of the tempered opposed tendencies by avoiding any predilection for the extremes — a lesson which is still respected in ethics under the form of an appeal to moderation.

Rigorous, rational thought applied to mathematics led not only to abstract scientific models constructed in incredibly subtle forms, but also to revolutionary theories concerning the universe, such as that of Aristarchus of Samos, subsequently marginalized through the system of Ptolemy until revived by Copernicus. Technology, that is, the conscious pursuing of the efficiency of the means, is rationally founded and developed as well. It is true that the constitution of a Christian religious dogma impeded for centuries further evolution of science. Nevertheless, during the Middle Ages, rational development of technology functioned as the basis of further theoretical scientific research which led to the growth of experimental sciences. This would never have been possible without the constant reference of medieval and early modern science to the Greek philosophical and scientific heritage. Rome, the ferocious conqueror of Greece, was conquered in its turn by it, according to Horace's formula. The author, even more strikingly, renders this idea by asserting that "Hellenistic culture found itself gradually swept into that of Rome". The long developments of the cultural role of the Byzantine empire in its relations with the West confirm the importance of this statement, and extend its validity to medieval and modern times. Had the religious oppositions not taken the form of a struggle for domination on behalf of either side, the cultural unity of Europe would have been deeper and stronger than it actually is. Greece has always been the source of knowledge and especially of philosophical thought, which it conveyed toward the West, either directly through Rome, or indirectly through the peripheral road of Syria and North Africa. There is a remarkable continuity of this process up to the middle of the Fourteenth Century. At this precise time one may notice an abrupt discontinuity, and a reversal of the flux of the long process of the transfer of philosophical knowledge, preceding a similar reversal in other fields. At that time, which may be considered as crucial, the first influence of the West towards Greece is recorded, namely by the translation of Thomas Aquinas's *Summa Theologicae* into classical Greek by Demetrius Cydones. It is well known that Aquinas strongly founded his thought upon that of Aristotle, and that he drew his knowledge of Aristotle's works through the translation of the latter by Moerbeke, known to be defective in several respects. Cydones made two parallel efforts: to be faithful both to Thomas and to Aristotle, the citations from whom he helped reformulate both rigorously and creatively. It is at just this moment that one should place the beginning of modern Greek philosophical thought, instead of placing it either at the Eleventh or at the Fifteenth Centuries. Greek philosophy started being "fed back" by its own creation, Western medieval culture.

In every corner of the world, except perhaps in animistic or shamanistic societies, the presence of these conceptions has become a common and self-understood fact. European cultural models, be they of Eastern or typically Western inspiration, share in common ideas and ideals created in the Greek world and forwarded by the European scientific, artistic, and political spirit. From such a viewpoint, these models tend to become planetary ones. Even those philosophers of culture who belong to extra-European countries, and who try to denigrate and reject the established European cultural models, for instance the theoreticians of "futurism" *(demainisme),* very contradictorily accept the economic aspects of these models, although the various aspects are not dissociable from each other. Directly or indirectly, the presence of the Greek spirit in our day has been widely accepted and continually further elaborated. Finally, it seems to me that Professor Gruender has given us an excellent methodical approach and a comprehensive view of the issue, and that he has made a contribution to a better understanding of the roots and, hence, of the essence of our cultural being. In valuing the knowledge of this being through its own models, Europe, as a cultural entity with a universal vocation, has a further important historical role to play. In order to better prepare for us a future in accordance with our past, we have to better accept the latter, and thus establish the best conditions under which to guarantee the continuity of our culture.

COMMENTS ON "THE GREEK AND CHRISTIAN HERITAGE OF EUROPE: LOOKING BACK WHILE LOOKING FORWARD"

Maria Golaszewska

Professor Gruender gave us an exhaustive analysis of the problem of the Greek and Christian heritage of Europe and showed the very beginning of the division of Europe. I have nothing to add as far as the facts are concerned. Therefore, I would like to extend one of the points mentioned by him as inherited by Europe over the centuries from the Greek tradition, *i.e.,* Greek cosmopolitanism. I am in a position, as a philosopher, to interpret it as a pluralistic attitude towards the world, especially towards the world of culture. I will present only the main lines of the problem. The question about pluralism has two fundamental dimensions: *i.e.* philosophical and socio-political ones. Pluralism, as one of the most general systems of thinking, appears in Ancient Europe and still functions and it gains importance especially in its social-ideological form. In European philosophy and also in theoretical thought, there are two opposite ways of arranging ideas and phenomena as well: monistic and pluralistic ones. Sometimes special intrinsic contradictories occur, *e.g.,* in monotheistic Christian theology, the notion of the Holy Trinity; then, in Leibniz's pluralistic monadology, we find an idea of pre-established harmony, monistic in principle, universal, and all-embracing. We are interested here in the social-ideological kind of pluralism. This problem belongs to philosophical anthropology, and the limits of the phenomena in question are outlined by the limits of the human world. The theoretical assumptions of pluralism, its origin and its structure come into play here. We admit an introductory definition: Pluralism assumes a system of values, intentionally created, put in order on the basis of the equal importance of all of the components which are subordinated to the unique idea; all the components, being sub-systems, form one system and do not loose their autonomy. The most important feature in pluralism is not only the variety but a special linking of the elements, so that they compose a whole. To show the substance of pluralism more fully, let us contrast it with other systems:

1. Monistic, totalitarian systems. The components of such systems, have hardly any autonomy. The whole of the system presents itself as one block, it is monolithic.
2. Hierarchical systems. The components are subordinated to one supreme value: the farther from that value, the less autonomous they are.
3. Centralistic systems: all the components are connected in the same manner with the central point, which guards its axiological neutrality, *e.g.* technocracy.
4. Lack of system dispersion. There are no links between the elements, no system at all *e.g.* various tribes in Africa.
5. Pluralistic systems, The subsystems are autonomous, self-dependent, independent, and voluntarily linked by the common ideas, and common goals.

THE MESSAGE OF ANCIENT GREECE.

Pluralism seems to be something characteristic of Ancient Greek culture. It applies both to the social-political systems and to the intellectual movements, that is philosophy and religion. So, the separate *polis,* town-states, had their own autonomy, but, at the same time, they had a sense of belonging to the greater, panhellenic organism, and that what linked the separate elements in the whole system were the cultural values in peacetime, and patriotism in case of the threat of war. The history of philosophy of Ancient Greece is a testimony of its pluralistic character: the different philosophical systems coexisted and they engaged in peaceful discussions rather than harsh encounters with one another. The consequence of such different systems of philosophy as the Platonic and Aristotelian are an example of the lack of totalitarian trends in the Greek tradition. Plato did not intend to persecute what did not conform to his view, and Aristotle was his disciple. Another suggestive example of Ancient Greek pluralism was religion: polytheism. The Greeks were religious, but their religion was non-monistic. They worshiped various gods and feared them, although all the gods had to share Olympus with the more powerful Zeus. In theoretical Greek thought we can find totalitarian and monistic elements as well. Plato, in his *Republic* outlines a model of a perfectly organized state, where he proposed absolute power and total subordination of all the citizens. However, the Platonic conception did not overstep the limit of a philosophical program: it was not realized. The achievements in the field of government in the Ancient Greek culture were imitated in Europe as a model of theoretical-historical analysis, as well as an inspiration to social-political activity. These pluralistic ideas functioned since Grecian times, although their realization was attempted in various ways with and without success.

THE CHRISTIAN MESSAGE.

As far as religious doctrine is concerned, Christianity belongs in principle to the category of monism, taken over from Judaism. However, it was a particular monism, different from the Judaistic one, allowed the infiltration of pluralism. The conception of God as a Holy Trinity has this element of pluralism. Moreover, universalism implies giving up the exclusiveness of elitism: there is no Greek, no Jew, before God, the Scriptures say. Another trait of Christian pluralism is the principle of love: *caritas*. These tendencies gave rise first, to Christian communities and, in our time, to the ecumenical movement. The departure from pluralism brought the Catholic Church to break from its fundamental teachings about love and forgiveness. This led to the Inquisition, with the death, among others, of Giordano Bruno, who could not find his place in the new totalitarian Church.

EUROPEAN PLURALISM NOW.

In contemporary European culture, and in social-ideological practice, pluralism reached the status of a universal postulate, in spite of being understood in different manners, in so far, as it is sometimes treated only declaratively, as a camouflage for the quite totalitarian reality. Making allowance both for the historical moment and the present state of European societies, and also the assumptions resulting from the Greco-Christian mode of thinking, we now make more precise part of the universal structure of pluralism in respect to the highest values:

1. Tolerance, and affirmation of the general attitude of tolerance.
2. Affirmation of Christian ethics independently of the accepted ideology; even the non-Christian and atheistic systems find a common ethical platform, inspired by Christian ethics.
3. An engaged attitude; radical ideological indifference evokes lack of motivation to make a given subsystem join the pluralistic system;
4. a rough equivalence between the particular systems: A radical opposition seems to be intolerable; *e.g.,* Fascism is radically totalitarian.
5. Manageability of systems, the ability of the subsystems to be directed to achieve the "state of pluralism" and realization of superior goals.
6. System-character: the subsystems voluntarily and consciously include themselves into the system as a pluralistic whole.
7. The hierarchical set of highest values must be accepted as common for all systems, along with the common universal goals and then the application of the uncontradictory elements with the pluralistic means of realization come into play.
8. The observance of the principle of good will.
9. There must be an openness towards coexistence with other, analogous systems.
10. The principle of common communication, and penetration of ideas must be observed. It seems to be obvious that a system like pluralism must be theoretically correct, and useful in practice. Two difficulties arise here: as social life in Europe shows, there are elements which cannot be assimilated by pluralism — these are the systems of totalitarian ideology, and those which are evidently contradictory to Christian ethics. The second difficulty consists in avoiding the danger of extremes: fanaticism, and scepticism. It seems that pluralism *ex definitione* — as it were — excludes fanaticism, but one can become a fanatic of pluralism. On the other hand, tolerance can lead to scepticism and indifference.

In the light of these remarks, the division of Europe reveals three problems:

1. Thanks to the division, we can consider Europe as a whole — if such a whole really exists — as pluralistic in principle, because the opposite viewpoints and ideologies coexist here.
2. If we agree that Europe is divided into two camps, one must agree that the West is more pluralistic than the East, where the tradition of the absolute power is still vital.
3. There may exist such divisions which can be fruitful and contribute to development and to strenthen the tendency for peace: the ideological disputes make people more aware of what truth they really believe in, and what kind of values they essentially appreciate.

DISCUSSION ON GRUENDER

Vassilis Karasmanis

I would make some comments. First Prof. Moutsopoulos focused on the universality of the Greek mind and civilization. There is a peculiar character of the Greek mind. Although Greece was defeated by the Romans, Greece won over the Romans, and the expansion of the Greek mind did not take place through wars. The same happened with the Arabs when they conquered Alexandria and all the south of the Byzantine empire, and with the western world before the Renaissance. This is reflected in the crucial notion of *logos*.

Heinrich Beck

I have two questions especially to Prof. Moutsopoulos. First, what do you think about the thesis of Heidegger saying that the particular view of being in Greek ancient philosophy is to objectivize being. According to Heidegger, this static view of being in the Greek mentality is opposed to the Jewish view which interprets and understands being as a process of encounter. What do you think about this Heiddegerian interpretation of Greek philosophy? Second, I have the impression that your understanding of Greek philosophy inclines to see the being as an order and as energy, ruled by *logos* as a rational order which comes from form: on the other side, there is matter which is to be ordered and formed by *logos*. And, therefore, Greek understanding of being occurs when dualism is understood as an encounter of two principles, forming and being formed. This entails in the Greek interpretation of the world a certain tragic moment, a moment of failure. I now would ask Prof. Golaszewska, whether the Christian influence intends to resolve such a tragic moment, in a conception of order in which the moment of plurality and the moment of unity in the conception of the holy trinity are connected in a synthesis, the Trinity one God in three persons.

Andrzej Werner

In political science world pluralism is quite a new invention. I wish to compliment Prof. Delgado for having drawn our attention more to the future than to the past, and to the wealth of ideas that are becoming more and more important. In the previous session Prof. van den Dungen drew our attention to the very negative fact that the present division between east and west Europe constitutes a threat to our common heritage. Prof. Golaszewska implies that the present diversity in the wealth of ideas can lead to a synthesis. I doubt about that. The basic philosophy of the east is based not on the contribution to the world of ideas, but on the substitute of those ideas by the only truly scientific system. I listened with great interest to Prof. Zeleny. Prof. Andreski correctly observed that in the Soviet Union and in our countries all over the world young people behave in the same way. This does not mean however that they also think in the same way. I therefore would like to draw again your attention to the statement made by Prof. van den Dungen, that the present divisions in the area of ideas constitutes a threat to our common heritage.

Alexander Shtromas

First I would like to ask Prof. Gruender: why, when talking about Greek tradition don't you refer to the controversy which has started maybe even before Nietzsche but which Nietzsche stressed so powerfully, *i.e.,* that the Greek tradition which really is valid to our positive heritage is the presocratic tradition? That view was taken up by Popper, that the Platonic intrusion into the Greek soul has really created quite a lot of damage because it removes the tensions. This view is very important to me. In Parmenides and Zeno one will be confronted with the idea of the dialogue. However neither of them was able to really conclude anything which reasonably presents the basic foundation of pluralism, whereas both

Socrates and Plato, and even Aristotle, really establish a new tradition. We have to think of that contradiction within the Greek tradition. Second, I will ask Prof. Gruender about the implications which he made when he discussed the divisions between Orthodox Eastern Christianity and Western or Roman Christianity. Would he really draw a line from that kind of division to the present divisions of east and west or not? Third, to Prof. Golaszewska, my question is the following: You said that the concept of Trinity introduces pluralism and that was the sort of "eurofication" of Judaism which ignores pluralism. To me pluralism is embedded in the concept of the freedom of will, the free will which God endowed people with, and that is a Judaic concept which Christianity inherited. Finally, that could be answered by Prof. Moutsopulous, but it was more precisely expressed by Dr. Karasmanis: what about Solon? Solon introduced not only laws, but also ideology. What Solon does represent in the Greek tradition is very much open to question. I would like some comments on that. Marx and some interpretations of Marx seem alien to the western tradition. Marx himself is very much in the western tradition and one shouldn't really exclude him. On the other hand, Marxism is an extreme expression of humanism.

Tamás Kozma

Just one question to Prof. Gruender: don't you think our understanding of Greek philosophy today is much more an understanding of the 19th century German philosophers of the universities, than the so-called real Greek philosophy?

Ivan Maksimovic

It is possible to discuss this problem of Greco-Christian heritage on the perspective of east and west today without any correlation to the orientation of the ideology and political context of present political bodies in the world. There is no direct influence of any philosophical movement on the perspective of world movements.

José Delgado

I have a specific question on the paper of Prof. Gruender,

(page 31). There is a contradiction that should be emphasized. You talk about the historic constant of the natural law and there is a quote "above the law of nations stands the law of all mankind". The law of mankind is the interpretation of human beings and this is precisely what I think is important. Therefore the contradiction resides in that you state that each human being is bearing the dignity of his creator. This is only an interpretation. In the same page you say something beautiful, *i.e.,* that thousands of years later, ideals of some man still inspire us while the buildings of the ancient cities lie in ruins. This shows that ideas are stronger than cities. However here again there is a contradiction concerning natural laws, and laws created and interpreted, by human beings. My contention is that perhaps what we are trying to do is to create new laws for the human beings.

David Gruender

I have benefitted from the comments of my panelists and from those of you who have commented further. Nothing has been said about my paper that I disagree with, so I will not respond in the sense of arguing about any of those points, but reply to these questions by going backwards in time. First, to Prof. Delgado, I would answer that the phrase in quotation marks: "above the laws of nations stands the law of all mankind" is in fact a classical quotation. The Stoic conception is that there was a law which stood above the laws of the various nations and that this law was made by the same god who created individual human beings. This view has the advantage of raising our eyes to look at such a possibility in the absence of a creator who has clearly spoken to all of us. The contradiction is not over the existence. Potential contradictions do not surround the idea of the possible existence of such a creator who would make such laws, but rather over whether we can find the courage and the tenacity to approach that topic ourselves. Second may I report to Prof. Kozma, that my own view of Greek philosophy was not filtered through nineteenth century German philosophy. I have a very high regard for Greek philosophy, with its contradictions, and I must, in all candor, add that I have a very low opinion of nineteenth century German philosophy. It has been a task of later twentieth century scholarship to attempt to resuscitate anything possible. Third with respect to Prof. Shtromas' question as to whether the split between east and west today is caused or related to the division between eastern and western Christianity, I tried to give a synoptical sketch of what Toynbee thinks it is. We can talk about this split and the reasons for it, and comment on what a heritage of mistrust and misunderstanding this leads to. I agree with Prof. Moutsopoulos that there were important influences of the Greeks from whom we learned enormously. I certainly agree with Prof. Golaszewska, that cosmopolitanism and pluralism were both important. I find fanaticism to be one of the difficulties that we have learned, and which we may or may not succeed in avoiding. What we can learn from this unhappy history of Europe, is that we can learn that bigotry carries with it a very high price. Love of domination also carries forward from our heritage and has been extremely harmful to us.

Maria Golaszewska

I have omitted certain passages in my comment. I will clarify that, ontologically, pluralism can be considered as the property of the structure of the world. Pluralism can be considered as an important value as far as peace and the order in the world is concerned and as everywhere in the human world this implies human free will. To Prof. Werner I would like to say that synthesis of the opposites is not impossible. Recent history teaches us about it. Politicians in the socialistic countries must agree that models of government change.

Evanghelos Moutsopoulos

I would first like to start with Prof. Werner's opposition between the world of business and the world of ideas by relating a story which has been reported to me by Harold Cherniss a few years ago. Two people are travelling by train — a philosopher and a sales representative of a fabric manufacturer. "Well, what are you travelling in?", the representative asked the philosopher, "I myself travel in notions." "What a peculiar coincidence!", the philosopher said. "I also travel in notions." Dr. Karasmanis, made a very precise qualification of Greek thought in general. It's true that in Plato's *Republic* we find the qualification of the philosopher as *synoptikos,* as the one who has a general view of the object of his thought. We also find the same idea in Aristotle's *Topics*: *synoran,* "to see together" I think that the Greek thinkers had stressed ideas such as equality, welfare, justice, *isomoiria* or *lukraisa.* Temper, yes, but good temper, which means that the prefix *eu-* means something more in this context: some kind of perfection of measure itself. I have related this to the notion of *matrum,* an excessive measure, which has to do with "kairicity", and to another word which etymologically is also very close to *kairos*: *Krisis.* The measure of Greek cities is conceived of by Aristotle. An excessively big city cannot be democratic, *etc.* I think we should find new means in order to preserve democracy within our big cities and our big countries. To Professor Beck who asked me about the kind of opposition between the static Greek conception of being and the dynamic conception in Hebrew thought which has to do with the process of encounter, I would say that Heidegger's conception of this opposition is "stylized". I particulary think of Aristotle's conception of energy and *dynamis,* and in this case I believe I have been able to show in a paper published in the *Festschrift* of Francois Meyer, in France, that the Aristotelian conception of being resides in the interpretation of the very core of that being. On the other hand, we can say that in this perspective, being, as conceived of by Aristotle is a structure and an order. Order within the core. To Prof. Shtromas, I would say that Plato did some kind of damage to Socrates, and I remind him of Whitehead's conception that after Plato, all philosophical thought is a kind of commentary on Plato's philosophy. In any case, with Socrates, happily Greek thought shifted from a cosmocentric perception to an anthropocentric conception.

THE RISE AND DECLINE OF EUROPE: FROM LIMITED GOVERNMENT TO UNLIMITED DEMOCRACY

Gerard Radnitzky

"Democracy's last dilemma is that the state must, but cannot, roll itself back."
(Anthony de Jasay, *The State*. Oxford: Blackwell 1985, p. 323).

1. THE "EUROPEAN MIRACLE":
— Europe as the exception among the advanced civilizations in history

So far as we know, most advanced civilizations have been despotisms, and the mass of the people have always lived in extreme poverty. A longitudinal performance comparison of economies and nations reveals that "the Rise of the West" is an *exception*. At the end of the middle ages Europe was lagging far behind Chinese and Indian civilizations. However, in the last 500 years it overtook all of them, and at the beginning of this century Europe ruled the world.[1] Today European civilization has become Western civilization, and one normally associates with it a technology-based way of doing things, as well as the basic elements of *Rechtsstaat*[2], *i.e.*, at least a certain amount of individual freedom, of individual rights, which are respected by the state. This European civilization has spread to other countries. Its center has moved from Europe to the United States, and countries like Japan, Korea, the Republic of China (Taiwan), and Singapore exemplify Western civilization in this sense. The European or Western approach to solving practical problems, including social and political problems, has been selected in cultural evolution. It has been selected because it has made those nations that have adopted it more prosperous than those who have adopted other approaches. Hence, rational people have imitated the successful ones. A comparison of the performance of the economies of the West (in that sense) with those of the Soviet bloc and the "socialist" states in the Third World confirms this appraisal. The totalitarian states have not been able to catch up. On the contrary, they are increasingly lagging behind; they have to rely on technological espionage, and to glean shadow prices from the world market in order to avoid calculational chaos in their inefficient, centralized economies. To summarize: the conspicuous features of "the European Miracle" are the economic success of those nations which have adopted the Western approach, and also the fact that these nations allow relatively more individual freedom, more "private rights" than the others do. The phrase 'Western civilization' is, normally, construed in such a way that these features follow from its definition. How did this tradition and the institutions embodying it come about? We can at best hope to give an "explanation of the principle". *Prima facie* the following three interrelated factors appear to be central:

1. limited government leading eventually to a *Rechtsstaat* (the Rule of Law that respects private rights),
2. the market order, and
3. autonomous science (Albert 1986, pp. 17, 30, 55).

Erich Weede sees the *evolution of limited government* even in an age of absolutism as the central feature (Weede 1987a, p. 2 *et passim*, 1987b). I agree. *It is the taming of the State that made possible the evolution of institutional arrangements that are wealth-creating,* where "wealth" is taken in the widest sense, including not only physical and economic wealth but also epistemic resources: knowledge and know-how. To be wealth creating, institutional arrangements must make possible, firstly, the efficient production of knowledge and the efficient use of knowledge; secondly, they must provide the incentives that set free the energy of the individual by making him accountable for his actions in terms of success and failure; and thirdly, they must secure free competition not only in the economic market but also in the market of ideas in order to facilitate inventions and innovations. An invention can lead to an innovation only if an entrepreneur is willing to invest in risky enterprises. In summary, the key factor in "the Rise of the West" is the emergence of "private rights" in combination with the evolution of the market order, which, in turn, presupposes a legal frame that secures property rights and thereby makes a first step towards a *Rechtsstaat:* to the taming of whimsical governmental power. To analyse this development we need a theoretical framework. For reason of space I can merely, give a rough outline. No attempt will be made to provide a detailed explanation, rather I will submit an "explanation of the principle" (as Hayek uses that term [*e.g.,* Hayek 1952, pp. 34, 43, 182]).

2. THE THEORETICAL FRAMEWORK NEEDED FOR THE EXPLANATION OF THE PRINCIPLE.

2.1. Explanation in Terms of the Economic Approach.

The following assumptions underlie such an explanation:

1. The methodological rule that the phenomena to be explained should, at some level of analysis, be reducible to the actions of individuals; only individuals can be agents in the full sense (Flew 1985, pp. 44 ff.). This principle is usually called *'methodological individualism';* the property rights analysis of social phenomena makes use of this microeconomic perspective on the institution or institutions being examined.

2. A general hypothesis about human nature asserting that *man attempts to maximize "utility" with constant tastes*. The common criticism levelled against the Economic Approach (property rights analysis or rational-action approach) claiming that it only deals with "financial" motivation (monetary profits, *etc.)* fails to recognize that "utility" is construed in the widest sense and that the arguments of the utility function remain open. From this perception of man it follows that people with the same motivation (attempting to maximize the same sort of utility) will act differently in different institutional settings, *i.e.,* that their action will depend on their perceptions of the constraints: on their "framing" of the situation. From this, in turn, follows the methodological precept that the historical analysis

should proceed by specifying the particular features of the institutional setting that lead people operating under such constraints to behave as we observe. There also follows a warning, namely that the official "function" of an institution or activity need not be the reason for the existence or the maintenance of that institution or activity.
3. The general hypothesis about social phenomena that asserts that a very large part of the social phenomena are *unintended* consequences of the actions of individuals, consequences that often are unexpected and even unpredictable. Karl Popper has, therefore, recommended that social scientists focus on such unintended consequences of social action. In a similar vein Friedrich von Hayek has always seen the most important of our social orders, traditions, institutions, *etc.* as *spontaneous, i.e.,* as orders that have evolved as the unintended effect of the actions of large numbers or generations of individuals who, while pursuing their own ends, created a certain order without ever intending to bring it about and even without being capable of doing so internationally. This implies that many of the institutions we find around us are not the result of deliberate design, that man sometimes stumbled across institutions that proved to be wealth-creating, that he often did not understand why, and that he did not need to understand this in order to be successful. Hayek also claims that group selection played a decisive role in the evolution of such wealth-creating institutions. His attempts to identify the principles that underlie them culminated in the trilogy *Law, Legislation, and Liberty* and in *The Fatal Conceit* (for an overview see, *e.g.*, Radnitzky 1987c).

2.2. Political Structures are two-faced: A Mix of Positive and Negative Sum Games.

Karl Brunner in (1985) and (1986) has convincingly argued that in any social order the individual has three basic options for investing resources and effort:
1. productive, wealth-creating activities: production and trade; and non-productive activities, directed to redistribution, either
2. extracting wealth from others, or
3. protecting oneself against attempts at wealth-extraction by others.

In a situation of relative anarchy within groups, the prevailing uncertainty undermines the link between productive effort and the returns, and therefore, wealth-creating activities remain low. The methods of wealth-extraction are violent (such as robbery), and therefore it is rational for the individual to invest part of his resources and effort in defense against robbery.[3] Since anarchy is not a stable state, some political structure is bound to emerge. Thereby the situation is improved. How much, depends on the particular mix of protective and redistributive aspects in the emerging political structure. Karl Brunner rightly emphasizes that *any* set of political institutions produces its specific mix of positive-sum games and negative-sum games. The two-faced character of the state is unavoidable, because there will always be incentives for those with better information and better access to political agencies than the mass of the population to manipulate these agencies in order to advance their own special interests (the Mancur Olson effect; *cf.* Olson 1982). The *positive-sum game* results from an increased expectation of capturing the returns of effort. Such expectations are rational only if *property rights* are protected, mutually beneficial contracts possible, and contracts enforceable. On the level of institutions, the positive-sum game is represented by wealth-creating institutional arrangements; and an institutional arrangement can be wealth-creating only if it is protective with respect to the productive activities of the individuals. Trade qualifies as productive in this sense, because a voluntary exchange takes place only if both parties think that they will be better off: that their wealth will have been increased after the transaction. Hence, protection of economic freedom and civil liberties will make it rational for the individual, household, firm, and so on, to invest in productive and economic activities. *The protective state enhances the positive-sum game.* What about the second and third options, the investment of the resources and effort in wealth-transfer? In an organized society the *counterpart to robbery is investment in political activities with a view to transfering wealth from others to oneself.* Examples are all sorts of rent-seeking behavior, such as lobbying for subsidies or monopoly prices in the market, and political processes designed to impose constraints on choices bearing on contractual arrangements and the tenure of private property, which eventually lead to an erosion of private rights. A good example from European history is the comparison between absolutist France, when entrepreneurs could escape from competition by buying royal favors and establishing monopolies, and parliamentary England which early overcame the mercantilist rent-seeking society, and could outpace the more populous France [Weede1987b, p. 8]. *The counterpart of defense against robbery is investment in defensive political measures,* such as tax-avoidance and tax-evasion, switching over to the hidden economy, or — as a last resort — emigration, the exit option. *The more a political system is dominated by the negative-sum game,* by the redistributive purpose of the state, *the more wealth-impeding consequences will ensue.* Protectionism and cartelization on the part of both the labor unions and the producers today are among the most important wealth-impeding and growth-hampering phenomena.

2.3. The Market and Knowledge.

The prosperity of a society or nation will be a function of the degree to which its political structure fulfills the protective function of the state, *i.e.,* to the extent to which it guarantees economic freedom — which in turn is a precondition for individual freedom and civil rights. In a modern, highly complex economy, if a society is to remain prosperous, the state must abstain from interventions in the market process. Friedrich von Hayek has demonstrated that only the market order can make an economy function satisfactorily.[4] An economic system functions properly if and only if it solves the following problems: it must be able to provide information about people's desires, preferences, skills, and so on; be able to handle this information so that creative and entrepreneurial activity becomes possible; and be able to create incentives for people to act on the information. Only if it achieves this can it coordinate the activities of very large numbers of individuals, households, and firms. Hayek shows that the market order is basically a discovery system, which tells man how to serve the wants of people whom he does not know in order to serve his *own* interest. The relevant knowledge for market operations is "local" knowledge: about fleeting circumstances and occasions, one's own resources, capabilities and aims, *etc.* Thus, it is widely dispersed, and some part of it is "tacit" in the sense that the individual himself could not articulate it, even if he wished. Centralized planning is, for *epistemic* reasons, unable to simulate the efficiency of the market order. Because it is impossible to transfer the local knowledge to a central planning board, the only efficient way of collocating the relevant knowledge and decision rights is to transfer the decision rights to individuals who possess the relevant knowledge. Besides functioning as a *discovery* system, the market order also *controls* human behavior by locating decision rights along side the proceeds of the exchange in such a way that the consequences of decisions are imposed on the decision makers themselves by providing the decisive link between effort and expected returns; it makes people accountable for their actions. Since the assignment of decision-making rights is a matter of law, the market order presupposes a legal system. In any economy, 'exchange' refers not only to physical articles or services *per se,* but to bundles of rights attached to them. Hence, every society is faced with the task of the enforcement of individual rights to property. Therefore, the market order presupposes an apparatus of law enforcement. Otherwise, it would be unable to eliminate the Prisoner's Dilemma, which arises when contracts cannot be enforced. This, of course, applies to groups or societies that are larger than a face-to-face group. Only in the face-to-face group, where individuals expect repeated transactions with the same individuals, can the Prisoner's Dilemma be overcome by personal mechanisms of trust. The development of European civilization, of course, concerns a plurality of societies which are relatively large, at least so large that they constitute anonymous societies.

To summarize: The market order functions as a discovery system; it ensures both competition and cooperation; it ensures that there are incentives for effort and risk-taking by making the decision makers accountable for their actions; and it provides the basis for the development of individual freedom. It does so by presupposing and reinforcing "private rights" or "property rights". In the context of an economic approach to history, the phrases 'property rights' and 'private rights' are used in a wider sense than in ordinary language (Radnitzky 1987c, proofs p. 28). The desire for private property is most intense insofar as it concerns control of one's own person and one's own time; possessions or, more accurately speaking, property rights with respect to material things, are valued also because they are guarantors of our autonomy from others. Private rights also essentially include the rights to the proceeds of one's work. This new form of obtaining a livelihood — from work — had an important liberating effect in European history: serfdom to the landlord began to disappear when wages appeared. The market order has made people independent of particular groups or tribes — but only so long as free entry to a labor market (at flexible prices of labor) is not hindered by the monopoly of organized groups ("unions" for example). After having outlined what, in principle, makes a society or nation prosperous, let us apply these considerations to our explanandum: the success story of the European civilization. The main contribution of Western civilization to the social evolution of man is that for the first time in human history an *Order of Liberty* has been developed. The science-based technology, which has enormously increased man's power over nature, the taming of nature, is a secondary achievement compared with the Order of Liberty, the taming of the state. This appraisal appears justified even if the technical achievement is given its full due and it is kept in mind that our stone age ancestors possessed the same natural resources as we do, for what has been the cause of the difference between our standard of living and theirs is the difference in knowledge.

3. WHY DID THIS TYPE OF CIVILIZATION DEVELOP IN EUROPE[5] AND ONLY THERE?

If, in addition to the rationality assumption we assume constant motivation which, in the case of absolute rulers means power and material wealth, then the observed differences between the behavior of the Asian and Islamic rulers, on the one hand, and the European princes, on the other hand, have to be explained in terms of the constraints. Erich Weede has offered such an explanation (1987a and 1987b, with many references to relevant literature).

The Rise and Decline of Europe

My own account is based on Weede's work. Why did certain wealth-creating institutions evolve only in Europe? The following natural circumstances appear to have been of decisive importance.

1. The European *geography:* European soils, geology, and climates vary from place to place, and *core-areas are comparatively small.* By contrast, Asian rulers operated in territories where it was easier to project military power from the core to the periphery, and they succeeded in establishing empires over vast territories. Their empires bordered on backward people, who were not real competitors; and, if it happened that such peoples conquered, nonetheless, an empire, the conquerers, having become the ruling class, would accept the superior civilization of the people they had conquered. By contrast, the European states faced neighbors with roughly equal military capabilities. In Europe the international game of power was characterized by permanent and fierce competition. Thus, the peculiar natural constraints of Europe lead to a *permanent fragmentation of political power.*

2. Weede also points out that the variety of European climates and soils made division of labor more profitable and led to *bulk trade in mass consumption goods* and to the formation of *interstate trade and markets.* I would add that interstate trade also led to flexible rates of exchange and also to *competition* among currencies (Peter Bernholz). Moreover, the mere existence of competing money should discipline the ruler's handling of their state's currency. Given the differences in interregional production opportunities and the division of labor, trade became more and more profitable. The rulers could get a larger income from a steady stream of protection rents than from robbing merchants. Robbery would induce traders to bypass the territory of the robber prince, who, in contrast to the Asian rulers, only controlled a relatively small territory. International markets became free to respond to changes in demand and supply. *Free competition in economic markets,* the autonomy of the economy, provided the seed for *an autonomy of technology and, later, of science.* Given the natural constraints, for European rulers it was rational to keep in check their predatory and kleptocratic appetites and to concede *relatively* safe property rights (Weede 1987a, p. 4; 1987b, p. 2). Property rights, private

rights, were in turn the growing ground for a moral system of individualism and personal responsibility. In a nutshell: the international system in Europe made possible the spread of the market order or capitalism; and, since the market ordet presupposes a legal framework guaranteeing property rights, it put Europe on the road to the *Rechtsstaat,* whose precursors are found in Greek and Roman law. Conceding property rights to individuals meant *limited* government; the protective purpose of the state became more and more pronounced. Thus, limited government could evolve in an age of feudalism and absolutism. *Limited government is a predemocratic achievement.*

3. *Competition* among holders of political power *within* a nation — a phenomenon common to Europe — *boosted capitalism and economic growth.* Thus, the less absolutistic countries, such as England and the Netherlands, were economically more successful than centralized France and Spain. England's economy profited from the rivalry between King and Parliament as well as between the Royal Courts and the Common Law Court (Weede 1987b). In other European countries the power struggle between the state and the church, which eventually led to their separation, boosted individual freedom and tolerance. Now the churches, too, profited from the rule of law (Albert 1986, pp. 20 f.). In general, the more limited a government, the less will the state be prone to protectionism and other follies which were favored by absolute rulers — and in our age by democratic government.

4. European *pluralism* had also the advantage of *decentralization: risk diversification.* The stupidity of a ruler or government could harm one nation, but never damage all of them. By contrast, in united China whimsical policies of the central government could ruin the prospects of economic growth for the entire civilization [see Weede 1987a], p. 2 for examples and references).

5. The competition between states, together with practicable opportunities for exit, facilitated the spread of innovations throughout Europe. Individuals could escape from religious and political persecution by emigrating to other countries, where they were welcomed if they possessed some superior skills. No single government was in a position to suppress an

innovation. In summary: *Europe became more inventive and creative and also more tolerant because of political and religious fragmentation and rivalry.*

6. Besides competition between states in the form of trade, competition in the form of power politics and wars was another factor that boosted economic development. If only for risk diversification, it is advantageous to enlarge a national territory. The richer a country is, the more tempting it will become for neighbors that are militarily strong to profit from its riches not by trade but through conquest. Hence, the richer a country is, the more it will rationally invest in defense effort. Military technology has always been the pacemaker for civil technology *(cf., e.g.,* Albert 1968, p. 14, Andreski 1968, Andreski 1969). The role which military competition between states played for European development can hardly be overrated. It is a mechanism of rule selection through group struggle, and even the preparation for aggressive war or for defense deeply influences the economic and political life of a nation. With increasing military effort, the rulers and the elites became more and more dependent on the common man as soldier. This is likely to have a positive effect. It widens the market of human capital such as skills and knowledge; it prompts the introduction of a reward system and a selection system that is based only on merit and achievement, and thereby it overcomes inefficient selection mechanisms, in particular, those based on characteristics that are irrelevant for military achievements such as, *e.g.,* aristocratic birth. Since the rulers become increasingly dependent on the loyalty of the common man as soldier, they will have an incentive to grant him certain rights in order to maintain his loyalty above all: equality before the law.

Weede points out that so long as popular participation in military events is fairly limited (as was the case before the French Revolution), interstate competition weakens the power of the rulers *vis-à-vis* the rising capitalist merchants and entrepreneurs (1987b, p. 16). These unintended effects of wars will favor the trend towards limited government and, thus, to individual freedom. However, the situation changes when, in an intellectual climate of nationalistic, egalitarian, and democratic ideologies, military competition between states involves a massive popular participation and forces governments to intervene in the economy and in the political life of the country (Weede 1987b, p. 16). In that new context, war and preparation for war or for defense will increasingly threaten economic growth and also individual freedom. Robert Nisbet has drawn attention to this phenomenon of "war-sprung egalitarianism" and "war-state-socialism (1976, p.18). It has been a major source of what Hayek sees as *"the two greatest threats to a free civilization: nationalism and socialism"* (Hayek 1979, p. 111, ital. GR). "War-state socialism" is certainly not limited to the European experience; and it has lost nothing of its topicality: Roosevelt's enduring political endowment to succeeding generations, an ever-growing welfare/warfare state, remains as intrusive as ever. In European history, "war-state-socialism" has been of central importance. Up to the so-called first world war, "the great European war." Europe's ruling class was an aristocracy with family ties between national branches; its main problem was that facing every dictator: how to stay in power. That ruling class destroyed itself and, with it, much of the European order in World War I. That war was the seed-bed of the two great socialist revolutions of our century: the Russian of 1917 and the German of 1933. Because the ruling class had lost most of its power, at the end of World War I, peace-making after the model practiced in Europe during the last two centuries that preceded it was no longer possible, and hence that war also set the stage for the destruction of Europe and for a coming world order dominated by two extra-European superpowers — a development presaged by such "Central-European" political writers as Constantin Frantz and Fieldmarshal Radetzki.

To summarize: "the European Miracle" teaches us the virtues of private rights, *i.e.,* of limited government and of the rule of law: the virtues of approximating the libertarian ideal of a minimal protective state. Moreover, the history of Europe shows that limited government emerged as a spontaneous order in an era of feudalism and absolutism, and that the taming of the state is a predemocratic achievement. It also shows that this exceptional development has its forerunners in antiquity, in particular, in Roman law, and that Russia had no part in "the European Miracle". However, when speaking of the European Miracle we should remember that today the main bearer of Western civilization is the United States, and that certain Asian countries, such as Japan, approximate the ideal type of Western civilization better than many of the states of contemporary Europe. The protective state has received its best codification in the American Constitution. It was a lucky accident in history that the United States could develop after 1787 without European interference. In 1789 the French Revolution broke out, and, for the 25 years that followed, the European powers and their overseas colonies were embroiled in war. Thus the 13 States of America were free from European interference for a complete generation, and could develop undisturbed. Perhaps, the year 1776 should be taken as the beginning of the chronology of "the Rise of Western Civilization". What this rise meant can be visualized when we remember that between 1. A.D. and 1776 A.D. men had available to them much the same income, travel means, life expectancy, and so on. It was 1776 when *The Wealth of Nations* was published (the first clear exposition of the market order), the American *Declaration of Independence* signed (that paved the way for first written Constitution of Liberty), and the steam engine discovered. From 1776 to 1975 the world population increased sixfold, real gross national product eightyfold, the amount of energy that can be released from a pound of matter over 50 millionfold, and other changes of similar magnitude were achieved.

4. Do ideas matter?

Every political philosophy has an epistemological base — even if both may be at a rudimentary level.

4.1. The Intellectual Origins of Western Civilization.

The most important source appears to be *Greek* tradition: The *Presocratics* (Popper 1962, chapter 5 "Back to the Presocratics"). As far as we know, this is the first tradition in intellectual history which not only allowed, but even *encouraged competition among ideas* — a market of ideas — and created what has been called 'the criticist tradition' (Popper, Bartley, Albert). It flourished in a climate of polytheism, and taught the *virtues of tolerance*. The second of the main sources was *Roman* law. It established *private rights* and protected the private sphere of the individual from intrusion by others, including the state.[6] The third of the main sources was the *Hebrew* tradition. Judaism early grasped the *social utility of competition, prices and profits,* and also identified some classic abuses and perplexities any community is likely to experience regarding these. "Despite certain talmudic sayings to the contrary, no anti-commercial tradition existed in Judaism as existed in Christian social thought." (Tamari 1987). The merchant and the entrepreneur play a legitimate role, and are morally entitled to a profit in return for fulfilling their function. Jewish thought on the nature of economics has been more penetrating than Moslem or Christian thought.

Of course, there has not only been progress but also regress. The criticist tradition inaugurated by the Presocratics was soon replaced by the essentialism of the Platonic Socrates; and, later on, tolerance has again and again been replaced by intolerance.[7] After the Fall of Rome followed a stagnation of about 1000 years. (Later on I will return to some disquieting similarities between the situation at the time of the Fall of Rome and in contemporary Europe.) As Max Weber has explained, *Protestantism* provided a religious legitimation of an ethic of achievement. This development within the Christian tradition was very important for the development of Western civilization. However, its influence was limited to a certain period, and there have been other sources of psychological motivation directed to achievement in addition to religious sources (Albert 1986, p. 26).

4.2. The Philosophical Base of the Free Society: The Criticist Tradition VERSUS Justification Philosophy.

The best articulation of the criticist tradition so far we owe to Karl Popper. The core of the criticist tradition or critical rationalism and hence of the *epistemological* base of the free society is *fallibilism* — i.e., the recognition that our methods of ascertaining the truth value of a statement, or the merit of a viewpoint, are necessarily fallible — in combination with the claim that rational theory preference is nonetheless possible, even if such an appraisal of the comparative scientific merit of two rival theories, viewpoints, criteria, *etc.,* also must remain in principle fallible, and hence revisable (for an overview see, *e.g.,* Radnitzky 1988). The classical tradition in epistemology, which even today is the dominant tradition in academic philosophy, is *justificationist philosophy.* It is guided by an ideal of knowledge according to which a statement should be accepted if and only if its truth value has been established, *i.e.,* if it has been demonstrated that it is true. This requirement is modeled on the idea of mathematical proof. Justificationist philosophy conflates and confounds truth and certainty. Thereby it creates a *dilemma:* either truth claims can be ultimately justified, or genuine knowledge is impossible. That dilemma cannot be overcome in the justificationist context. It can be overcome only by abandoning the quest for certainty, *i.e.,* by adopting the maxim to hold all positions (statements, viewpoints, criteria, and so on) open to criticism — including this maxim (Bartley 1962/1986, Radnitzky 1987a).

The dilemma that confronts justificationist philosophy in epistemology has an offshoot in ethics in the alleged dilemma: either substantive moral judgments and norms can be ultimately justified, or nihilism must be accepted. This dilemma can be overcome by an application of the criticist philosophy: fallibilism combined with the possibility of cognitive progress. From pervasive fallibilism it follows that an *ultimate* foundation of a value judgement or a moral norm is as impossible as giving a proof for the truth or for the falsity of a descriptive empirical statement. Since rational theory preference is possible in spite of fallibilism, critical discussion of fundamental *(i.e.,* noninstrumental) value judgements or norms appears to be not only possible, but, if we are to act morally, necessary (Popper 1945, Andersson 1984a). Critical rationalism also stresses that it is an individual who adopts values and sets himself aims, not society; and that the ultimate values adopted by an individual are solely his business and his responsibility, not that of "society".

The dilemma that the justificationist philosopher faces in epistemology has an offshoot also in political philosophy in the alleged dilemma: either we adopt a politics of goals with a view to realizing a common aim, or anarchy will reign — by implication, "either a politics of goals, *i.e.,* a paternalistic, interventionist state, or anarchy". This dilemma can be overcome with the help of two insights, which we owe to Hayek.

1. Hayek showed that the market order makes possible the evolution of an "extended order", an order which extends peaceful cooperation beyond the boundaries of the small group or the tribal horde, and thus enables us to transcend what we perceive: to transcend our experience of people and circumstances with which we are acquainted. When personal exchange has been replaced by impersonal markets, a special order has been brought about by many individuals, who need not, and normally do not, know one another but who, nonetheless, benefit from each other's effort in spite of differences in their several aims, and often even because of such differences (Hayek 1976, p. 110). People can now cooperate peacefully *without* having any common purposes, apart from the purely instrumental aim to secure the formation of an abstract order that will enhance for all the prospects of achieving their own (individual) aims.
2. The second insight is that, in history, the spontaneous evolution of order has been, by far, more important than "instinct" and design taken together, that the most important of the social patterns we see around us can be explained by the "invisible" hand. Moreover, it can be shown that a politics of goals is bound to have totalitarian implications (*cf.*, *e.g.*, Brunner 1986).

4.3. The Image of Man and the Conception of the State.

The present controversy about the proper role of the state and the proper relationship between individual and state can be traced back to two opposing traditions of thinking about man and the fabric of society: the Scottish moral philosophy of the 18th century, and the tradition that emanated from the French Enlightenment (Brunner 1983; 1985; Brunner and Meckling 1977). The Scottish tradition of economic analysis and philosophical anthropology sees man as a chooser: as a search organism responding to incentives and engaging in rational problem solving. Man wants to improve his lot under the constraints facing him; he recognizes that all resources are scarce, above all his time, and that he has to act on imperfect and incomplete information (fallibilism). The "Scottish" model emphasizes the uniqueness of each individual.

The image of man that grows out of the French tradition, the so-called "sociological man" model, sees man basically as a rule follower. Man plays social roles; he is infinitely malleable, and hence, in an important sense, a product of his environment. According to that model it is therefore possible that, after successful indoctrination by "socialist" institutions, self-seeking man can be replaced by "political" man. Planners and politicians thus "educated" or "re-educated" would act in accordance with what they perceive to be the public interest, in spite of changes in the incentive structure; and they would do so even if it is detrimental to their self-interest. This model of man has inspired the three great socialist revolutions: the French in 1789, the Russian of 1917, and the German in 1933 (Kuehnelt-Leddihn 1985). The contemporary public-interest theory of government behavior is based on that conception of man.

These two models of man provide the basis for competing theories about the evolution of human society and the functioning of social organization. The Scottish tradition with its model of man as a "resourceful, evaluating, and rationally-behaving" being explains how our most important social structures emerged or evolved as unintended consequences of the actions of individuals who pursued their own interests. It supplies the descriptive part of what has become known as the "Economic Approach" to human behavior *(cf., e.g.,* Radnitzky and Bernholz 1987). The model has also helped us to recognize that the wealth of a nation essentially depends on its human capital, including its epistemic resources, and that therefore those institutions are wealth-creating which facilitate the improvement of human capital. The model can also explain why the "sociological" model of man — man as a rule follower — has a particular, limited realm of applicability where it can provide good explanations and testable consequences, *e.g.,* conduct in the tribal horde, in a society governed by tradition, or in a social institution governed by strict conventions and rituals.

The French tradition of sociological analysis claims that the most important of our social structures are the result of collective actions directed to bringing about these structures. It serves as the basis of a tradition of thought that combines a romantic picture of a self-denying politician, who is whole-heartedly devoted to what he perceives to be the public interest, with a hubristic belief in the capability of government to acquire and handle the knowledge necessary to shape economy and society to its benign purpose — what Hayek has recently labeled *'the Fatal Conceit'*. The "socialist" tradition that grows out of the French enlightenment succumbs to the justificationist dilemma in political philosophy: either a politics of goals, or anarchy. *The politics of goals* works with an end-state principle of justice (as Karl Brunner calls it); it is a secularized counterpart of the doctrine of salvation: redemptive egalitarianism in this world. The end-state that the socialists have in mind is "social justice" conceived under the egalitarian paradigm. It is the official aim in the Marxist-Leninist doctrine of salvation, and in the Protestant secularization of the Sermon on the Mount, and it also underlies the concept of *"Volksgemeinschaft"* of the National-Socialist German Workers Party (in the 1930's admired by Swedish socialist thinkers like Gunnar and Alva Myrdal). Historical examples demonstrate what an economic analysis with the help of the "Scottish" model suggests: that the institutions required for implementing a politics of goals are necessarily wealth-reducing or poverty-creating. Increased state activity, which is required to implement a politics of goals, must lead to a persistent shrinkage in the choices available to the individual. Contemporary Sweden is a choice example of such a development in a full democracy.[8]

Adam Smith pointed out that we would do others more good if we behave *as if* we were following our self-interest, rather than pursuing altruistic purposes. From Hayek's analysis of the market order as a discovery system, it follows that even in a community of pure altruists — if that community is larger than a face-to-face group — people would produce the best situation for all by behaving as if they were following their self-interest. This is so for epistemic reasons, because the market order is the only efficient mechanism of collocating relevant knowledge and decision rights. Politicians who honestly intended to serve the public interest and did so by fostering governmental intervention, would be "led by an invisible hand to promote" some special interest group —

"which was no part of their intention" (Friedman 1986, p. 138). It follows that, if the aim is the well-being of the individual citizen (chosen at random) — their wealth and their freedom — *a society is better off with a minimal government than with a Big Government, even if the government honestly intends only to serve the "public interest"*, to do good, and to make people "happy". In politics, the wish "to make people happy" appears to be the most dangerous of all possible points of departure. Thus, it transpires that the issue at stake is "the free individual *versus* interest groups" or "the protective state *versus* the re-distributive state". Since — as we have learned from Karl Brunner — every political structure is a mix of protective and distributive features, the scope of constitutional protection locates the individual on the freedom-slavery spectrum (James Buchanan). Leftists often deride the libertarian ideal of a minimal protective state as "the night-watchman state". However, the protective state can function only if it is very strong. Considerable resources and effort are needed to protect the citizens' freedom and private rights. Only a strong state has the capability to defend itself against outside challengers; and only a strong state can effectively guarantee security in daily life, and can, among other things, effectively protect citizens, against criminal attacks on their persons and property. Hence, it is absurdly false to equate the minimal protective state with a weak or powerless state.

While the nineteenth century was the century of private rights, a century that emphasized the protective aspects of a state, the twentieth century has seen the cancerous growth of the redistributive welfare state — the impact of the perception of man and the conception of government which have grown out of the French Enlightenment. The rhetoric of the statists claims that the state is an instrument of progress — a claim that presupposes constructivist rationalism. The statists embrace the public-interest view of government. Hence, they cannot appreciate the two-faced character inherent in all political structures. The statist rhetoric provides the excuse for the attenuation of private property rights, last not least by the judiciary *(cf., e.g.,* the special issue of *The Cato Journal,* Spring-Summer 1986). In the United States, the Supreme

Court has eroded the line between legislative and judiciary, and has been prone to use the law as a tool to shape and reshape society — all, of course, in the name of "social justice". This goes back, to President Franklin Roosevelt's "court-packing" plan of the late 30s [*cf., e.g.*, McDonald 1987, p. 19] Instead of acting as a tribunal deciding cases according to law, it has become a super-legislature that has eroded the constitution (Dorn and Manne 1987). In this disquieting situation — with such a judicial activism — the constitution may indeed be likened to a chastity belt of which the lady herself possesses the key so that she may herself decide whether or not the temptation is sufficiently strong to warrant using the key. West Germany, too, suffers from judicial activism. The statist rhetoric also claims that such things as protectionism in economic life, state intervention in the market order, and the process of political intervention are indispensable in the service of "social justice". But there are wealth-reducing methods which emphasize the negative-sum game aspect the state. They are inimical to competition, hamper the market selection mechanism, and retard economic growth. The mirage of social justice and its concomitant rhetoric camouflages the encroachment of the state first on economic freedom and then eventually on civil liberties. Socialism as a world-wide trend of the twentieth century has been fairly successful in putting us on the *road back to serfdom.* Hayek's warning of 1944 is today as pertinent as ever.

4.4. Beside an Epistemological Base, a Substantive Philosophical Doctrine that Defends Private Rights is Needed for a Free Society.

The American Constitution is not only the first written constitution of liberty, but is regarded as a paragon. Such a constitution is the result of a long process of intellectual evolution. It is primarily the product of experience, but, nevertheless, certain publications that had influenced the thinking of the educated portion of society in Europe and America also helped the framers of the American Constitution of 1787. Russell Kirk (in 1987) points out that, at the Constitutional Convention, the framers obtained from Montesquieu a theory of checks and balances, and of the division of powers. He shows that, in contrast to what typical American school textbooks in history have asserted, it was not John Locke who influenced the signers of the Declaration and the framers of the Constitution. David Hume in his *Enquiry Concerning Human Understanding* (1748) had demolished Locke's myth of the social contract and the notion of a primitive social compact. Hume was extremely important. Kirk also draws attention to the importance of William Blackstone's *Commentaries on the Laws of England* (1765) and of his idea that "natural liberty" consists of three articles: "the right of personal security, the right of personal liberty, and the right of private property". He makes it plausible that Edmund Burke's ideas influenced the American Framers, since they took for their model the English constitution as it stood between 1760 and 1787, and these were the years when Burke loomed so large in the House of Commons (Kirk 1987, p. 14). The contributions of Western civilization to human history are primarily the order of liberty, and only secondarily material wealth. The taming of the state and the emergence of individual freedom for the ordinary man are even more important than the "taming of nature". Many economists tend to blur the distinction between wealth and freedom. For the constitution of liberty, a negative concept of freedom is indispensable. Hayek defines 'freedom' as the absence of interference by others, including the state, in particular, as "freedom from the arbitrary will of others". What is at issue is the absence of constraints that are not required to secure the like freedom of others and, ultimately, one's own future freedom.

This suggests the following definition of 'totalitarianism'. A regime is non-totalitarian to the extent to which there exist effectively rule-protected spheres within which the individual has liberty of choice and action. The socialist states exemplify totalitarianism insofar as in none of them are even the most fundamental economic and civil liberties protected and respected in the practice of the daily life of the citizen. They do not even permit persons to retain exit options — something the market always does.

The concept of 'wealth' or 'power' refers to the set of choices available to the individual because of his resources, including his abilities, technological expertise, and so on. Thus, *e.g.*, an ordinary citizen of Soviet Germany is not free to leave the country, even if he is able to do so in the sense of having the necessary financial means. He is unfree, even if he is not poor or disabled. All this shows that it is imperative to distinguish between wealth and freedom. An increase in the authority of the state to "do good things for us collectively" imposes necessarily a cost in individual freedom. (A summary of Hayek's thinking on this topic is given, *e.g.*, in Radnitzky 1987, pp. 31 ff.). The case for individual freedom, for limiting the role of the state, has been made on empirical grounds, with reference to the innovativeness and efficiency of a social order based on privacy ethics. However, for many people freedom of choice has an intrinsic value. Freedom is the shadow of serfdom; like health it is appreciated only when it is absent or threatened. The maintenance of individual freedom is a public good. Normally, an enlargement of freedom means restricting the scope of government, whenever that can be done without injury to the freedom of others and to security. A key problem of classical liberalism is how to defend private rights against the organized professional guardians of those rights *(sed quis custodiet ipsos custodes?)*. Of course, the constitution of liberty can be effective in the practice of daily life only so long as there exists enough will on the part of the citizens to defend it. It is, in this respect, much like a medieval fortress: It cannot *per se* guarantee security (freedom). If the garrison is sleepy, the fortress would not help. But normally, a garrison with a good fortress had a better chance of defending itself successfully than an army without a fortress. If one adopts a political philosophy that gives priority to liberty, to the autonomy of the individual, then the crucial test for the merit of a political system is in which of them an individual chosen at random has the best chance of achieving his unknown purposes, provided only that equal freedom is conferred upon all, *i.e.*, that the individual's aims are compatible with the prevention of infringement of the protected domain of one's fellow men (Hayek 1968, p. 13; Hayek 1979, p. 168).

5. Does Democracy Matter

5.1. Limited Government is a Predemocratic Achievement.

Erich Weede has convincingly argued that the key factor of "the European Miracle", or "the Rise of the West", was the emergence of limited government. Limited government evolved in an era of feudalism and absolutism; it is a predemocratic achievement. Weede's analysis of the European success story also shows that, for the sake of military efficiency, European rulers and elites had to involve more and more sections of the populace in military service, and that this development, in turn, created an incentive for the rulers to make various concessions to the common man, for becoming more "sensitive" to popular demands. This development appears to have prompted the first steps towards democratic institutions. Strangely enough, many educated people believe that democracy *per se* can secure individual freedom. However, democracy is not a sufficient condition and may not even be a necessary condition for individual freedom. If 'autocracy' or 'tyranny' is defined as a regime that does not need to take pains to secure the renewed approval of the governed and hence is relatively indifferent to their demands, then in such a regime the governed can improve their income only by investing in productive activities. In that situation it is not possible for them to enrich themselves through the political process (Jasay 1987, p. 325). Hence, an autocracy or tyranny is compatible with a minimal protective state, in which many spheres of activity are free from state intervention. It forces the citizens to conduct "the pursuit of happiness" outside the political process; and hence a society thus governed will be less prone to becoming a rent-seeking society than a society with a "sensitive" government. This appears to be the main advantage of "insensitivity" on the part of government. By contrast, it is unlikely that a modern democracy, *i.e.,* democracy as we are now practicing it, will *not* become a rent-seeking society. In other words, it appears unlikely that the modern democracies will advance towards the libertarian ideal of a minimal protective state in which the forces of the market are allowed more room to play and the massive apparatus that characterizes the welfare state is dramatically reduced in size, scope and power. "No such result emerges from any plausible model of the workings of democratic decision-making." (Buchanan 1986, p. 34). As de Jasay points out, the main drawback with an autocracy or tyranny is the risk that, since it can afford to disregard the wishes of the governed, it may suddenly embark on a politics of goals, and that it may be even more susceptible to this temptation than a democracy. At any rate, for most ordinary people it is by far more important whether government is limited or unlimited than whether it is elective or non-elective: Hong Kong is an example of a government that is non-elective but limited. Sweden is the choice example of a democracy with a Big Government that leaves the individual scarcely any freedom of choice; hence, it has been apostrophized as "the new totalitarians" (Roland Huntford) or *"le Goulag avec le confort"* (Thierry Moulnier). The Swedish example shows that the phrase 'elective dictatorship' is not an oxymoron.

5.2. Democracy and the "Sensitivity" of Government.

The expressions 'democracy' and 'democratization' have acquired a cloud of new semantic overtones, since they have been used as weapons in political debate and in the egalitarian rhetoric of politicians like Willi Brandt of West Germany. 'Democracy' originally means a particular kind of decision-making, which is codified in a particular kind of constitution, *i.e.*, a meta-rule for rule-making which prescribes that rules should be selected with the help of some sort of majority vote. This leaves open the way in which the democratic method is to be practiced. Hence, we have to find out whether a particular consequence of our use of the democratic method is due to a built-in characteristic of the democratic method, or to the way we have practiced that method in the case at hand. Every method has a limited realm of applicability and, normally, when a particular sort of problem has to be solved more than one method is available. Thus, the first question is: In what sorts of problem situation is the democratic decision-making method superior to methods competing with it? To clarify what is meant by 'superior', we have to make explicit the value position. If the primary aim is approximating a system that provides a maximum of freedom and wealth for an individual citizen chosen at random, in what sort of situation is the democratic method preferable to rival methods of decision making? If there are such situations, which way of practicing the democratic method is the most efficient means for achieving the aim? The economic theory of politics views democracy as essentially a vote-producing and vote-buying system, in which the politician is an entrepreneur in votes, and the voter a consumer of competitively marketed political merchandise. This means that, if democracy is practiced under a simple majority rule, the costs of effecting a particular policy would typically be those of obtaining the vote of fifty percent of the populace plus one, and rational voters would act in accordance with the perceived benefits of the handouts. In the foregoing section I proposed to regard a regime as an autocracy or a tyranny to the extent to which it can afford to be insentive to the demands of the governed. The sensitivity of government is maximal in a democratic system. Sensitivity has a positive aspect: democracy is claimed to be the only non-violent method of getting rid of a government which has not fulfilled the wishes of the governed. This is generally regarded as its decisive advantage. However, the sensitivity of government is two-faced. The negative aspect is that the more sensitive a government is, the more susceptible it is to being blackmailed by special interest groups. So long as politicians have unlimited power to enrich sectional interest groups, so long will they be tempted to buy votes with other people's money and freedom. This behavior is not only rational but indispensable for the politician's survival in the next election under the majority system. Given this way of practicing democracy, a cynic may perceive a general election as a future's market in property to be stolen. Every political structure is a mix of positive and negative sum games. If democracy is practiced in the above-mentioned way, the state will relentlessly develop into a re-distributive state, and economic and political life will concentrate on the negative-sum games. De Jasay (in 1987) has demonstrated, by game-theoretical arguments, that in any democratic system there exists a sort of Prisoner's Dilemma situation which makes it rational for the voter:

    (a) with respect to public goods to practice "free riding",

(b) steadily to demand more benefits from the state, and
(c) to practice a mixed strategy, *i.e.*, to demand benefits while at the same time demanding lower taxes.

Anthony de Jasay's conclusion is that the democratic system is *self-destructive* — I would add, at least if practiced in the way in which we are now practicing it. It has a built-in tendency towards cancerous growth of state activity. The meaning of 'self-destructive' in this context has to be clarified. I do not know whether de Jasay will agree to the following proposal. I take it that it is assumed that a regime deserves the honorary title of 'democracy' only if, in daily life, it respects individual freedom, and if the rule of law prevails. Hence, if it loses that property, it may be said to have been destroyed or to have destroyed itself, even if the facade of democratic procedure has remained intact, *i.e.*, even if the government remains elective. If so, an evaluative semantic overtone has been added to the descriptive meaning of 'democracy'. Thus, for example, a state like contemporary Sweden is certainly democratic in the sense that the government is elective. On the other hand, *de facto* Sweden has become a state where the individual's freedom of choice has been drastically restricted, as mentioned above *(cf., e.g.* Maulnier 1977, p.422; see also Radnitzky 1982, pp. 52–62 with reference to further literature on that topic). The state is formally a democracy, and the individual has the exit option (although, if he happens to possess a fortune, he has to leave it, or most of it, behind — witness the Wallenberg case); but the state decides, for instance, to which doctor he has to go, to which dentist, to which hospital, to which school his children have to go, and so forth; and the taxes and other compulsory levies are confiscatory (marginal taxes sometimes reaching 100%), so that one feels tempted to speak of a "social cleptocracy" *(sit venia verbo)* rather than of a democracy. However, most important of all, is that the Rule of Law has been completely eroded. This can be seen, *e.g.*, by the massive complaints of human rights violations *(cf., e.g.,* Sundberg 1987a, pp. 961 ff.). Sweden's Social-Democrat government has implemented the basic Marxist philosophy that the Law should not be used to protect the individual's rights, but rather should operate as the motor to move society to the ultimate end-state, namely to create the new classless society *(cf.* Sundberg 1987a, p. 968). This program is made explicit in official declarations by the government, and implemented in the practice of daily life. Hence, Sweden should qualify as an example of a democracy that has in the relevant sense destroyed itself while retaining the facade of a full democracy, *i.e.,* while retaining elective government; it has become an example of an elective dictatorship.

Strong government interference with the economy is a predemocratic phenomenon and may well survive democracy (Weede 1987, p. 7). In socialist countries, interference is so strong that economic performance is deplorable. That stultifying economic policy is followed because the socialist states pursue a politics of goals, which grows out of the "sociological" model of man, and also that the ruling class cannot afford economic democracy for it would undermine their position. However, that others are worse off than we are is cold comfort; and, moreover, here our concern is only the West. In the case of the Western democracies the cause for the rampant encroachment of the state in more and more areas of the economy and of "private space" is that the sensitivity of government has been carried to its extreme. Sensitivity will be extreme — and in consequence make the system self-destructive — if the democratic method is practiced in the following way:

1. All restrictions on suffrage are eliminated, and no account is taken of the fact that in all realms of activity, decision making requires considerable experience of life;
2. The system fifty percent plus one vote is practiced, which may invite the greatest of democratic dangers: the potential tyranny of the majority. With Burke, one may claim that the tyranny of the multitude is a multiplied tyranny.
3. Proportional representation is practiced, which allows a tiny party to function as a procuror of an artificial majority, and thereby to play a disproportionate role in politics (as, *e.g.,* in West Germany the so-called "Free Democrats" have done for decades) — a situation which is a mockery of the idea of democracy.

The growth of the franchise has given the masses the opportunity to use the public sector as a means for redistributing property rights, to their assumed advantage. If a democratic government is extremely sensitive, then a tendency towards a run-away redistributive state is unavoidable. The growth of government diminishes the everyday freedom of the individual, and also reduces the relative power of the private sector to maintain its independence and diversity: the pluralism and the freedom of economic democracy, which have produced "the European Miracle". It is bound to undermine limited government, hinder economic growth, and reduce individual freedom, and by doing so it would ultimately destroy itself.

In certain respects, European democracies appear to be worse off than democracies in other parts of the world, because, as Mancur Olson (1982) has shown, *aging* democracies suffer more from well-established special interest groups than younger democracies do. Hence, this illness or disease has been labelled 'Eurosclerosis': too much of the negative-sum games of political structures, too much of the transfer society, the bargaining society. At this point it may be permissible to draw attention to some disquieting similarities between Western Europe of today and the Western Roman Empire during the period of decay until the last emperor, Romulus Augustulus. Probably the main factor in the fall of the Roman Empire was the state of the Roman economy. In the West, a terrifying high rate of taxation was inflicted, which led to an enormous increase in bureaucracy, which, in turn, virtually obliterated the middle section of West Roman society (a phenomenon which we now could call a case of chronic "Swedenitis"). Western Rome left the defense of its borders to domesticated Teutons. Similarly, many European political parties today obstruct defense expenditures and would prefer to leave the defense of their countries to the Americans. Another major factor in Rome was the extraordinary failure of those natural allies, the Western and the Eastern Roman Empires, to cooperate in the defense against the common enemy across the northern frontiers. Future historians will perhaps regard it as equally strange that today's Western allies, facing the Soviet block, find it equally hard to unite. A policy of defenselessness is also advocated in the well-known Pastoral Letter of the United States Catholic Bishops on war and peace *(cf., e.g.,* Brunner et al. 1986; Berns 1986, chapter 3). Physical and financial wealth and civilization itself rapidly decline when the moral core of a nation withers.

5.3. The Practicality of Constitutional Reform Depends on the Climate of Opinion, and that Climate can be Influenced by Education.

Are there means of correcting the special-interest bias in democracy? Eminent economists and political philosophers like Friedrich von Hayek and James Buchanan place hope in constitutional reform. Others, like Arthur Seldon of the Institute of Economic Affairs (probably the most successful and influential institution of this kind in the world), appears to believe more in educating the public. The constitution can be a framework of liberty, but it cannot be more than a framework for rule making. Moreover, a constitution is something living, and it reflects "a political order already accepted, tacitly at least, by the dominant element among a people" (Russell Kirk 1987, p. 11). The practicality of implementing constitutional reforms depends on the existing climate of opinion. Politicians will — rationally — be unfavorably disposed to any such proposals until or unless the public is strongly in favor of them.

In the United States and in Great Britain the climate of opinion has drastically changed since the 1960s. Milton Friedman (in 1986, p. 128 f.) points out how much the intellectual climate has changed in the past quarter-century in favor of more market effective and greater freedom of choice; and he also provides many observations that support his assertion. He claims that the change was produced by experience, not by theory or philosophy: even the devotees of big government (such as Russia and China), and, in the United States and in Great Britain, the devotees of the welfare state, became disillusioned; and the ordinary man felt the consequences of the welfare state in the form of inflation and high taxes. But, as Milton Friedman emphasizes, changes in the climate of opinion affect policy only after a long delay. In my opinion, the change in the intellectual climate in the United States and in Great Britain is, to a considerable extent, due also to the success of such institutions as, in Great Britain the Institute of Economic Affairs ('IEA' for short), and, in the United States the Hoover Institution, the Cato Institute, the American Enterprise Institute, the Heritage Foundation, the Liberty Fund, and so forth. The educational task is to make explicit the costs of political democracy as opposed to the open-ended democracy of the market with a view to controlling those costs and to preventing the extension of democratic coercion to activities that can be better conducted by consent in the market and regulated by competition (Harris 1985). The above-mentioned institutions have succeeded in educating the sector of the population that is capable of learning, and those politicians who are not prevented by commitment to ideological dogma to appreciate arguments. Nonetheless Milton Friedman is right when he claims that the key factor is personal experience. Not until the fashionable expedients for inflation and unemployment, for welfare and poverty had failed, did politicians and ordinary citizens begin to recognize that the so-called "politically impossible" proposals in IEA papers were politically acceptable and even politically overdue. Education and experience worked in the same direction and reinforced each other. In 1962 the IEA stood almost alone in its courageous, principled, and ultimately effective defense of the market and a free society. Since then, the numbers of such institutes has multiplied. In the United States and in Great Britain some of the market has been restored and state interventionism reduced — even if most of us are disappointed in how limited that extent has been (Friedman 1986, p. 138).

NOTES

1. The dominant position of Europe in the international game of power was shattered only through the First World War. However, that was a world war only in the sense that at that time Europe was still the center of the world in terms of power politics. Moreover, up to WWI, Europe, apart from the technology-based approach to practical problems, had also a certain *cultural unity.* At least up to that time it was *one of the main purposes of higher education to give the upper portion of*

society a common background. This gave them similar social talents so they could get along well with each other, at least in the sense of being able to communicate with each other, at least in the sense of being able to communicate with each other even in a situation of conflict (Gordon Tullock). In contemporary tertiary education in the West, this purpose has been abandoned and with it the cultural unity has been lost.

2. It might be advisable to write *'freiheitlicher Rechtsstaat'* — although this is pleonastic — because in English texts the concept is often construed as asserting not more than the existence of an effective law (*Gesetzesstaat*). But this is just one necessary condition. In a *Rechtsstaat* the private rights of the citizen are guaranteed by the Constitution, and, to achieve this the *Rechtsstaat* is a constitutional system that incorporates federalism, separation of powers, independent law courts, and multiple checks and balances, so that the citizen is protected not only against interference from others but above all against an interference by the state that is not in accordance with the Constitution. In short, a *Rechtsstaat* means a Constitution of Liberty.

3. A fascinating illustration of the working of the three economies that, in the context of anarchy, correspond to the three options: productive activity, transfer, and defense against transfer is Kurozawa's masterpiece "*The Seven Samurais*". The village community, whose economy is based on subsistence farming, employs a group of unemployed samurais, who are paid in kind for defending them against a band of robbers, which regularly takes the major part of their harvest. These three groups exemplify the three economies that correspond to the three options which an individual has in the absence of governmental power. From our own life experience we know how the three activities interact in the context of industrialized Western democracies. The twentieth century has seen the cancerous growth of the re-distributive purpose of the state. Probably the best example in history is contemporary Sweden, where differences in factor income before taxes amount to 1:70 whereas after taxes purchasing power is equalized to 1 -2.

4. Hayek introduced these ideas in a seminal 1984 *American Economic Review* artlcie entitled "The use of knowledge", and previously in *Economica* in 1937.
5. The European experience, which begins in Roman law with its recognition of private property and of spheres of life in which the individual is protected from interventions by the state, is limited to what we now call Western Europe. Russia, where throughout its history the rule by fear was operative and the Rule of Law never played a significant role, has never had the political experience of Europe (Albert 1986, p. 18 with further references; Bernholz 1985, p. 54). It may well be that this difference reflects the heritage of Rome, which ends at the eastern border of Poland and Hungary, on the one hand and the heritage of Byzantium on the other.
6. Very likely the Roman aristocrat enjoyed more individual freedom than a citizen of what we today call a free society. However, this extent of private rights was reserved for a minority; it was not for the masses.
7. Trier may be symbolically associated with important paradigms of intolerance in European intellectual history. When in the fourth century Symmachus, an educated Roman aristocrat, appealed to the authorities that, in the name of tolerance, at least private worship of the older gods be tolerated, this plea was rejected as "empty talk of freedom and tolerance" by St. Ambrosius, who at the court of Valentinian in Trier played the role of an educated Bishop. Abouth fifteen centuries later Marx (probably the most famous son of Trier) likewise claimed to be in possession of absolute truth; and his secularized eschatology is an example of the most fierce intolerance. These two very different men had in common that they both wished *to rule out competition in the realm of ideas*. Dogmatization is the intellectual counterpart to protectionism in economics; both are an attack on competition. Each of them will hamper and eventually stop growth in the respective sphere of life. *Cf.* also (Albert 1986), pp. 23, 27, and (Albert 1986), pp. 24 and 29.
8 Sociological studies show that the latest general elections in

Sweden have been decisively influenced by the state-controlled national television. If the government can rely on the electronic media and the media enjoy a monopoly position, then it should not be too difficult for the government to influence public opinion in its favor. In Sweden the official politics of goals is "social justice" under the egalitarian paradigm. Hence, if 50% + 1 voter of the population can be convinced that they will gain by the next round of redistribution, the government will stay in office. Incidentally, the Swedish social democrats have been so afraid of the possible influence of foreign television programs that the general labor union tabled a proposal in the parliament (the *Riksdag*) that a law should be passed forbidding parabolic antennas. (*Cf., e.g.,* the article by the former parliamentary undersecretary of state [*statssekreterare*] Bertil Levin entitled "*Förbud mot antenner?*" [prohibition of antennas?] in the Swedish daily *Expressen* of 5 December 1980; see also, *e.g.,* [Radnitzky 1982, pp. 61 ff.].)

REFERENCES

Albert, H. 1986. *Freiheit und Ordnung*. Tübingen: J.C.B. Mohr.

Anderson, M.J. (ed.). 1986. *The Unfinished Agenda: Essays on the Political Economy of Government Policy in Honour of Arthur Seldon*. London:Institute of Economic Affairs.

Andersson, G. 1984a. "Creativity and Criticism in Science and Politics", in (Andersson 1984b), pp. 1-14.

Andersson, G. (ed.). 1984b. *Rationality in Science and Politics*. (*Boston Studies in Philosophy of Science,* Vol. 79). Dordrecht: Reidel.

Andreski, St. 1968. *Military Organization and Society*. Stanford: University Press.

Andreski, St. 1969. *The Uses of Comparative Sociology*. Berkeley/Los Angeles.

Bartley, W.W., III. 1962. *The Retreat to Commitment*. New York, NY: Alfred A. Knopf; 2nd ed. with 100-pgs Appendix, La Salle, IL: Open Court 1984.

Bernholz, P. 1985. *The International Game of Power*. Berlin/New

York, NY: Mouton Publishers.
Berns, W. 1986. *In Defense of Liberal Democracy*. Chicago, IL: Regnery Gateway.
Brunner, K. 1983. "The perception of man and justice and the conception of political institutions", in Machlup F. et al. 1983. *Reflections on a Troubled World Economy. Essays in Honor of Herbert Giersch*. New York, NY: St. Martin's Press, pp. 327-355.
Brunner, K. 1984. *Technological Change: Challenge and Consequences*. (*Working Paper Series*, No. GPB-84-4). Rochester, NY: Center for Research in Government and Business, University of Rochester.
Brunner, K. 1985. "The poverty of nations", *The Cato Journal* 5:37-50.
Brunner, K. 1986. "The ambivalence of political structure: Illusion and reality", in (Brunner and Wagner 1986), pp. 25-36.
Brunner, K. et al. 1986. *Economics, Theology, and the Social Order*. (*Center Symposia Series* CS-19). Rochester, NY: Center for Research in Government and Business, University of Rochester.
Brunner, K. and Heckling, W. 1977. "The perception of man and the conception of government", *Journal of Money, Credit and Banking* 9:70-85.
Brunner, K. and Wagner, R. (eds.). 1986. *The Growth of Government*. (*Center Symposia Series* CS-19). Rochester, NY: Center for Research in Government and Business, University of Rochester.
Buchanan, J. 1986. "Our Times: Past, Present, and Future", in (Anderson 1986), pp. 29-38.
Dorn, J. and Manne, H. (eds.). 1987. *Economic Liberties and the Judiciary*. Lanham, MD: George Mason University Press.
Flew, A. 1985. *Thinking about Social Thinking. The Philosophy of the Social Sciences*. Oxford: Blackwell.
Friedman, M. 1986. "Has Liberalism Failed?", in (Anderson 1986), pp. 125-140.
Gabriel, L., Radnitzky, G. und Schopper, E. (Hrgb.). 1982. *Die i-Waffen: Information im Kräftespiel der Politik*. München:

Herbig Verlag.
Giersch, H. 1986. *Liberalisation for Faster Economic Growth.* (*Occasional Paper* 74). London: Institute of Economic Affairs.
Harris, R. (Lord Ralph Harris of High Cross). 1985. *What price democracy?* (MS of a lecture given at *Centro* "Luigi Einaudi" in Torino on 6 Dec. 1985).
Hayek, F.v. 1944. *The Road to Serfdom.* Chicago, IL: University of Chicago Press.
Hayek, F.v. 1952. *The Sensory Order.* Chicago: University of Chicago Press, Midway Reprint 1976.
Hayek. F.v. 1960. *The Constitution of Liberty.* Chicago, IL.: University of Chicago Press.
Hayek, F.v. 1973, 1976. 1979. 3 Vols. *Law, Legislation and Liberty.* London: Routledge and Kegan Paul.
Hayek, F.v. 1979. *Social justice, socialism and democracy.* (*CIS Occasional Papers* No.8), St. Leonards NSW (Australia): Centre for Independent Studies.
Hayek, F.v. 1987. *The Fatal Conceit. Part One: Ethics: The Taming of the Savage.* (*The Collected Works of F.A. Hayek,* Vol. 14; General Editor: W.W. Bartley, III), London; *in press.*
Hoyningen-Huene, P. and Hirsch, G. (eds.). 1988. *Wozu Wissenschaftsphilosophie?* Berlin: Walter de Gruyter.
Huntford, R. 1971. *The New Totalitarians.* London: Allen Lane The Penguin Press.
Jasay, A. de. 1985. *The State.* Oxford: Blackwell.
Jasay, A. de. 1987. "Pour une tyrannie paresseuse", *Commentaire* 10: 317-325 (Eté 1987).
Jensen, M. and Meckling, W. 1983. *Democracy in Crisis.* (*CIS Occasional Papers M.8*) St. Leonards NSW (Australia): Centre for Independent Studies.
Kirk, R. 1987. "Burke, Hume, Blackstone, and the Constitution of the United States", in *The John M. Olin Lectures on The Bicentennial of the U. S. Constitution.* Reston, VA: Young America's Foundation, pp.17-23.
Kuehnelt-Leddihn, E. 1985. *Die Falsch Gestellten Weichen. Der Rote Faden 1789-1984.* Wien: Böhlau.
McDonald, Forrest. 1987. "Interpreting the Constitution: Judges

versus History", in *The John M. Olin Lectures on the Bicentennial of the U.S. Constitution.* Reston, VA, pp. 17-23.

Maulnier, T. 1977. *Les Vaches Sacrées.* Paris: Gallimard.

Nisbet, R. 1976. "The fatal ambivalence of an idea. Equal freeman or equal serfs", *Encounter* 47:10-21.

Nisbet, R. 1986. "Roosevelt and Stalin (I): The infamous courtship of a patrician and a revolutionist", *Modern Age* 30:103-112 (Spring 1986).

North, D. 1981. *Structure and Change in Economic History.* New York, NY: Norton.

North, D. and Thomas, R. 1973. *The Rise of the Western World.* Cambridge, MA: Cambridge University Press.

Olson, M. 1965. *The Logic of collective action.* Cambridge,MA: Harvard University Press.

Olson, M. 1982. *The Rise and Decline of Nations.* New Haven, CT: Yale University Press.

Popper, K. 1945. *The Open Society and Its Enemies.* 2 vols., London: Routledge and Kegan Paul; 11th ed. 1977.

Radnitzky, G. 1982. *"Die Unfähigkeit zur ideologischen Auseinandersetzung"*, in (Gabriel *et al.* 1982), pp. 10-90).

Radnitzky, G. 1985. *"Sul fondamento epistemologico della filosofia della societa aperta"*, in (Ricossa e di Robilant 1985), pp. 21-49.

Radnitzky, G. 1987a. "In defense of self-applicable critical rationalism", in (Radnitzky and Bartley 1987), pp. 279-312.

Radnitzky, G. 1987b. "The constitutional protection of liberty", in Butler, E. and Pirie, M. (eds.). 1987. *Hayek on the fabric of human society.* London: The Adam Smith Institute, pp. 17-46.

Radnitzky, G. 1987c. "An economic theory of the rise of civilization and its policy implications: Hayek's account generalized", *Ordo* 38 (1987), *in press.*

Radnitzky, G. 1988. *"Wozu Wissenschaftstheorie? Die falsifikationische Methodologie im Lichte des Ökonomischen Ansatzes"* in (Hoyningen und Hirsch 1988), *forthcoming.*

Radnitzky, G. and Bartley, W.W., III. (eds.). 1987. *Evolutionary Epistemology, Theory of Rationality, and the Sociology of Knowledge.* La Salle, IL: Open Court.

Radnitzky, G. and Bernholz, P. (eds.). 1987. *Economic imperialism: The Economic Approach Applied Outside the Field of Economics*. New York, NY: Paragon House Publishers.

Regnery, H. 1979. *Memoirs of a Dissident Publisher*. New York and London: Harcourt Brace Javanovich.

Ricossa, S. e di Robilant, E. (eds). 1985. *Libertà, Giustizia e Persona nella Società Tecnològica*. Milano: Giuffrà Editore.

Stigler, G. 1979. "Why have the Socialists Been winning?", *Ordo* 30:61-68.

Sundberg, J. 1987a. "Human rights in Sweden: The Breakthrough of an Idea", *Ohio State Law Journal* 47:951-983.

Sundberg, J. 1987b. *Human Rights in Sweden*. Littleton, CO: Fred B. Rothman & Co.

Tamari, M. 1987. *'With All Your Possessions'* : *Jewish Ethics and Economic Life*. New York: Free Press.

Topitsch, E. 1985. *Stalins Krieg. Die sowjetische Langzeitstrategie gegen West als rationale Machtpolitik*. München: Olzog Verlag.

Trapp, P. 1987. "West Germany's Economic Policy: What Direction?", *Cato Journal* 6:837-850 (Winter 1987).

Tullock, G. 1987a. "Autocracy" in (Radnitzky and Bernholz 1987), pp. 365-381.

Tullock, G. 1987b. *Autocracy*. Dordrecht: Nijhoff Publishers.

Vaubel, R. and Barbier, H. (eds.). 1986. *Handbuch Marktwirtschaft*. Pfullingen: Neske.

Weede, E. 1984. Democracy, creeping socialism and ideological socialism in rentseeking societies", *Public Choice* 44:349-366.

Weede, E. 1987a. "From 'the rise of the West' to 'Eurosclerosis': Are there lessons for the Asian-Pacific region?" *Asian Culture* 15:1-14.

Weede, E. 1987b. "Ideas, ideological basis and political culture as the mainsprings of politics", in manuscript; *forthcoming*.

"THE EUROPEAN MIRACLE": EUROPE AS THE EXCEPTION AMONG THE ADVANCED CIVILIZATIONS IN HISTORY

Ljubisa Rakić

With refined criticism, Prof. Gerard Radnitzky introduces us into the world of modern Europe via its past in an inspired, appropriate, wise and engaged manner, revealing the roots of Europe, which should explain how it happened that it became the forerunner of the most prosperous civilization in the modern history of mankind, without despotism which used to accompany the progress of each previous civilization. Only a half millennium ago, European civilization was behind China and India, to become, already at the beginning of this century the leading civilization of the world. Attributing only features of Western civilization to the whole European civilization, the author points out that its inclination towards solving practical problems, including both social and political ones, has been crystallized in the course of cultural evolution. Indicating the importance of Rome for the development of European civilization, the author accentuates the significance of historical and cultural roots of this ancient civilization and its inheritance for conceptualizing and expressing essential characteristics of European (Western) civilization, which he opposes to Byzantine influence. However, the author adds other more specific and significant characteristics to these fundamental ones, related to European soil, climate, geology and, especially, the permanent fragmentation of political power, which has led to competition among the subjects of political power within a nation, European pluralism, *etc*. The most important part in this article is undoubtedly its interpretation of the philosophical basis of a free society: the tradition of criticism *versus* justification in philosophy, which the author elaborates competently in the light of numerous modern philosophical postulations. It also applies to problems of democracy, its current status and future. Dr Radnitzky generally follows the European tradition of decentralization and pluralism in the best possible manner. He perceives the tradition as the solution for the preservation of European civilization, for which the future decision makers should be permanently educated.

The authors mechanistic approach to the spreading of European civilization into other countries is an inferior part of the article, and it probably resulted from political pragmatism more than from scientifically documented attitudes, since it is difficult to accept the logic of the author's attributing European civilization to countries with a completely different cultural background, such as Japan, Korea, Thailand, or Singapore. As to the United States of America taking over European civilization this is more firmly based, since American civilization was formed as a direct European offspring. Supporting the basic postulates offered by Prof. Radnitzky related to the problem of the rise and decline of Europe, I would like, as a physician, to accentuate the position and role of human personality in these trends. Decentralization with a purpose of attaining social harmony and welfare on higher levels of association does not only characterise social communities, but primarily each human being: an individual, and his psychical and social welfare. This is the function of human personality in creating and developing modern civilization in the context of the permanent promotion of individual freedom in accordance with biological, psychological, and social characteristics of optimal expression of his democratic liberties and, consequently, some health aspects of human rights. In the context of individual, cultural, and political interactions among people from different meridians, besides general principles of human freedom, differences related to geographical features should also be comprehended and understood. The basic question that arises is: What is a man; what do we know about his nature, his contradictions, capacities and limitations; his rise and fall, magnitude and tragic qualities; ideals and flaws? What is today, in what time do we live, in what world? What is it that enables us to produce tomorrow based on today, and how can we understand what happened yesterday? What is it in the present that we can change according to our vision of future and knowledge of the past?

Owing to his technical knowledge, man quickly increases control over natural forces and is on a fair way to get free from hunger, various diseases, poverty and natural catastrophes. The level of real political freedom has significantly increased simultaneously with expansion of literacy and elementary culture, especially related to the development of gigantic means of communication. After the Second World War, the world system of colonialism collapsed. Dozens of Asian and African peoples successfully attained national liberation, and became active participants in international politics. Our century witnessed extensive emancipation of women and young people from patriarchal restraints. But at the same time, man experienced an apparent loss of interest for some forms of freedom which once were of primary importance. Numerous nations which have only in this century entered history, or returned to it, encountered an alternative: political democracy of a civil type in conditions of private proprietors' economy, or some of the varients of a socialist way with nationalization of the means of production, central planning, state strengthening, insisting on discipline and loyalty to the common aim, and unavoidable suppression of personal liberty. It turned out that the masses are far more interested in material goods than in political and other freedoms. Freedom that does not bring along other values but offers only the strain of decision-making and the unpleasant burden of responsibility does not appear all that attractive to the masses as theoreticians of liberalism would like to believe. This situation, however, comprises a permanent risk of establishing political and economical tyranny. Indeed, the twentieth century generated a group of "leaders" that are among the greatest tyrants in the history of mankind. A philosopher should be intrigued by the fact that the masses in these countries peacefully witnessed the extermination of hundreds of thousands of their countrymen, and that a decisive impulse of the masses to prevent such terror has never been noted. Now, apart from poets and philosophers, a man is still mainly a being highly appreciating only some forms of freedom, and even those under certain conditions — at least in some parts of the world. Nevertheless, even when he appears more free, a man is not so in numerous aspect — for he is finite, limited in his capacities and in the time and energy available. A man of today, for example, has surrounded hiself by miscellaneous devices in order to become free: for manipulating all kinds of mechanisms, for rapid transfer in space, for launching new projects, for all kinds of new forms of organized leisure. He simultaneously lost his freedom for love, natural beauty, rearing of his children, and contemplation of himself and his primary aims and values.

After all these words, a question arises: shouldn't we be surprised that the unanticipated sparkles of rationality were not more numerous, instead of our amazement at their sheer occurence, since the twentieth century, on the other hand, has brought about unimagined eruptions of human irrationality — eerie both in character and extent. The man of the last decades of the nineteenth century, who believed in permanent peace and progress, in spite of all local disagreements, must have considered the First World War a mass insanity. The insanity appeared the more inexplicable since it affected even the progressive forces in which some level of basic rationality was presumed *a priori*. International intellectual cooperation that had been built for decades was destroyed in a moment by the fury of the meanest chauvinist passions. The Second World War brought even more bloody outcomes. Nationalism was accompanied by racism, unheard of in history for the kind and extent of its crimes. This war brought also moments of triumph of human solidarity and heroism in the struggle against evil. But the question remains: How could evil be so great? How was it possible that all nations with blind devotion and fanaticism strived for completely irrational aims and eagerly used irrational means to reach them? Are the people of these nations characterized by different biological and psychological structures? Or are there some real capabilities of human beings in question, manifested in certain historical conditions, for which each individual is at least partially responsible, since it could have been different? Should we, then, strive to completely eliminate human irrationality, promoting men who will neither judge nor act before critical consideration and defining of the issue in question? We are faced here with antinomies established by anthropological thought which are only an expression of existing contradictions of human nature. Man is both cerebral and sensitive, capable of the most abstract meditations in thought, as well as more concrete and intimate experiencing of fellow-men. The majority of philosophers point out only a pole of these antinomies. We, therefore, encounter overaccentuated rationalism and intellectualism on one hand; mystic intuitionism, and romantic protest against reason, the philosophy of life and existence, on the other. Modern technical civilization has brought along new forms of human alienation. Serial, scientifically organized production reduced the possibility that the producer could find his human purpose in the work itself. The discrepancy between his intentions and accomplishments, initiative, and routine, has became larger than ever. The activities of immediate producers have lost all traces of creativity.

The liberated times failed to help men become free, owing to the promoting of artificial human needs — the cheapest forms of entertainment, increasing the quantities of all kinds of commercial goods. These goods are not only alienated from man in the sense that he has lost the power to control their production and exchange — they start ruling over man since he is subjected to a kind of compulsion to buy even when he actually does not need it — sacrificing other life opportunities (the consumatory society). Gigantic means of modern communication produce a mass culture which, although it provides first contacts with science and art for many, is usually shallow, directed to *kitsch* and surrogate goods, sometimes with destructive effect on the most primitive and uneducated layers of society. More than ever, these colossal means will be used not only to inform, but to disinform — they will be able to connect and unite one man with another, but they will also be used for inspiring hatred towards ones fellow-man. Need for a more rational, organized administration over things and human activities has led to the generation of huge institutions: state, party, and other social systems which promote creation of a special type of man, the so called organization, operator, or ruling man, striving to identify his being with his function, for whom power over people becames the basic value, who does not see an integral human being in his fellow-man, but perceives only a possible means for accomplishing his operational interests. Generally speaking, in a highly developed industrial society a tendency of natural, amiable, noncalculated relations among people to disappear is quite obvious. When the ideology of success has taken root, and when possession of as many commercial goods and as much power as possible has become the measure of success, alienation from other people becomes unavoidable. Friends are now people with whom the exchange of goods and services is done. Everybody has a lot of friends — and maybe not a single true one! It is a simple fact that a man, owner of his car and house, in search of a better place to live and higher wages — commonly lives far from all the people he cares for, and his social contacts become restricted and formal.

Another problem arises — the relationship and balance between the individual, and general values and interest. Who is the one to define general interest; how is an individual supposed to know what is the general interest? In a strictly centralized society, an individual is faced with a specific state-party apparatus claiming to speak on behalf of a society as a whole. The attitude of an individual will depend on his conviction that the single center of power is the true representative of the society, or he will continue to suspect that it is only a group of bureaucrats with particular repressive interests. The moral situation of an individual is relatively simple in that respect. In a partially decentralized social community, however, where competition, initiative and relative freedom for resistance to central representatives of power do exist, an individual is faced with a series of centres of power — from local to federal — all claiming to act on behalf of the society, but which confront each other to a greater or lesser degree. The question what is the social interest cannot be answered by a simple acceptance or rejection of the official line of the central bodies. No single central line can be discerned, occasionally. The dogma that the highest authority is always right, has been rejected. More and more an individual is forced to find out what the general interest is. Without it, he cannot decide either what should be supported, or what should be resisted and opposed. Moral dilemmas, therefore, remain permanently unsolved. In the creation of integral human freedom, the important prerequisite for its realization and affirmation are the health aspects of human rights, as the condition for the adequate adjustment of an individual to his living environment. The adaptation of human beings to the constantly changing conditions of the environment represents the great problem facing the humanity of our time. Different professions in social and life sciences — the psychologists, the economists, the sociologists, and the physicians, carry the most important responsibilities in protecting and guiding the individual, the community, and the society as a whole — to help the people adjust to their environments, including the environmental fact of constant, profound, and all-inclusive change. It includes proper adjustment to the changes in the physical, psychological, and social environments. All these adjustments require a development of special conditions for detection, treatment, and investigation, as well, of new disorders which represent a specific response of the organism to the novel noxious agents (maladaptation disorders, genetic, psychosomatic, malignant diseases, *etc.*). In the pursuit of these goals and the creation of effective functioning of the system, broad cooperation on the national and international levels represent a *conditio sine qua non*. Cooperation in the broadest way, as from a philosophic and humanitarian point of view, would help very much in solving many of the open world problems in this field. Unfortunately, today they do not exist in an optimal condition for this cooperation: we have based our modern societies on competitive rivalry, rather than cooperative association. Competition in its industrial, commercial, and nationalistic manifestations has stimulated a material progress, but at the same time carried to extremes all the worst elements in human nature. As a basic operating principle for society, competition is not acceptable because it is not ethical, and because in the long run it is self-defeating. Cooperation exercises those human qualities that are in accordance with the moral law, and it is as wise as it is virtuous.

Without going into great detail, I shall only point out some of the aspects of health as a human right. When referring to health as being a human right, it is essential to consider what is the exact significance of this right, what it involves, and what is its true perspective, while avoiding as far as possible the study of the problem as an abstract concept. It must be demonstrated that the right to health has obvious limitations, and it will likewise be necessary to show in the light of advances in biology, medicine, and science, what benefits and what parallel potential risks new developments may entail as far as the right to health and, possibly, other rights are concerned. Historically, and in contrast with the early introduction of a number of other rights, the right to health was one of the last to be proclaimed in the constitutions of most countries in the world. There are no references to the right to health in eighteenth and nineteenth century constitutions, whereas a number of other rights are specifically mentioned. At the international level, the Universal Declaration of Human Rights established a breakthrough in 1948, by stating in Article 25:

1. Everyone has the right to a standard of living adequate for the health and wellbeing of himself and of his family including food, clothing, housing and medical care and necessary social services and the right to security in the event of unemployment, sickness, disability, widowhood, old age or other lack of livelihood in circumstances beyond his control.
2. Motherhood and childhood are entitled to special care and assistance. All children, whether born in or out of wedlock shall enjoy the same social protection.

The Preamble to the *World Health Organization* Constitution also affirms that it is one of the fundamental rights of every human being to enjoy "the highest attainable standard of health" and that "governments have a responsibility for the health of their peoples which can be fulfilled only by the provision of adequate health and social measures". The right to health must also be considered from an international point of view. It is clear that countries have a duty to protect their citizens from communicable diseases, dangerous drugs, and pollution originating in other countries, as well as their own. Various international agreements have been reached in an attempt to secure such protection, examples being the International Health Regulations, the Single Convention on Narcotic Drugs

(1961), the Convention on Psychotropic Substances (1971), and the International Convention for Prevention of the Pollution of the Sea by Oil (1954). The right to health has to be considered in relation to a number of other rights, such as the right to food, clothing, and housing and the right to freedom and privacy, and consequently one may state that in particular circumstances specific human rights may sometimes conflict with one another. In a number of situations, the right of health may involve a number of obligations that may entail limitations of personal liberty. This is the case where, for instance, such measures for the control of communicable diseases as quarantine or vaccination may be considered as constituting an infringement of personal liberty, but must be accepted for the sake of the protection of the community. The right to health may thus involve duties to preserve the general welfare and the rights of the community, duties that may override the rights of the individual citizen. Moreover, because of differences in standards of living and economic and educational conditions, the attainment of the right to health may vary considerably. If all the factors that may influence legislative provisions dealing with health protection are studied, it is clear that differences exist owing to factors other than the level of present scientific knowledge. These include religious, moral, ethical and traditional attitudes that differ from country to country with respect to matters such as abortion, sterilization, and contraception, although such attitudes may well change in the course of time. While advances in biology and medicine may promote the attainment of the highest possible level of health and, thus, benefit to mankind, a number of examples in this study will illustrate how they may sometimes involve a risk to the physical and mental aspects of the right to health. Furthermore, the benefits of recent discoveries in the medical field may still be limited to a few persons. A number of reasons may explain why a general application of the benefits of such discoveries is not feasible, and why stringent selection of beneficiaries might be necessary even in highly developed countries — obvious examples being renal dialysis, and organ transplantation. The cost of equipment, other financial constraints, and lack of highly skilled personnel may constitute powerful barriers to the exploitation of new medical discoveries.

In summary, there exist, in the field of human rights and health, positive aspects which the State and the community have a duty to ensure that the individual citizen benefits from, but those rights may entail negative elements in that the individual citizen has the duty to limit his right to freedom for the benefit of the community, as in the case of pollution and immunization. There can be no doubt that further ethical problems will emerge as progress continues in medicine and biology, and that these problems will affect an increasing number of countries.

COMMENTARY ON PROFESSOR RADNITZKY'S PAPER

A. Shtromas

My first problem is with the so-called economic approach. I have grave doubts about it. It seems to me that, to sum it up, Professor Radnitzky says that the most conspicuous feature of the European miracle is the economic success of those nations who have adopted the western approach, and only then mentions the fact that these nations allow relatively more individual freedom or private rights than other nations do. So, the economic success is the core, the basic attractive feature of the European miracle. It seems to me, however, that exactly the opposite is true. The basis, the foundation for that economic miracle consisted, first of all, in the amount of rights, the private rights the people acquired in European societies. The economic miracle was the result of these rights, not *vice versa*. The amount of firm guarantees for personal success, which they struggled for and received, encouraged the Europeans to engage in all sorts of productive activities, including economic ones, and create the free market, not only for commodities but also for ideas and cultural and spiritual values. It seems to me that the position, which also was emphasized by Professor Rakic, according to which people are more interested in material well-being than in freedom, is not entirely right. People actually look for a good life, which also includes their material well-being, but which in the first place enables them to live in a meaningful way — in a way in which their personal contribution to life could really make a mark: leave a lasting trace. I think that is what human beings are seeking, above all. They want to be able to exercise some real influence, as individuals and in groups and thus to acquire both respect and self-respect. I would say that the concept of a good life is the central one here, and, first of all, consists in spiritual comfort (impossible of course in conditions of poverty), rather than material wealth. Material wealth following from such comfort, is a bonus result of it. Just take an example. The French Republican order, after many squabbles, was finally consolidated by 1875 with the adoption of the Constitution of the Third Republic; and who agreed about that republican arrangement? The monarchists. Everybody who authored that republican French constitution was, practically, a monarchist. But since one group among these monarchists was legitimist, the other Orleanist and the third Bonapartist, they could not agree on any other order than the republican one with which they all disagreed but which provided them with the only consensus-based compromise. They found that the democratic republic accommodated them all with their own preferences, views, and allowances for further continuing the debate as equals. And that was a sufficiently comfortable arrangement for all of them. The fact that this arrangement would also produce some economic benefits was not known at that time. But it produced them indeed. In 1875 France was a rather poor agrarian country with a militaristic bias fostered by the Napoleonic tradition, and then it quite quickly became a wealthy country which naturally assumed the function of the banker of the world, beating England at its own game. To sum it up, my suggestion is to overcome the narrow horizon of the economic approach and enlarge it to the concept of a good life, which includes spiritual comfort in the first place, and that means personal and collective liberties and rights; tolerance, coexistence and cooperation in a pluralistic society; meaningful participation in government and equal justice for all.

The second doubt I have about this paper has to do with the opposition it propounds between limited government and democracy. I do not think the two could exist without each other. I do not think that a truly limited government could persist for a long time without democratic checks and balances, without democratic institutions. I completely agree with Professor Radnitzky's thesis that limited government is a pre-democratic achievement. I do not know of any fully "unlimited" government in history except maybe for the despotisms in ancient Egypt, Babylonia and Peru. Every other government was to a certain extent a limited government as it presided over what Hegel termed the 'civil society' which, in its basic functions, was autonomous from the state and which was served by the state as accorder and protector of rights. Without a state no society could become a civil society, according to Hegel. But a state could also devour the civil society, thus becoming "less limited" or even "unlimited"; and the only reliable instrument preventing this kind of development is western liberal democracy. Of course private property, the right of ownership, is one of the major rights which create a civil society and allow it to function. Civil law is the main law, and, as long as it functions properly, any state will remain a limited one. But to effectively preserve civil law against all the attempts of the intrusive state — and each state is intrusive — to become the sole subject of that law, or, in other words, to protect the society and all its members from the state, one needs democracy. For a *Rechtstaat* without a political machinery able to protect that very *Rechtstaat* cannot remain a *Rechtstaat* for too long. So I do not see how Professor Radnitzky could separate the limited state from democracy, its only reliable guarantor. For a limited state to be secure and to be really protected, the only real mechanism is democracy.

DISCUSSION ON RADNITZKY

Anthony de Jasay

There is a misunderstanding and Prof. Radnitzky was going to get attacks other than from Prof. Shtromas. The economic approach, the expressions used, don't at all mean concern with food, concern with materialist forces. The economic approach is — its a logical term which bears the relation between ends and means. What Prof. Radnitzky is saying is that what drove the European upswing, was that law bound action gave way to purposive action, which equals the economic approach.

José Delgado

Prof. Radnitzky gives answers but also sets many questions. Freedom is not genetically determined. It is a capability that must be learned, like language, like music. Freedom depends on culture. Either in the capitalistic or in the socialistic society, people think: "we are free", but the concept of freedom is cultural, it is not genetically determined. If there are strict limitations of freedom, this is due to first expanding technology, and second to the biological limitations of human beings. We must learn freedom and therefore freedom will come from the outside, from the sensory input shaping our brains and determining the way we interpret reality and freedom itself. I think we must propose to the individual: "this is your choice".

Tamás Kozma

First I would like to raise some questions to Prof. Radnitzky. You say in your title "From Limited Government to Unlimited

Democracy." I quite understand limited government from your paper, but I cannot catch the idea unlimited democracy. What do you mean by unlimited Democracy? In your paper you summarize your ideas in this way: "the secret of the European miracle was the evolution of limited government." I feel this is a typical sentence when, to my mind, you changed the tools in aims. I think that limited government was a result of the European miracle. I think that it was a special balance of political powers.

Ivan Maksimović

I think that the problem of restriction of government activities is a political problem. What we have to restrict indeed, is the bureaucracy and the technique of governmental life. As an economist I cannot understand any modern society and any modern government which has no responsibility for macroeconomic life. One has to be cooperative, to work within the society in order to get a social welfare function. Also I am not in agreement with the evaluation of planning systems and planning matters in a democratic society. Planning is something which is also a result of rationalization of economic life. Modern planning is something which is very necessary. I am speaking of democratic planning, not central planning. But planning cannot evolve as a problem, as a means to which we reduce the rationality of our economic system. Today there is no market system which could work without planning. If you don't plan the system as a whole, you cannot play the game of the market. A market without planning is impossible to conceive today.

Stanislaw Andreski

I propose that the chairman provide enough time for free discussion. The worst thing is that the commentator summarizes what the speaker already said.

Andrej Werner

I think you know that Prof. Radnitzky left us a lot of place for debate and discussion. We should eliminate competition to the benefit of cooperation. I think, that we should think twice about such a proposal. Coming to the other points that were raised here by Prof. Maksimović, I think that he is right, although partly. We can ignore neither the great depression, nor the rising expectation of people to increase their welfare. I like very much Prof. Radnitzky's criticism of the welfare state. He abstains from all the criticism of the state controlled economy, but I think that we could stick for the moment on the criticism of the welfare state concept. Prof. Maksimović is right, when he stresses that governments should intervene into economic life one way or another, but also that we should make it perfectly clear what that kind of intervention can achieve. What Marxist economists expected to achieve was that, just as capitalism developed the enterprise as the most perfect economic institution, they could obtain the same results through nationalization, *i.e.*, by optimizing the economic effects on the national scale. What they did was that they just killed the enterprise.

Nansen Behar

There is a sort of shift in the institutional structure of society, from some market mechanisms toward some more centralized system. After World War II, the rise of Europe was due to programming in western European countries. After that, due to some process of democratization, the market mechanism became more active. Of thinking and decisions — I am not bearing in mind the bureaucracy which is making this process a little bit insufficient — but in the future again a new wave towards centralization will occur in respect to the ecological policy, resource policy, social policy. And finally, reading the paper of Mr. Radnitzky, on one side we have limited government with limited democracy and so on. On the other side we have unlimited democracy which means market sufficiency. In reality however no pure system exists.

Gerard Radnitzky

I will reply to Prof. Rakić that competition is indispensible (discovery mechanism; selection mechanism). There is a mechanism or process in which a small number of people makes it necessary for many people to make a greater effort than they otherwise would have made; To Prof. Shtromas my answer is that limited government is the main cause of economic growth. The policy of eastern countries was that of an imitation of the successful. In their case, the successful was imitated without the imitators knowing why our people are successful. As for limited government and democracy, I would refer to page 91 where I quote Prof. de Jasay and define autocracy or tyranny of an ideal type as a regime that does not need to take pains to secure the renewed approval of a government and hence is relatively indifferent to their demands. In answering Prof. Delgado's question about freedom, I would like to refer to page 89, and say that freedom is negatively defined as the absence of interference by others, including the state: "freedom from the arbitrary will of others", freedom of others and ultimately one's own future freedom. So freedom can only come about by restraints, and exactly, your thesis is the cultural public good which has to be learned, and freedom is only possible through restriction. As for unlimited democracy I would refer to p. 92, where I quote Buchanan. The idea is that if we practice democracy in such a way that a majority becomes a ruler, we have the phenomenon of a so-called totalitarian democracy. The market order provides the goods that people want. Those who make it work cannot really explain why it does so. The central planning system does not provide the goods, but the people who operate it can easily explain its failure.

Ljubisav Rakić

I am trying to find a balance between existing possibilities in society and the position of the human being. In my approach, the human being is in the centre. I did not try to eliminate competition; competition is a very important step in the development of our civilization and will still be such in the future. I wish however to advocate cooperation as a higher level of the development of human being. It has a feeding function, it has an excretion function, it has a reproductive function, *etc*. But the opposite, too much competition, produces the most detrimental diseases of the human being. Multiplication of representation and representatives is, in many cases, followed by the reduction of democracy. This morning Prof. Werner stated that no more than 700 people can express democracy. If you have more (forum romanum or some other form), there are no possibilities for democracy, because you have to deal with a representative, but the representative, at every level, always frustrates you from a part of your freedom and your democracy. This is an important problem for the future of civilization, especially in the technologically most advanced societies.

Alexander Shtromas

My comment is addressed to Prof. de Jasay and to Prof. Radnitzky. You talk about utility as an economic approach in general terms. I disagree with that approach. I do not think it helps to answer the questions we want to understand. The approach should be broadened even beyond the Weberian scope of cultural determinism. About limited government and unlimited democracy, the problem is that there be democracy. This is far more important than whether the government is limited or unlimited, elective or non elective. As long as people want the state to regulate their lives, it is fine, let's have the consensus, provided they could revoke and change their opinion by democratic methods of election. That is what Britain has demonstrated. To Prof. de Jasay, I would like to say that for the rulers, utility is maximization of their power. It is their utility. As for competition, and cooperation, cooperation is the framework for competition. Finally, to Prof. Delgado, I would say that freedom, unlimited freedom, the will to power as formulated by Nietzsche, is genetical. What is cultural is the ability to limit and correlate one's striving for freedom with that of the others.

MAN, SOCIETY AND THE STATE: CHRISTIAN AND MARXIST PERSPECTIVES

Milan Damnjanović

The connected triad: man — society — state, belongs to and is settled in the historical *world of man* that will be interpreted in the present essay, firstly from the christian *theological* viewpoint, and then from the marxist *anthropological* viewpoint in order to show their formal congruent ideas, and also their apparently very different positions. The world of man is, of course, not to be necessarily interpreted in an anthropological sense, but the *compositum:* man — society — state, is possible only as a structure of the world of man: the point of departure is *man,* and the *state* is the formal organisation of the *human society,* but the supposition is always the being of the world. Not only an anthropological orientation, but also the supposed concept of the world — "man, this is his world" according to Marx — was the essential *constitutivum* of the marxist philosophy, long before the "world" became the "supposition of all suppositions" in modern phenomenology, in Husserl's *Lebenswelt* (world of life, *monde vécu*) or in the early Heidegger's position of *In-der-Welt-Sein* (being in the world). The triadic structure: man — society — state, resembles the triad within occidental metaphysics: man — world— God, in modern language, *anthropos — kosmos — tó theion,* in ancient Greek, *homo — mundus — Deus* in Latin. The term of departure is relative to the cosmocentric, theocentric, and anthropocentric orientation (cosmos, *Deus* and man). The meaning of 'world' is not quite the same in the different terminologies and positions: it is firstly "nature" (cosmos), then the "creation" and finally the world of man (history).

So within the given anthropological frame of the triad: man —

society — state, the first question concerns the *world* as the formal supposition of the triad, firstly as the *creation* in the theological Christian view, *mundus* as the work of *creator mundi,* and then as the *world of man* in the philosophical marxist view: man as producer of his own world (history) and not as a *creatura,* not even as *creatura creatrix,* in the Christian view. But in both world views, the possibilities of change in the world and of transformation of the world itself are accordingly assumed.

Marxist philosophy, to begin with, is essentially the theory of change or of transformation of the world, *i.e.,* of instability of meanings, values, and realities, of all historic dynamics of the world, supposing that man is the creative being *(animal creans)* able to bring changes and radical changes, *i.e.,* revolutions in world history. The Christian theological philosophy implies *formally* the same idea as the metaphysical decision concerning the creation and providential development of the world, including radical change, the *revolution,* already completed with the revelation and the appearance of Christ as the end of history.[1] To bring the *revolution Christi* in the world means the end of history, and not the beginning of "Christian history" in the supposed continuity of world history. So the revolution as a creative act belongs not to man as *creatura,* who can act only within the limits of God's salvation plan, of his *providentia,* and, *gratia.* The message of the New Testament is not a call to an historical act, but to repentance. Man is neither enabled nor authorized to bring (radical) changes in the world as creation. Finally, man has no right to creativity; it does not exist among the human rights.[2]

So the very point of departure here is the *world* (encompassing man, society and state), firstly in the meaning of the Christian supernatural *creation,* and then as the historical *world of man* produced by himself — in both perspectives the creativity *supposed* as possible, firstly as an anthropologic philosophical supposition, and then as a metaphysical theological supposition. The world as *nature* is not yet considered here, but it will be later argued that the allience between history and nature, between humanism and naturalism, is important for the recently acknowledged Marxist ecological interest.

We are coming from the central concept of 'world' englobing man, society, and state in the contrapunctual composed worldviews of Christian metaphysics and Marxist philosophy. The juxtaposition is parataxic and not hierarchically minded, not only as a confrontation of opposite positions, but also as possible dialog and cooperation in the present situation and perhaps in the next or further futures. Is the dialog in principle possible? The discussion of the three concepts 'man,' 'society' and 'state' has to be introduced methodologically by working out the extreme opposition of the Christian theological and Marxist philosophical and anthropological perspectives. The exposed contradictory meanings of 'world' in both considered world-views will be confirmed by the categorial triad to be discussed later. Moreover we have not only to make comparisons between both theories: convergent or divergent, theological and philosophical, but also to see critically the other orientations and new possibilities of thinking: the "alternative thinking" beyond both considered viewpoints, because the thinking "has to become more thinking," *das Denken muss denkender werden,* after Heidegger, or has to be reoriented, *Um-denken,* in the present situation of mankind facing the real possibility of self-destruction.

The historical origins and systematic forms, the central metaphysical or ontological ideas and basic experiences, and finally the opposite methods of the Christian and Marxist viewpoints have to be recognised methodologically, and some formal congruent points will disappear as insignificant beside the radical differences. Therefore it is quite important, in the first step, to see the apparently insurmountable distance, the very abyss between both worldviews, where no mediation is possible.[3]

The diametrical opposition, the very antitypical worldviews of Christian theocentric metaphysics and Marxist anthropocentric philosophy can be expressed as follows: theology *versus* philosophy; faith *vs.* reason; transcendence *vs.* immanence; mythic *vs.* scientific; dogmatism *vs.* criticism; mysticism *vs.* enlightment; irrational *vs.* rational; value metaphysics *vs.* the fact finding approach; supranatural *vs.* natural; eternity *vs.* temporality; providence *vs.* natural laws; indeterminism *vs.* determinism; *philosophia perennis vs.* historicism; illusion *vs.* reality; passivity *vs.* activity, revelation, and grace; providence *vs.* historical act; the engagement of man, hopeful, and optimistic, *vs.* hopeless and tragic; religious *vs.* profane (mundane); *civitas Dei,* realm of Christ *vs. civitas terrena,* realm of man; absolute faith *vs.* radical atheism; the destruction, collapse of human society, and discontinuity (the end) of history *vs.* the continuity of world history; the divine creation *vs.* creative activity of man, *etc.*

A more *ad hoc* and rhapsodic than systematically construed opposition, representing the Middle Age religious Christian worldview *versus* the New Age rational, Marxist worldview, or the "Christian world" *vs.* the "modern world", tacitly supposes the historical continuity of the world history. Nevertheless the thesis of historical continuity must be revisited here, for many reasons. The appearance of the modern world was possible just after the "break with tradition" *(Bruch mit Tradition,* are Nietzsche's words), including the Christian tradition, after the revolution of modern science inseparable from the industrial and technological revolution, and also after the social and political (French) revolution: it seems that radical historic change conflicts with the presupposed thesis of continuity. In the Christian view, "Christian history" is neither possible — the very expression is an oxymoron — nor history at all. After the end of history, the *apparition Christi* is a revolution not within the world of history as a metaphysical turn, but a total personal transformation for the *Realm Christi.* In the Marxist view, revolutions are possible as discontinuities and as dialectical continuities within history (world history). The changing of man is always dialectically necessary for the changing of the world. It seems that for the Marxist philosophy, historical changes were, one and all, after all scientific, industrial, and social revolutions in the New Age and the universe of history absolute, so that the nature of man would be radically transformed, and nature itself (the cosmos) methodically annihilated (the Fichtean *motiv* in Marx). It presupposes the turn from *prehistory* to *history* the radical change of man and his actual surroundings, so that conciliation with the existing reality was not possible, *i.e.,* no historical continuity was granted and acceptable; the proletarian revolution, introducing the new society, named 'communism' and 'socialism', was linked to Marx with the radical transformation of class society, and with the emergence of a "new man" *(der neue Mensch)*. On the other side in his dialectical, historical thinking, Marx considered humanism and naturalism in their interaction and mutual dependence, supposing Nature and the nature of man (the Schellingian *motiv* in Marx), so that an ecological perspective of Marxist philosophy became evident nowadays. But the thesis of historical continuity and also of dialectical discontinuity is in question: was the nature of man indeed enabled to survive all historical changes, even the atomic era and atomic war? After all historical experiences, each destruction was always linked with and followed by a new construction. Maybe the possibility of a real apocalypse does postulate some alternative thinking.

When one speaks about the "break with (Christian) tradition" in the modern world, it is necessary to give criteria of the "break" as a historical discontinuity. As an anthropological matter of fact, man is essentially the "being in-the-tradition" *(In-der-Traditions-Sein)*,[4] not just in the sense of conservativism: as a creative being, *i.e.*, in bringing something new in the world into being, man needs a tradition. But how is it possible, then, to "break with tradition"? The Christian world was not simply followed and succeeded by the other world in a diachronic sense, in the course of world history: Christian and modern worldviews are also and are, even now, synchronic and coexistent. According to K. Löwith, in the modern post-Christian all was Christian, and equally non-Christian, Christian in its origins, and non-Christian in the results of the process of secularization.[5] In other words, the Christian worldview was not abandoned, giving its place to the next one, but secularized.

The effect of the process of secularization was a change or shift of meanings of all categories, including the triad considered here: man — society — state. The process of secularization is conceivable within the change of the worldview, and within the social and technological change of the world in a New Age, or in other words, within the change of the cultural paradigm. For the thesis of this paper it is very important to see that the modern world is not more religious, not Christian, but throughout, profane (mundane) and progressive, yet it is a secularized Christian world. It was Marx's historical effort, and the effort of Marxist philosophy, to abolish the ambiguous situation in favor of a radical this-side and immanent anthropological perspective by redefinition of basic categories, first of all 'men,' 'history,' and 'world'. The critical triad: man — society — state was, *eo ipso,* and inevitably concerned in this project and undertaking.

To avoid misunderstandings, I have in mind Marxist philosophy as *philosophy,* not as ideology, Marx as the critic of ideology and not ideologist, and last but not the least, Marx *contra* Marxism.[6] For the, at first sight, odd idea of Marxist philosophy as a philosophy of creativity in the anthropological mind, and also for the Marxist concept of man as a creative and selfcreative being, not at all as creature, was the process of secularization of the necessary, but not sufficient, historical condition. In the same way, modern profane and mundane philosophy sees the origin of Marxism arising from the general process of the secularization of Christian culture. In the history of philosophy, the turn from Hegel to Marx, for instance, in their different interpretations of the phenomenon of estrangement (alienation), is an example of the process. In the same way, the concept of man as a creative being and the Marxist philosophy of creativity is also to be considered. In the very beginning of the New Age, it was *Nicolaus of Cusa* who conceived, still within the Christian tradition, the creative, *i.e.,* non-imitative, non-mimetic nature of the new system of technical and artistic production, anticipating modern activities in the Western world (H. Blumanberg). The great enthusiasm for the technological transformation of the modern world, the lively spirit of investigation and exploration, the ambition to be "creative", the tendency toward fullfilment in the horizon of the future, all reveal, according to Löwith, the secularized faith in creation having an imanent religious ferment, even if revelation and creation are taken only as insignificant myths (K. Löwith, *ibid.)* So in the modern worldview and, *a fortiori* in the Marxist view, creation was accepted without a Creator in the naturalistic and humanistic scientific minded-philosophy, but also in the transcendental metaphysics of subjectivity;

the goal had fullfilment in history and was also accepted without a live faith in revelation and in the next *eschaton,* and was interpreted as progress in history. So, emancipated from the Christian confession, the modern profane *bourgeois* world without a religious perspective, still depends on it. The hope for a better world, for a future realm of God, Jewish messianism, and Christian eschatology are still recognizable in secularized forms, in material production and in well being, in the idea of a general progress. The essential traits of this *bourgeois* world were a striving to gain (profit), and a will to power (according to Jacob Burckhardt), both insatiable and derived from the eschatologic hope for the last fullfilment. Christian in its origins as it was, the modern world became antiChristian in its results. The revolutionary christian culture set in motion enormous energies and creative activities in the western world; in effect, the Christian world was undermined by applying Christian principles to mundane affairs, the generative idea (S. K. Langer) of Christian culture degenerated in Christian civilization, conquering the whole world in its imperialist tendency.

The ideal of modern man in the progressive, secularized, Western world was not only to rule over *nature,* to be *"maître et possesseur de la nature"* (Descartes), to increase its knowledge, that means its power inseparable from technics and industry by modern science, but also to rule over *history;* that means over society and state within the "master culture" *(Herrschaftskultur),* over other people and cultures following the Christian order to expand the truth of revelation for a better world as the way of salvation and redemption of all mankind. No more restricted by antique cosmological metaphysics, the emancipated man in a state of modern hubris puts himself in the position of an absolute as a creative and selfcreative being, as a "root of himself" *(Wurzel seiner selbst,* after Marx). Later, still at the time of Marx and after him, *i.e.* at the end of the Modern Age, and especially in our century, it became evident that modern man, with the effects of his knowledge and power, of his absolute power, was endangered by scientific and technological progress, menaced by himself on the way to possible selfdestruction. To give a summary of the situation, there is no better formulation than the one given by the poet

Paul Valèry in the Twenties: *"On peut dire que tout ce que nous savons, c'est á dire tout ce que nous pouvons a fini par s'opposer à ce que nous sommes"* [One may say that all that we are, that is to say all that we are capable of, is, in the end, opposed to that which we are].¹¹

The process of secularization was, for Marxist philosophy, the necessary, but not sufficient condition: necessary for many reasons, all concerning the turn from the theological-minded Christian metaphysics of transcendence, to the scientific-minded anthropological metaphysics of the Marxist philosophy of immanence. But the Marxist thinking can't be reduced to a secularized form of Christian metaphysics, for instance, contrast Marx's conception of history with that of a primary state of innocence, the sinful fall of man, his redemption, and return to the eternal life.⁸ In the realm of secularization, there is no dependence of Marxist philosophy on Christian metaphysics, from which it was emancipated. Also one should not understand *Umwertung* in Nietzsche's mind as reorientation in value judgement by maintaining the same problem-level: Christian — antiChristian. Marx's thinking was *beyond* the modern Christian and antiChristian perspective, and also *beyond* the modern metaphysical and antimetaphysical orientations, just as *radical historicism (geschichtliche Denkweise)* and *radical criticism* are.

We have now to explain the meaning of Marxist historicism and criticism viewing the three categories of man — society — state also within Christian thinking, and within present day "alternative thinking".

The radical historicism of Marxist philosophy does not mean that historical relativism *(e.g.,* evolutionism) takes as absolute some relative historical phenomena, processes, or epochs. Historicism does not mean more or less the theory of absolute historical necessity or historical laws ruling the history of mankind. Speaking in positive terms, Marxist historicism is an open thinking, facing actual historical experiences throughout historical categories *(e.g.,* the category "proletariat") by maintaining in principle the "historic difference" between an act *(Handlung)* and an event *(Ereignis);* between social conditioning, economic being, and interest, and dialectically dependent, conditioned, consciousness in history. The history that exceeds all projects, all programs of man, so-called historical laws and rational predictable development, remains always an open process with possibilities of productive failure (even in the construction of socialism), and of the successful or antiproductive commitment of man as a creative being.

The apparently paradoxical position of man as a creative, and even selfcreative being must be explained, because radical Marxist historicism does not imply any form of absolutizing of the *world of history* (as for instance by *Vico* or *Hegel*) in relation to the *world of nature*. The anthropological Marxist viewpoint is not at all anthropologism, taking man as absolute in producing history and himself. Man is neither a Christian creature in his supposed extramundane civic origins, nor has he brought himself into the world as *alter deus* making history *ex nihile* in his mundane origins. With his capability to transform nature and to produce the *other, human world of history,* man belongs also to the general history of nature.[9]

It was important in my view to stress the principle of the *other* within the *one and whole world,* against the theory of the two worlds: the physical world and the world experienced by man, the world of nature and the world of history, the two worlds as the result of disintegration, and, in fact, of the lost world of modern man. Man can't abolish or leave behind him his natural suppositions nor except himself as *logos* from *physis,* as occurred in all idealist traditions, *e.g.,* with the "transcendental difference" (E. Heintel), but he is enabled to exceed his natural suppositions producing in principle *something other (heteron, allon, anderes, autre chose)* in his historical existence, and in the one and whole world. That means to be creative within the world of nature and within the general history of nature, in the imanence, and not the transcendence of the one and whole world. In this sense, I have proposed the *heteronotological viewpoint* within the Hegelian and Marxist tradition.[10]

Marxist historicism, therefore, does not discover or state "historical laws", nor authorize one to apply the laws to concrete situations *in praxi*. First it supposes as dialectical theory the inseparable connection of *theoria cum praxi*. Second, concerning as philosophical theory the whole of the world of history, history itself cannot be exhausted by relative viewpoints and interpretations and reduced to a meaning in history. The Marxist philosophy of history needs history as a science supposing the rationality of human historical existence, *i.e.,* recognizable "tendencies and latencies" (E. Bloch) of the actual historical process, but does not suppose "reason in history" *(Vernunft in der Geschichte,* after Hegel): rationality but not rationalism. Third, for the Marxist historicism, the world of history is not absolute, yet is dialectically coming from and connected with the world of nature, supposing the alliance of nature and history, of naturalism and humanism. In his early yet abandoned project of *"One* historical science" *(Eine Geschichtswissenschaft,* stressed by Marx), he overrides methodologically the difference between the natural sciences and the social sciences (humanities). The One science is, to be sure, philosophy of history, and Marx accepts *eo ipso* the Hegelian dialectical difference between *Geschichte* and *Historie,* between the objective historical fact-finding approach, and a selfreflexive considering of the world of history as whole. Fourth, the "making" of history by man in his subjectively motivated *praxis* is not at all acceptable for Marxist historicism, in spite of the Marxist concept of man as a creative being, because history itself, and the world of history goes beyond human *praxis,* and, also goes beyond the consciousness of man, his programs, theories and projects. — "they do it but they don't know what they are doing" *(Sie tun es, aber sie wissen nicht, was sie tun, Das Kapital I).* The leveling of history and *praxis* of man is the exact definition of ideology as "false consciousness" (Marx). Fifth, Marxist radical historicism postulates philosophical criteria, *i.e.,* the *essences* of considered relative historical phenomena, applying backwards to past occurences, and also forward to the future. But Marxist historicism has nothing to do with the general viewpoint and historicism of the last century, nor with essentialist metaphysics, with Platonism of any form. Essences are to be taken *ex post facto* dialectically from history itself, from the historical process, or epoch, *etc.,* just in the moment expressing logico-ontologically the entire development: in the history of organic nature, *e.g.,* the anatomy of man is the key for the anatomy of the monkey (Marx), but, also, prospective remains of man are the criterion, *e.g.*, against neodarwinism, *etc.* Capitalism and *bourgeois* society were criteria for all class-organised societies and their economics, applying back to the ancient Greek epoch, the Middle Ages and also prospectively going beyond all class existence, *etc.*

The concept of man as a creative and selfcreative being is the point of departure of Marxist historicism viewing the history of mankind as an epochal process releasing its creative potentialities in the production and reproduction of his life in the exchange of matter with nature *(Stoffwechsel mit Natur)*, in class history, and, finally, in the history of communism and socialism, *i.e.* in the abolished organised society for the sake of community *(Gemeinschaft instead of Gesellschaft)* and in the abolished state finally as a dictatorship of the proletariat for the sake of an association of free producers — under the guiding idea of the fullfiled human right to creativity at the widest democratic ground.

The Marxist philosophy representing the Modern Age and modern thinking is obviously not so relevant in its historical form as in the mentioned representative function, and moreover in its prospective value. In this sense, it may be employed as the operative criterion for the actual meaning of the (antique) Christian tradition, and also for alternative possibilities of thinking — of course, in considering the three categories: 'man-society-state'.

In a systematic shortened form I have, therefore, to show from the viewpoint of Christian metaphysics and that of Marxist philosophy as a philosophy of creativity in the anthropological sense, first the idea of man and the ideal of man as *saint*, as *creative being (animal creans)*; and second, the idea and the ideal of society as a *Christian community*, and the communist society, *viz. community (Gemeinschaft)* as an association of free producers, *i.e.* creative persons; and, third, the idea of the state as a provisional *civitas terrena* and as an eternal *civitas dei*, and as an absolute idea of a class-organised society, provisional as a socialist state to be replaced by small communities of creative persons (mentioned above).

It is not possible, of course to discuss the ideas in an historical or logically exhaustive way here, but only in a representative ideal-typical manner. To get the idea of man, *e.g.*, in the Christian tradition one does not need all known reflections *de homine*. It is sufficient to take one or two operable definitions from Thomas Aquinas, or, in the Marxist tradition, from Marx.

In his first writing, *De ente et essentia,* Thomas formulated two definitions of man, in both of which antique themes within the frame of a new philosophy are recognizable. In other writings, especially in his *Summa theologiae,* both definitions are *in actu:* the first one aims to distinguish man from other living beings, and the second to fix his place within the totality of all things, or the whole of being *(tota universitas rerum)*. The first definition, of Greek origins, *zoon lógon echon* was *animal rationale,* meaning: reasonable (rational) living being. In the definition both hemispheres of the aggregate human being are considered: the spiritual, or logoid, and the material or sensory part, as it was still put in ancient Greek philosophy on other metaphysical grounds, in its prevailing rationalist orientation. The antique Christian tradition also systematically neglected the material, sensory part, or natural existence of man, not only in the high form of Scholastic philosophy, but in all forms of Christian mysticism.

The second definition of man as "boundary *(confinum)* and horizon" had to fix the exact point of contact of both principles: of the material and spiritual one. Man is far and also near to both of them: neither angel nor animal. The spiritual principle was identified as rational, and the material one as animal. The definition had not only to confine the place of man within the all-existing, but also the position of his soul, to confine the space of his free decisions. Shortly, man is singled out and separated from all, and at the same time he is in touch and in community with all existing things. In his extreme possibility as a boundary horizon, he is enabled to conceive the All as an order, as the image of God. In modern Christian philosophical thought, man is conceived as a free being, guiding his experimental existence under the one sole condition of knowledge, that one is addressed by God.[11]

For Christian morality and humanity, the ideal man was a saint, and no longer a *wise* man, as in ancient times. The very nature of man, the twofold structure: spiritual and material, rational and animal, is denied, and replaced by the existence of a saint. The inverse is valid for all Christians, because they are not children of this world. The saint as a living paradox is beyond the boundaries of the human world as a human being, being a nonhuman being. Not *"confinum et horizon"* any longer, he belongs to the other world, in spite of his human existence. Every Christian is *potentialiter* saint, and the *imitatio Christi* the way to the realm of Christ, or to the *civitas Dei*.

Society, in the eyes of the founders of the Christian religion, was worth destroying as a natural, "this-side"–oriented material-interested form of human common life and group (social) existence: it had to be replaced by the Christian community. After the ancient *polis,* the Christian community was a new historical world: both of them as small communities in their democratic forms of life based on different grounds, were opposed to the modern (mass) society, in Marx: *Gemeinschaft* as opposed to *Gesellschaft*. The Christian community essentially had a preparatory and transitory role of guiding and ascending to the realm of Christ, to the *civitas Dei*.

So we have attained the Christian idea of a 'state' from Augustine as a *civitas Dei* at the beginning of Christian philosophy, and of the important still not-finished history, the different Christian forms of the *civitas terrena,* all of them rejected by Marx as class-organized societies ideologically justified by the Christian doctrine.

In order to focus on the tradition of Christian social and political philosophy it is perhaps plausible to consider the situation in Hegel at the end of the Christian-antique tradition, with the possibility of addressing immediately afterwards Marx and Marxist philosophy, and, finally, concluding with the alternative present day thought.

Within the system of Hegel, and in his modern philosophical language, we meet all the important Christian-antique ideas of equality and freedom, of rationality and consciousness, *viz.,* self-consciousness of man, of progress and historicity of his existence, *etc.,* on the traditional metaphysical and theological suppositions. In his doctrine of the absolute spirit *(absoluter Geist)* and in his

Science of Logic (Wissenschaft der Logik) we are, thanks to Marx, enabled to see — without the lecture of Marx it is not possible to understand and interpret Hegel — not only his logic as metaphysics, but also as *socio-logic,* not only the theologico-philosophical dialectics of the revelation, but also the dialectics of social antagonism and contradictions. Theunissen interpreted Hegel's doctrine of the absolute spirit as his "theologico-political tractatus" *(op.cit.).*

Marx carried out his "break" with the philosophical tradition in his criticism of Hegel's philosophy. At first he recognized in Hegel's *Logic* the logic of contradiction conceived as socio-logic *(Widerspruch)* in the concrete and real historical form of the class struggle. At any rate, *Hegel* knew social and economic motives, needs, and interests in the existence of man, expressing these in systematical form in his writings about society and the state, but also in his criticism, especially, of the Modern Age. In his theory of the state,[12] Hegel described the idea of the state as the "reality of the moral *(sittlich)* idea", as "substantial will reflecting on itself and knowing itself" executing the idea as something reasonable *(Vernünftiges), etc.* In present day perspective, the Christological interpretation of history as the dialectics of the revelation, *etc.,* is not important for quite other reasons. Faced with a real apocalypse, but also with a real utopia (Bloch) in our century, we must establish the positive relation between morality and politics for the first time as the historical unique "responsibility for the whole" *(Veranwortung für das Ganze,* after C. F. von Wiezsäcker).

The "responsibility for the whole" is here, of course, not intended from the viewpoint of "transcendental subjectivity", of the "great J" Fichte, nor as *cogito*-philosophy at all. But the problem of intersubjectivity and of the "social ontology" of the *cogitamus*-philosophy was performed by Hegel, according to the new interpretation of Hegel by V. Hösle.[13] Hösle revisited the central problem of the relation between *Logic* and *Realphilosophy* in Hegel. In the conclusion he stated that there is no correspondence through-out between them: logic remains a philosophy of "absolute subjectivity", whereas the philosophy of the "objective spirit" is now, for the first time, interpreted as an intersubjective process.

The "social ontology" is, of course, the matter of Marxist philosophy. But in Marx the Fichtean theme was important for his activism, for his *praxis*-oriented philosophical thought. Moreover, his apparent individualism (still in his dissertation, or later: the freedom of each man, individual freedom as a supposition of the freedom of all men) seems to deny Marx's "social ontology" or his "we-philosophy". It is only apparently so, because the point of departure in the *cogito*-philosophy remains a necessary point of departure in the *cogitamus*-philosophy as well, in the dialectical sense of Marx's thought. Formally, the same is valid for class consiousness as a form of "we-thought" conditioned by the social being. *Praxis* is, for Marx, general social *praxis,* encompassing dialectically individual *praxis, etc.*

The last point in Hegel to be mentioned here is the idea of dialectic concerning logical thought and being as absolute spirit, interpreted by Marx as the dialectics of reality, and as the logic of contradiction. It was evident for Marx's dialectics, especially of class struggle, *viz.* the struggle of social and economic interests within the class existence of mankind and the world of history submitted to the logic of contradiction. There is no "dialectic of nature"; the dialectic remains in the world of history, supposing the surrounding world of nature as partner, and the dialectical processes of the humanisation of nature and of the naturalisation of man as a human being. Therefore, the logic of contradiction is not universally valid, there are no cosmic struggles, no cosmic dialectics, there is no "brothersplit amidst the things", *pólemos,* in the Heracleitian sense as "the father of all things", as all encompassing war. Is the war indeed one of the ground-phenomena of human existence?[14] Dialectic thought was not dialectic in failing to see its own limits. Within the world of history, beyond the logic of contradiction there is "dialogic" as the *logic of mutual recognition,* there is equality of different human communities at the cosmopolitan level in the present day situation, as it was in the case of the *polits* (citizen*)* in the ancient Greek *polis.*[15] The Marxist idea of ideal man as a creative and selfcreative being (scientist, explorer, artist, *entrepreneur),* man opposed to himself, has in principle no limitations for his critical thought and for his work, save selfrestriction. Faced with possibility of a real apocalypse, *i.e.* of selfdestruction, man is directed to selflimitation, not to doing all that he can do. The ethical postulate is not to be conceived as the Christian virtue *humilitas,* nor as the antique virtue recognizing cosmic norms, but as critical insight and as a creative act of man. So man does not have to accept a situation of any form of fatalism in the present day: he does not have to abandon reason, history, and reality for the sake of new myths and new forms of irrationalism.

Beyond the antique Christian tradition of philosophy, we have to argue for the "we-philosophy" as a new form of thought, which does not replace *cogito*-philosophies, and the *I* as a point of departure, but denies the role of the *J* and its function, rejecting philosophies of unity and identity, viewing nature as a partner of man. The other and the difference (Th. Adorno, U. Guzzoni), the equality of different human communities and their mutual recognition beyond the Marxist logic of contradiction are suppositions for a new commitment in philosophy: philosophy is to be abolished *(aufgehoben)* by fullfilling it *(verwirklicht).*

REFERENCES

1. For the christologic interpretation of Hegel's philosophy of history, esp. the idea of revolution, *cfr.* Michael Theunissen: *Hegels Lehre vom absoluten Geist als theologisch politischer Traktat,* (Berlin: de Gruyter, 1970). For critical remarks on the central role of christology in Hegel in Theunissen's view, see Wilhelm Weischedel, *Der Gott der Philosophen. Gruendlegung einer philosophischen Theologie im Zeitalter des Nihilismus* (Darmstadt: Wiss. Buchgesellschaft, 1971), Bd. I, p. 312–15

2. In my contribution to the International Seminar Philosophical Foundations of Human Rights (Ankara: Hacttepe Univ., 1980) p. 79–87, "Droit a creer", I tried to give some plausible arguments for a reasonable conception of the "right of creativity". My central intention was an outline of the lacking philosophy

of creativity as the task of Marxist philosophy. For the grounds of a yet not written philosophy of creativity, for its historical and systematical foundation see the important contribution of Carl R. Hausman, "Philosophy of Creativity", Ultimate Reality and Meaning, 2 vol.1 (1979): 143–162. See also the Congres Proceedings of the IX Intern. Congress for Aesthetics, "The Problem of Creativity" (ed. J. Aler and M. Damjanović, 1980). I do agree completely with Hausman's thesis: "Within the main line of the Western tradition, creativity as a topic has not been singled out for sustained, systematic attention. With few exceptions, there are no philosophies of creativity, in either the systematic or critical forms of philosophy" (Introduction).

3. Karl Löwith, *The Meaning in History* (Chicago: Chicago Univ., 1949) and in German *Weltgeschichte und Heilsgeschehen. Die theologischen Voraussetzungen der Geschichtsphilosophie* (5. Aufl., Kohlhammer, Stuttgart 1952).

4. After Michael Landmann, *Der Mensch als Schöpfer und Geschöpf. Geschichts und Sozialanthropologie,* (Reinhardt, München-Basel, 1961).

5. Karl Löwith, *Meaning in History* (Chicago: Chicago Univ., 1949).

6. Julius J. Löwenstein, *Vision und Wirklichkeit. Marx contra Marxismus* (List Gesellschaft, Suhrkamp, Frankfurt, 1970).

7. Cited in Hannah Arendt, *On Violation* (New York: Harcourt Brace, 1970).

8. In his *History of Western Philosophy and its Connection with Political Circumstances from the Earliest time to the Present Day,* 1946).

9. *Cfr.* K. Löwith, "Geschichte und historisches Bewusstsein" in *Zur Kritik der christlichen Überlieferung.* Voträge und Abhandlungen, (Stuttgart: Kohlhammer, 1966).

10. In accordance with Th. W. Adorno and U. Guzzoni, and also with Vittorio Hösle in his new Hegel interpretation, in a few projects, first of all in the three books ed. W. Oelmüller *Kunst und Philosophie* (UTB Schöningn Verl., Paderborn, 1981-83).

11. E. Heintel in the sense of *philosophia perennis,* and in Hegelian tradition.
12. See *Grundlinen der Philosophie des Rechts,* (ed. J. Hoffmeister, 4. Aufl, F. Meiner, Hamburg, 1965; 3. Abt. "Staat" [257-59), where Hegel experssed the idea of the state as the "reality of the moral [sittlich] idea.")
13. Vittorio Hösle, *Hegels System. Der Idealismus der Subjektivität und das Problem der Intersubjektivität,* (Stuttgart: Frommann-Holzboog, Bd. I. uII., 1987).
14. *cfr.* Eugen Fink, *Grundphanomene des menschlichen Daseins,* (Freiburg München: Alber, 1979).
15. *cfr.* Heinz Kimmerle, *Entwurf einer Philosophie des Wir.* Schule desaalternatien Denkens, Germinal, Bochum, 1983.

COMMENTS ON PROF. DAMJANOVIĆ'S PAPER

Gordon L. Anderson

In a discussion of the common heritage and future of Europe, Christianity and Marxism both play a major role in shaping thought about human nature, society, and the state. Christianity and Marxism have both had their dogmatic and their open expressions, they have both existed as marginal systems of thought, and both had experience with political power. Both have also been more attractive as ideals than in their political expressions. They have also, in my judgement, expressed partial views of human nature, with Christianity focusing on the spiritual nature and Marxism on the material. This difference is particularly acute in the dogmatic expressions of these philosophies. As is the case for most adherents of one group, they tend to have stereotyped views of one another.

However, as I read Professor Damjanović's paper, I realized that many of his concerns are the same as my concerns, even though his educational background and world of thought are quite different from mine. Some of these concerns are:

1. a philosophy which promotes creativity;
2. Eastern and Western cooperation for the prevention of nuclear war; and,
3. the establishment of a positive relation between morality and politics which is based on "responsibility for the whole." There are too many stimulating issues raised in this paper to comment on all of them; I shall limit my remarks to the most basic.

A Stereotyped View of Christianity

One of my main concerns with Prof. Damjanović's paper is what seems to be a stereotyped view of Christian thought. The description of Christianity appears to be based on the 19th century critique found in the German idealists from Kant through Nietzsche (interpreted by Marxists), and, perhaps, familiarity with the traditional Catholic church in Europe. However, I would like to suggest that the German idealists have also profoundly transformed the thought of many protestant thinkers. In fact, the movement of "Social Christianity" at the end of the nineteenth and beginning of the twentieth centuries offered a de-emphasis on otherworldly salvation, and a stress on building the kingdom of God on earth. It took up many of the same issues of social justice as the Marxists; in fact, some of these Christians became Marxists. Like Marx, these Christians acted on the basis of advances in science and social re-organization based on industrialization. This movement was primarily composed of German and American protestants.

Jesus and Marx Differ on Conflict Resolution

There is one essential difference, nevertheless, that I see between Jesus and Marx. This is in their respective methods of conflict resolution. Jesus' social revolution was brought about by forgiveness and love, which melted differences between individuals. This idea is necessary when one's worldview holds all human life as sacred, and all actions accountable to a higher creative power that loves each person unconditionally.

Marx's stress on class conflict led to a social movement which justified the use of violence against an oppressor to obtain liberation. This is a natural consequence of a philosophy of human nature which places a stress on human control over one's economic destiny.

The integration of the partial views of human life of Marx and Jesus would lead to the creation of a healthier political philosophy. Marx could stand to be baptised with the spiritual view of human life which teaches reconciliation with the "enemy". Jesus, on the other hand, conscientized by Marx, could have taught physical salvation on the present earth. As a result of the partial views,

Christian Churches have been unable to escape the charge of ineffectiveness against this-worldly oppression. Marxist society, on the other hand, has been unable to fully liberate human life.

Tradition, Ideals, and Institutions

Christians cannot accept the notion of a radical severance from the Christian tradition or the concept of God, nor could they accept the notion that the founding of Marxism was an advance from *prehistory* to *history* as some Marxists believe. For Christian socialists, like Reinhold Niebuhr and Paul Tillich, critical thinking enabled the discernment between what falls into the realm of reason, and that which can only be held as an article of faith. There are, accordingly, insights from critical philosophy which could be applied equally in analyzing Marxism and Christianity. The Marxist idea of the emergence of a "new man," for example, is seen as an article of faith, and not a scientific truth claim. Rather than making a radical break from the Christian tradition, modern (as opposed to traditional) theologians would prefer to speak of *pre-critical* and *critical* history. It is maintained that essential truth, though certainly not all of the truth, about human nature, society, and the world can be obtained from pre-critical history.

Reinhold Niebuhr, in his *Nature and Destiny of Man*, stated that,

> The modern mind interprets man as either essentially reason, without being able to do justice to his non-rational vitalities, or as essentially vitality without appreciating the extent of his rational freedom.[1]

While Professor Damjanović has been careful not to ascribe reductionism or rationalism to Marx, I believe he follows a general tendency among Marxists by linking mythical and non-rational modes of thought to "false consciousness." We can see, for example, that at the end of his paper Damjanović argues that we do not "have to abandon reason, history, and reality for the sake of new myths and forms of irrationalism." While I agree with the letter of this statement, I see a danger in any conclusion that new myths and forms of irrationalism cannot contain new and useful truth. In fact, just as an artist may be able to express the spirit and problems of an age before they can be articulated by philosophers, so, too, all human beings organize and integrate their lives with non-rational modes of thought.

The idea that Marx's ideals have not been realized in the institutions created by Marxists, which seems central to Damjanović's paper, is an argument which has also been used by Christians and against Christians. A Hindu philosopher made the often quoted statement; "I can believe in your Christ, but not your Christianity." Furthermore, it is a double standard to compare the followers of one movement with the founder of another, or, in the case of Marxism, to relegate Jesus' teaching to false class consciousness because Christian institutions served vested class interests.

In my article "Ideological Convergence of the US and the USSR", I argued that "one of the major errors in Marxism and the Enlightenment in general has been the rejection of the inherited world view because inconsistencies with realities were observed."[2] Further, Marx's focus and insights were based on the human being *qua homo economicus*. While economics play a central role in human life, one cannot simply reduce all other aspects of human life to superstructure. Christianity, with its emphasis on the human spirit, is not disproved by truth about economic injustice.

Sociologist Edward Shils has concluded: "The renunciation of tradition should be considered the cost of a new departure; the retention of traditions should be considered as a benefit. In short, Marx's philosophical "break," which Damjanović wisely put in quotation marks, could not be complete, even if it were desired. People thus obtain more benefit from a transformationist, rather than a violent revolutionary approach to social change. They would both do less damage to the society, and suffer less chance of being co-opted by self-seeking opportunists.

Creativity and Christ

Perhaps creativity is an answer to Nietzsche's question of the "Why of man." Creativity is closely related to the Marxist idea of the right to work. For in Marx, the product of one's labor is a reflection of oneself. An individual receives personal fulfillment in creating. I have no quarrel with a philosophy of creativity. However, while this may remain undeveloped in Marxist circles, such philosophy is not new in the United States. For example, Professor Alfred North Whitehead who was for a time, chairman of the philosophy department at Harvard University, developed a theoretical outline of a philosophy of creativity in *Process and Reality*. In the introduction to this work, Whitehead wrote:

> 'Creativity' is the universal of universals, characterizing ultimate matter of fact. It is that ultimate principle by which the many, which are the universe disjunctively, become the one actual occasion, which is the universe conjunctively. It lies in the nature of things that the many enter into complex unity.
>
> 'Creativity' is the principle of novelty. An actual occasion is a novel entity in the 'many' which it unifies. The 'creative advance' is the application of this ultimate principle of creativity to each novel situation which originates. The many become one and are increased by one.[3]

From Harvard to the University of Chicago, creativity was a central part of indigenous philosophy in the United States. Christian theologian John B. Cobb, Jr., who was taught the philosophy of creativity by Charles Hartshorne at the University of Chicago, writes of a creative Christ that provides material liberation for the poor in the modern era:

> Christ is not seen as the symbol of suffering as such but of redemptive suffering. Christ is not to be seen in the miserable as such but in every impulse to overcome that misery. He appears in the creative transformation of consciousness from hopeless resignation to the demand for justice. He appears in especially in sustained and effective efforts to transform the structures that produce misery.
>
> Further, oppression and misery are not limited to particular classes. Women have come to new consciousness of their oppression, and in the powerful surge of self-liberation they have raised the consciousness of men as to how

they too are oppressed. Even the rich are oppressed by their wealth and the powerful by their authority. And we now recognize with Paul that the whole of creation groans in travail waiting for liberation. The drive for redemption is universal, and Christ appears in the creative transformation of all life everywhere.

Finally, we now realize that no new order into which liberation might lead us would be free of new forms of oppression. Utopia does not lie ahead as an actual future. Whatever we accomplish, the need for liberation will continue. In the unending drive for liberation, yesterday, today, tomorrow, we discern Christ.

This recognition of Christ in the liberation movements is now widespread. It is also widely recognized that these movements are essentially transformations of consciousness and understanding which then express themselves in new organization and overt action. To identify Christ with these movements is to see Christ as the creative transformation of thought and imagination even more than of economic and political structures.[4]

While I agree with Cobb's transformationist approach to a politics which seeks liberation from all forms of oppression, the understanding of Christ as the personification of creative transformation does little to explain the whole picture we have received of the historical Jesus of the Bible. Cobb seems to lose the historical Christ in the attempt to make him relevant in the world today.

This phenomenon is not new, however, for Marxist thinkers continue to rewrite Marx and reinterpret Marx for their time as well. This process is the basis of the so called "Creative Marxist-Leninism" officially announced by Leonid Brezhnev in 1975. In short, while it was the goal of Feuerbach and Marx to show the way in which Christian theologians projected their class interests onto sacred symbols, their followers are using the same type of justification for the legitimacy of Marx in their own era. I am not so sure that Prof. Damjanović is, in principle, operating much differently from many of the great Christian theologians.

Avoidance of Nuclear War and Conflict Resolution

Conflict resolution requires a result different from the elimination of one party by the other. It requires the parties to accept the existence of the other and to either resolve or accept their differences. In the Bible are paradigmatic stories of elimination, such as Cain killing Abel, and of conflict resolution, such as Jacob's reunion with Esau. It is impossible to imagine men and women resolving sexual conflicts by murder of one by the other. Damjanović is correct to emphasize a *logic of mutual recognition* which is beyond the logic of contradiction. The realization of self-limitation is for the necessity of self-preservation.

In his *Irony of American History,* Reinhold Niebuhr noted that the threat of nuclear anhilation was an "ironic climax of history"[5] It is in the situation of nuclear standoff that nations may finally have come to recognize that the fate of one nation is not controlled solely by itself. Just as Cain could never experience fulfillment as a brother by killing his brother, the West cannot experience fulfillment without the East, and *vice versa*. It may be that such a final irony of history will force the Marxist to realize the truth of Jesus and the other worldly Christian to realize the truth in Marx. There must be a mutual recognition, and ultimately the hope that the "reunion of the estranged," to borrow from Tillich, can be *aufgehoben* into a new union. It is only such *praxis* which can save us from nuclear destruction.

The Reunion of Politics and Morality

The lack of congruence between ideals and politics in both Christian and Marxist states is a reflection of the inability of either system of thought, as manifested in political parties, to address the totality of human needs. With the advance of science and modern philosophy, the application of reductionistic forms of analysis has led to a fragmentation of human life. To the biologist, man is an extension of the animal world; to the social engineer, man is a product of social-structural relations; to the logician, man is a rational and free agent; and, to the Christian, man contains a spirit which is an extension of God. In all four of these examples, specific cause and effect relations are writ large onto the totality of human nature.

However, we know from human experience and other traditions that the human being is a complex made up of numerous dimensions, each subject to its own causal relations, yet because of the higher order creative unity in the individual "the many become one and are increased by one." Human beings are equipped with integrative faculties to provide direction for constructive behavior that will lead to enhanced life. However, these integrative forces, by definition, do not divide and analyze like reason; they are non-rational modes of experience, modes which integrate rational experience with all other forms.

Tillich called this a "depth dimension" in human life. Here is where intuition, narrative, art, story, myth, imagery, and other non-rational modes of experience attempt to describe integrative human behavior in terms of morality and virtue. The complexity of human nature is such that morality can never be solely derived from reason or biology or analysis of social structure. The totality of life is *perceived* through images which, as Whitehead states, come to us as "drops of experience." The main debate between christians and communists is not whether man has both a body and a spirit but, rather: which is the starting point of philosophy? A wholistic approach starts from an integrated view of human nature that rejects any single aspect of human nature as the proper basis of political philosophy.

Political parties, which have the role of providing values for the society, must contain metaphors, myths, symbols, and narratives of the good society and virtuous people if they are to lead to "responsibility for the whole." To accomplish this goal they must go beyond the reality as naively perceived by pre-critical, pre-scientific thought, without reflection on concrete historical experience. They must also go beyond that level of monocritical thought which substitutes some form of narrow self-created ideology for the former naive view. Rather, mature wisdom of thought, to paraphrase Ernst Troeltsch, is to subject that naively perceived reality to criticism and transform it into a higher context of thought by discarding only what can be replaced by reflection on experience.[6] This moves beyond the ideological level of action and reaction, which has divided East and West, to, what he called, *thinking*.

It has often been said that Eastern and Western European thought reflect a schizophrenia in modern civilization; the one with a passion to fulfill one part of human life, and the other to fulfill another. Only when these two views of human life come together to form a more total picture of human nature can civilization be healed. This means the subjection of ancient and whole perceptions of life to the criticism not of a permanent "break" from the old but a temporary scientific suspension for the sake of critical analysis which can transform those common roots of Europe into a common future, free of the threat of nuclear anhilation.

In conclusion, while I come from a different background from Prof. Damjanović, looking ahead we have much to work for together. If I dwell on the difference between particular cultural histories, there may seem unbridgeable gaps between East and West. However, as I explained in my article on philosophical convergence, there is great reason to see that in common shared experiences in these nuclear times we will see an "ideological epigenesis," a superseding world view which will stress more common agreement than disagreement.

NOTES

1. Reinhold Neibuhr, *Nature and Destiny of Man* (NY: Scribners, 1964), p. 123.
2. Gordon L. Anderson, "Ideological Convergence of the US and USSR," *International Social Science Review,* 60:2, Spring 1985, p. 31.
3. Alfred North Whitehead, *Process and Reality* (NY: Macmillan Free Press, 1978), p. 20.
4. John B. Cobb, Jr., *Christ in a Pluralistic Age* (Philadelphia: Westminster Press, 1975), p. 57.

5. Reinhold Niebuhr, *The Irony of American History* (NY: Scribner's, 1952), p. 39.
6. Ernst Troeltsch, *The Absoluteness of Christianity and the History of Religions* (Richmond, Va.: John Knox Press, 1971), pp. 132–135.

DISCUSSION ON DAMJANOVIĆ

José Delgado

I think that this was a very fascinating paper, but there are a few aspects that I would like to question or discuss. I think that, perhaps, some of your positions are phrased in such a clear way that I doubt that they are acceptable. For example you talk about the Christian theocentric metaphysics versus Marxist anthropocentric philosophy and then you list a variety of oppositions: transcendence *vs* immanence, mythic *vs* scientific, indeterminism *vs* determinism, *etc*. Is that really true? Why do you identify anthropology with Marxism? This is not correct. Because some of the Christian authors were anthropologists. For example, Teilhard de Chardin. As you know evolution is accepted today — it is denied by some Christians but accepted by many others. So, question number one: why identify anthropology with Marxism. I don't feel that is correct. Question number two is the reverse. Why identify the transcendental concept of man, with Christianity? Because, you see, the transcendental conception of man is also to a great extent to be found in materialism. The ideas, the material creations of man, will overlast his own existence. So there is something which is transcendental from the materialistic point of view. The new biology will support the transcendental biology, that means, materialistic biology will support transcendental values in the existence of man.

And then question three: The blue collar worker, the exploited workers, today are being replaced by skilled labor. So, we have a new situation. Because of the technological evolution of the world, the struggle of classes is very different from what it was in the nineteenth century. Today what we have, really, are highly qualified technicians, and therefore we are thinking about a future world full of machines, with skilled labor and therefore not the unskilled labor, using these machines. And therefore the social situation has changed completely. And, even more, what we really need in the near future is the possible humanization of human beings. These are new ideas, and you see it even in the present Soviet Union. Now we are talking there — and I say we, because I am involved in some business with the Soviet Union. We have started a venture enterprise. This is really surprising. This is Gorbachev and his new ideas. Venture capital! We are allowed to withdraw our profits from the Soviet Union in USA dollars. This is really new. We have the competitive presence of the Soviet Union in the world markets, and, as you know, there has been talk today that the ruble, perhaps, is going to go into the foreign market, becoming a convertible money. And we talk about efficiency productivity, and some of the reasons they are not effective. Then they are going to be modified, because the Soviet Union needs efficiency. There are even some private businesses. You see, the whole thing is changing. I conclude my brief questioning. Anthropology cannot be identified with Marxism; transcendental philosophy cannot be identified with Christianity, and Marxism itself is recognizing the need for fundamental changes.

Tamás Kozma

This was the message. Because Jesus is coming, or had died for us, and at the same time he is surviving. And when Paul came to Europe, this message has been transformed into the ancient Middle Eastern philosophies or religions. This was the story of Christianity. So it started as that political philosophy, and this is close to the Marxism, because Marxist political philosophy has an eschatological point, which tells us that the proletariat is close to the next world, and we should fight the last battle. This is what is told. It is even the hymn of the proletariat movement. Now, the question for me is not really this philosophy, but how the original Christian message has been transformed into a philosophy of the establishment, while this Marxist philosophy has been transformed into a philosophy of the party establishment. So this is my question. How far you feel this transformation of a revolutionary idea into a philosophy of establishment has gone. This is my question.

Ljubisav Rakić

I would like first to congratulate both Professors Damnjanović and Anderson for very nice and rational presentations. And something I like very much in both presentations is the real rational-scientific approach, more than a pragmatic political approach to the problem. And the question to Professor Damnjanović is: could you explain a little bit more about one of the very important differences between Marxist and Christian approaches. This is about human immortality, especially life after death. It is the main difference in the philosophical approach between Christianity and Marxism. And Dr. Anderson, you know, I like very much your explanation about the convergences and divergences between Marxism and Christianity. And I would like it if you could kindly try to explain the convergences between the two philosophical approaches on the basis of unification theology and philosophy. And it seems to me, you know, that this unification philosophy helps very much in the explanation of similarities and dissimilarities between Marxism and Christianity. It seems to me up to date, you know; a more rational and more sophisticated explanation.

Vassilis Karasmanis

I would like to ask two questions. First, I note that Professor Damnjanović starts from the parallelism between two triadic structures and one world goal: Marxism and the Christian philosophy. I cannot understand this parallelism. I would like an explanation. I don't see really in which sense they are parallel. Another question: he said at the end that he proposes instead of a dialectic, a dialogical, say, approach or solution. In which sense is this dialogical, because the first sense of 'dialectic' is dialogical again. In the Platonic sense it starts from the dialogue. I would like an explanation.

Milan Damnjanović

I would like to begin with the philosophy of creativity. It is an old topic, and has to do with the history of the idea itself of creativity. In old Greek tradition, there was no word, no concept, and no philosophy of creativity. It does not mean that a Greek world was not created itself. It was in the first place the possibility, the creative possibility. The Greek world was unique in the history of culture. So, it is, perhaps, possible to explain the fact by psychoanalysis. For a man who creates something knows it is not necessary that it be materially created. So it is a world. But to say it in a word, it was the idea, in the sense of an ontological metaphor. It was not indeed the philosophy of creativity in the critical sense of the word. And I found it in the American author named Carl Hausman, of the Pennsylvania State University. He wrote a book, a discourse on creation, and also an important article on the philosophy of creativity, and in this article I found the following information: that in the western tradition, creativity as a topic has not been singled out for sustained, systematic attention, with few exceptions. There are no systems of philosophy of creativity in either the systematic or critical forms of philosophy. That was the word of Carl Hausman. The question of an idea of a systematical critical philosophy of creativity was not answered, and my supposition was that it can be supposedly the philosophy of Marxism in our time. That is the main idea. So, for instance, Whitehead is indeed important to the philosophy of creativity, but in the systematic and critical sense, there is no one undertaking it in the history of philosophy. It is, in my view, the place for Marxist philosophy. It is not interesting for me to say something already said. It was not my intention. What does it mean, 'creativity'? To bring something not in existence into the world. And this is the only, the main trait of the human being, in the sense of self-transcending being. It is also the conception of man, and in the Marxist view of the self transcending over the world. It is possible to give a reply to the question of what is man. It is the creation of man in the moral sense, and this is the point of the moral, of morality and politics. I have the possibility in the next few days to go to hear and to speak about morality and politics as posed by our colleagues in Vienna, concerning the president, Waldheim. The name of Austria has changed now, it has become Waldheimat. I had in mind, in the history of Marxism, the idea of Austromarxism. It was the day of social democracy in Austria. It was the relation, the necessary relation between Kant and Marx, in the sense that Marx and the theory of personality lacked ethical theory. It was criticized as neomarxism, as the attempt to bring together something that is not possible to bring together, and so on. But I am convinced now that it is necessary to have a solution of both, and to understand, in a productive manner, the relation of ethics and politics. It was in my exposition linked to the theory of the possibility of new values. This is an old topic. We have in the axiological-philosophical discipline the possibility to support cases of the eternal values, the logical values. *Caritas* was mentioned here this morning. *Caritas* is *agape* in Greek, and it is *liebe,* and there are innumerable meanings connected with the category of love. It is a term, or category that entails modification, historical modifications of the category, but in the platonic sense of metaphysics it always has the same value: it is love. But in Nietzsche it is also love for the future generation. This is central to the creation of our conference. It is the creation of survival, of the possibility of survival of mankind today. Then we have modifications, but creation is the possibility of new values, it is the great possibility of the adult. It is Nietzsche's creation. There are new values and the historical modification of values. I have stated the possibility of new values. For instance, there is a political category of coexistence, but we have had in the past the category of tolerance. But then the meaning shifted. It became a new category of coexistence. This must be conceived as the coming of dialectics. It is the creation of dialectics and I know it when they say again that it was a dialogue; it was one manner to, in a platonic sense, discuss, to discourse. But, you see, we have the idea of contradiction. It is very good to take Hegel as focussing on both Christian and Greek traditions. And it has proved that the prediction of Hegel is to be important. I found the solution in Theunissen, who said that contradiction is the expression of power. And it is now in the soul. We have no possibility to use power. The situation has changed nowadays. And we are obliged perhaps to face a new situation. I was a few months ago in West Germany and I saw the graphics on the walls in Bremen, the university in Bremen. The idea of the resistance is viewed in the graffiti. But indeed I would like to underscore the thesis of the philosophy of creativity, in the sense of critical philosophy and systematical philosophy. The topic was in the history of philosophy, in the European history of philosophy. But there is no critical and no systematical philosophy of creativity. It is most important that this be understood. Mr. Delgado mentioned the identification of anthropology and Marxism in this context; also de Chardin. I have not made an identification between anthropology and Marxism. It was no solution for me to deal with both enormous traditions lasting even today. It would have obliged me to have Marxist philosophy as the representative of the new age, and of the anthropological point of view. But I have not based the anthropology of Marxism in contradiction to Christian philosophy. I have not tried to make the philosophical archetype of both viewpoints. That was my idea. Concerning class struggle, I know very well that the desperation of nowadays is radically different to that of the last century. And I have the impression that it is necessary to overcome the contradiction in that sense that is used from the idea of the class struggle. There are different modifications of the class struggle, I know very well, but I was not interested to explain the situation of the known facts concerning Marxist theories and Marxist philosophy at all. As to the question of Mr. Kozma, concerning the future in the sense of eschatology in the Jewish and Christian tradition, it was not in my opinion the idea of Marxist philosophy to secularize both historical ideas. I spoke in the sense of radical histories. The transformation of the original Christian idea to the establishment is is an idea, a process, very known in the history of culture, and I have in mind the declaration of the so-called revolutionary idea of Marxism in Russia after 1917. In the few years after the revolution, the October revolution in Russia, there was indeed a flourishing of the culture. It was the possibility of different ideas and a fruitful period of a few years. That is enough. In that sense, the product of epochs are not lasting. It is proof that it was indeed a revolution. And it is not exciting to explore the establishment. It is also the establishment in my country, which has the same problem. It is the establishment that is a state, and made things impossible for creative life. We had no political life, nothing democratic at all. That was the idea of my country, and what we have now is the consequence.

Heinrich Beck

I would like to put a little question, not last but not least, but last and least. I think in order to compare within the problematic of a philosophy of creativity, the question of the origin and foundation of the faculty of man to create history, of the power of man to produce history, is important. And it seems that in both cases, in the case of Christian metaphysics and the case of dialectical materialism of Marx, this ultimate and finite origin is an infinite being, an unlimited being. In the case of Christian metaphysics, it is the unlimited being of God, in which man participates as an analogy and partner of the creator God. It is a personal being, God. It is intended, it is understood as a personal being and this participation and partnership is a dialogical one. And in the case of dialectical materialism, of Marxism, this infinite being as the ultimate foundation and origin of human creativity is an impersonal being. It is matter, which is an impersonal being. And human being is understood in Marxism as part of matter, and this participation or being part of matter, is understood in a dialectical manner. Not in a dialogical, but in a dialectical manner. And dialectics is understood as anonymous, as impersonal in its foundation, and this gives rise to my question. Must we not introduce necessarily this understanding of the ultimate origin of the creative power of man in Marxism as an anonymous and impersonal moment in Marxistic understanding of man and history?

Gordon Anderson

I would like to have a closing comment, I think, starting from Professor Delgado's question, because it prompted me to notice that the difference isn't that Marx lacks a transcendental view, or Christianity a material view. It is what they choose as the starting point of philosophy. For Feuerbach, which Marx picked up, theology is anthropology. This was a reversal, whereas Christian anthropology is rooted in a theology which has a view of a transcendence. Now I think if you really want a world view that is responsible for the whole, you must have a starting point that deals with the whole. And the problem with modern science is that it has tended to look at partial views of human life. So Christianity, influenced by modern science, reduces human life to spirit. Marxism in reaction to that, reduces human life to the material. A biologist will look at the animal nature of the human being, a social engineer will look at social structures, a logician will look at the rational free agent. All of these are important aspects of a very complex being. I don't think you can just add creativity under Marxist thought. I don't think you can just add it under Christian thought. I think you need a starting point in philosophy which deals with a view of human beings that is whole, because I think that any political philosophy is ultimately derived from a view of human nature. Those are my closing remarks.

THE QUALITY OF LIFE IN CAPITALIST AND SOCIALIST ECONOMIES

Anthony de Jasay

I do not propose to compare the quality of life in Switzerland and Byelorussia. Real-life, real-time comparisons prove little for my present purpose. In cases of multiple causation, with indefinitely many historical phenomena interacting over hundreds of years, who is to say why life in Byelorussia differs from life in Switzerland in certain ways? The true causal origin of such differences would forever remain open to pointless and inconclusive dispute.

In the United States and, to a, perhaps, lesser extent in Great Britain, there has emerged, over the last twenty years or so, an almost unemployable, ghetto-dwelling, helpless "underclass" made up largely of fatherless quasi-families and disoriented youths. They are maintained at public expense. Public support encourages recruitment into this "underclass". Its members become, in time, permanently unable to help themselves. It is a matter of conjecture whether the this phenomenon is intrinsic to capitalism, or to capitalism's attempt to be "social", or is due to non-systemic causes. Likewise, in the Soviet Union and some other socialist countries, alcoholism, suicide, infant mortality and problems of public health and housing appear to be particularly acute. It is conjectural to what extent this is due to the "system", and I have no intention of arguing it.

My undertaking here is of another type. Instead of proceeding inductively from particular evidence to a general hypothesis, I will try a limited exercise in partial deduction. I will single out three variable characteristics of socio-economic systems which seem to me important in conditioning people's lives, without claiming that there are no others. My choice is determined by the ease of passing from a typical systemic feature to a typical feature of the lives of individual persons living under that system, for I take the "quality of life" in my title to refer to personal lives. The characteristics I propose to discuss are present to some degree in any system; they are not contingent on time or place, and seem largely independent of the historical conjuncture. However, they take different shapes and intensities in the capitalist and socialist economic system. I will treat these differences as axiomatic. That is to say, I will take it that the terms "capitalist system" and "socialist system" have commonly understood core meanings on which no *bona fide* disagreement is possible. The argument will be limited to the corollaries, *i.e.*, to showing why, if the economic system is such-and-such, people's lives are liable to be thus-and-so. I must add, in all honesty, that anything I deduce is at best a probabilistic quasi-corollary; social science can have even less pretension to determinism than the more serious branches of knowledge.

Let me also say, in rounding out this explanation of what I am setting out to do, that my approach steers clear of certain vitally important systemic determinants of the quality of life. One is the mechanism by which political power is secured, kept and lost. Another is the built-in predisposition of an economic system to help generate peaceful or warlike "political" policies and to impose its ways on others by force. Yet another, no less important, is the "sociology" of information inherent in an economic system: how information is generated and disseminated, its monopolistic or competitive character. My reason for avoiding these areas, as far as I can, must be obvious. The partisans of each system consider that theirs is free, peaceful, and open and the other is, to put it politely, less so. Though I do not share the view that these questions are relative to "values" and cannot be discussed in terms of "true or false", I do not think this is the right occasion for doing so.

1. LINEAR VERSUS TRIANGULAR SYSTEMS.

Social organisation has manifold structures, based on affection, interest, or authority. Some of them are customary, others contractual, yet others straightforward command-obedience relations. Most of them exist under any economic system, and it is not really obvious that capitalism or socialism is a major determinant of their configurations. There is an organisational feature which is at the core of capitalism and socialism, respectively, and which the spokesmen of neither would want to disclaim. It is what Marx used to call, and some of his followers still call, "the relations of production". It is a term shrouded in metaphysical cloud and it takes the brutality of the profane to strip it down to its everyday meaning. I take it to mean the predominant form of ownership. It is sufficient for my purpose to identify only two forms: *private*, predominating under capitalism, and *public*, predominating under socialism. Hybrids and compromises between the two exist here and there, but I have no time to consider them. (Purely as a personal parenthesis, I do not think they are destined to a long and succesful life.)

Two aspects of ownership concern us. One is the power to appropriate the income accruing to the entity owned. The systemic "acid test" is the ownership of the equity, *i.e.* the right to the residual income left after prior charges. Under capitalism, it is consistent with the system for certain prior charges to be publicly owned *(i.e.,* the state might lend money or rent a building to an enterprise), but alien to it *("systemfremd")* for the equity to belong to the political authority. Under socialism, it is the other way around. There are interest-bearing savings accounts and a few privately held prior charges *(e.g.,* inventors' royalties, bonds, and rental contracts with enterprises), but private owhership of the equity of productive enterprise is *systemfremd* and, if tolerated, remains precarious.

The other relevant aspect of ownership is control. Under socialism, control belongs unambigously to the political authority. Trade unions, workers' councils, consumer associations and professional bodies may provide feedback, guiding to some extent the exercise of this control, but are never allowed to supersede it. Under capitalism, residual ownership (held by thousands of shareholders of an enterprise) and control (exercised by a few managers) look separate, and a certain "pop" sociology (Berle, Means, Galbraith), used to make much of this to prove "the convergence of the two world systems" *(i.e.,* both ruled and run by professional bureaucracies). We hear less of this since the rise of a market for corporate control has proved the ultimate inseparability of the income and control aspects of ownership.

The logical implications for the "quality of life" cry out to be noticed. In a capitalist economy, residual ownership of each enterprise belongs to a separate subset of persons (sometimes to a single person), though these subsets may partly overlap. Hope of gain and risk of loss impinge upon this subset; its members get rich or lose their money; the effect of uncertainty, of lack of perfect foresight, are largely borne by it, and it has pressing reasons as well as responsibilities for coping with and, if possible, overcoming them. The future needs watching; forecasting, mobility, a readiness to shift positions and to react instantly are called for. At its epitome, this is the life of the stock market speculator, selling an investment and buying another at the drop of a hat, his actions in the limit provoking changes of control and steering capital investment in an "invisible-hand process", whose more or less satisfactory working has been well researched in recent decades. Under socialism, the fortunes of separate enterprises do not influence the fortunes of separate subsets of owners (though they do influence the bonuses of key employees, just as under capitalism). Instead, as in a gigantic insurance scheme, the successes or failures throughout the economy are pooled over the entire set of society as a whole. No fortunes are made or lost (unless in illegal, grey-market, anti-systemic ways), and the range of variation between purely economic success and failure is no more than the one or two percentage points by which the growth rate of the whole national product varies between good and bad times. The extreme type of life generated by such a system is the life of the civil servant. He may be surprised by fate and treated well or badly by his political masters, but he has little to hope or fear from economics.

The second obvious implication of the ownership structure is that in capitalism, some people's livelihood is independent of any relation with an employer; if they do not work for wages, their capital is still working for them. The existence of such people has an impact on the quality of lives other than their own; it provides a morally respectable excuse for the politics of envy (as witness the widely voiced distinction between "earned" and "unearned" income); it furnishes much that is colourful, picturesque, and eccentric for the vicarious enjoyment of the public; and it is the economic base for the somewhat greater intellectual, artistic and political pluralism that capitalist countries seem to display. Needless to say, whether greater pluralism improves or worsens the quality of life may be contingent on time and place, and is a matter for argument. What is certain is that it matters.

All of this is familiar ground, necessary as it was to cross it. Let me venture to a less widely understood consequence of the "socialist relations of production". The capitalist organisation of society is triangular, with capital, labour, and the state at the three angles. Equilibrium among the three, such as it is, is potentially maintained by balance-of-power type politics: temporary coalitions on specific issues between any two against the third. Such triangular balancing is older than capitalism; its prominent examples are the shifting alliances made by European royal governments with the commoners against the nobility, with town against country, with the great estates against the commercial interest, or with manufacturers against slave-owners. In the modern era, the typical pattern is for the political authority to lean toward either the employer or the employee interest, assuming a role of conflict-resolution, notably in major wage disputes or in matters of social welfare. But it sometimes happens that it is groups of employers and employees who jointly stand opposed to the state on some issue, such as price control, credit, anti-trust action or consumer protection, the state having to yield or find support among other groups. In general terms, a loser in a conflict between two poles of the triangle can look for support, and if need be run for shelter, to the third, which greatly reduces the risks of taking a stand, of sticking one's neck out. Above all, the triangular design of society lends the state a modicum of impartiality, — I should like to call it positional or existential impartiality, echoing the thesis that "existence determines consciousness".

A classic example is environmental protection. Anti-pollution measures increase industrial coats, and may weaken export competitiveness. On the other hand, they are favoured by large sections of public opinion. In a triangular system, the state has no built-in bias either for industrial efficiency and plan fulfilment, or for cleaner rivers and purer air. It will lean on one side or the other, depending on the pressures that happen to be exerted. Where it owns and runs industry, it has a vested interest to resist environmentalist pressure, to claim that such pressure is ill-informed, demagogic, or, indeed, to deny it altogether. It is a fair supposition that the woodpulp or the chemical industry is just as noxious and polluting in socialist as in capitalist hands. If so, the relative weakness of environmentalist movements in socialist economies is likely to have something to do with the structural "design" of the respective social systems.

Socialist ownership eliminates one angle of the triangle. It can be seen as a straight line, connecting labour to capital, employees to the universal owner-employer who is, at the same time, the political authority. If such a system allowed major conflicts over wages or working conditions to break the surface, the state would be drawn into judging a dispute to which it was a party. It might well seek to be impartial in intention, but could not be impartial for "positional", "existential" reasons. The linear, socialist system is driven to deny the existence of serious employer-employee conflict, and to brand it as treasonable, anti-social, if not downright criminal if, by some mishap, it does manifest itself in strike or sabotage.

Psychologists are more qualified than I to go into the specific effects upon personal lives and characters, workplace atmosphere, *etc.,* of a state of affairs where a show of happy harmony is a civic, patriotic duty, and where some of the most basic conflicts in human existence, those over work and wages, find no open outlet but must, for all practical purposes, be ruled out of existence by a redefinition of terms. This is not to say that strikes are good, or that organised discontent is to be encouraged. Very likely it should be no more encouraged than suppressed. All my argument really claims is that a system that has no place for it, generates a style of life and breeds a type of man that the founding fathers of socialism might regard with dismay.

Before the system of royal jurisdiction gradually forced its way down to the humbler walks of life, most of Western Europe from the eleventh to the mid-fourteenth century ran on what I would call a linear system, not unlike the socialist economy. The lord was the sole "employer", he alone "owned" land, (the predominant asset in the village economy), and he was also the political and judicial authority of last resort. The lack of balance in this "linear" system connecting lord and serfs, with no third party to play the role of arbiter and judge of appeal, was mitigated by custom and Christianity, just as the effect of unifying in a single authority both political power and capital ownership is mitigated today by the fraternal-egalitarian aspects of the socialist ideology. Nonetheless, the same causes seldom fail to produce the same consequences; across centuries and continents, the concentration of all political and economic power in a single institution, whether the feudal manor or the socialist state, has always deeply marked the lives and behaviour of the people subjected to its double authority.

2. THE AGENCY PROBLEM.

When an apple-grower takes a load of apples to market, he will transport and sell them so as to do the best he can for himself. When he sends somebody to drive the truck and gets somebody else to sell the apples, there is a "best" for the grower, a "best" for the driver and a "best" for the seller, and these "bests" do not coincide. There arises what economic theory calls an "agency problem". The distortions it produces depend on the incentive structure. If the driver is paid by the weight he transports, the apples may arrive badly knocked about, while the man charged with selling them may go for the quickest deal instead of working for the best, or accept a favour, a bribe from the buyer, *etc.* Prodigious ingenuity goes into devising particular reward-incentive systems to suit particular agency problems. There are work norms by time and by gross output, value added, and quality; there are pay structures linked to the norms by complex difference-equations; there are commissions on sales, participations in results defined in various ways, and bonuses governed by convoluted formulae. There is, in any economic system, always a race between the evolution of agency problems, which change with technology and usually tend to become more subtle, and the design of new incentive systems supposed to cope with them. Human inventiveness cuts both ways: in new economic steering mechanisms, and in the clever adjustments and fiddles by which agents, defending their best interests, accomodate themselves to them. The agency problem is intrinsic to the separate identities of principal and agent; it is a cost of delegation, and hence a function of centralised ownership. Only in the one-man firm is there no agency problem between the owner and those he delegates to carry out various tasks, for they are one and the same person. The distortions of agency only stop where delegation stops.

The capitalist economy, like any other, is beset by a maze of micro-economic agency problems arising from the simple fact that not everybody is self-employed. These problems are numerous, but individually fairly small-scale, usually confined to the inside of a firm where functions are carried out by delegated agents of the owners. Towards the whole outside world, the firm acts as a principal. This is constraint — and in competitive industries a severe constraint — on the extent to which agency problems can get out of hand. It is impossible for very long to take it easy, to waste materials and fuel, to lie about quality, to innovate too much (for fun), or too little (by sloth), or to be rude to customers, and so forth, in a competitive situation, without financial alarm-bells alerting the owners. The firm whose agency problems the owners prove unable to keep within tolerable limits, will go under or get taken over.

Socialist economies have micro-economic agency-problems just as capitalist ones do. Additionally, they are punished with some others due to habits of quantitative targeting, the nature of socialist pricing, and all the inconsistencies that result from making production serve both "needs", defined centrally, and "demands", generated in spontaneous markets. These handicaps are well known to economists in socialist countries, and I need not enlarge upon them.

My purpose is to add that the socialist economy also faces a separate higher-order, macro-economic agency problem which deeply conditions lives and characters. This is simply a logical implication of the unified ownership of all, or practically all, "firms". The agency problem, instead of being confined within each firm, extends to interfirm dealings, and even to dealings of firms with households. A clear symptom of this higher-order agency problem is the periodic urge of socialist systems to decentralise themselves, to bring back markets, shorten chains of command, and reduce the distortion of delegation. However, after each decentralisation campaign, the fundamental forces of central ownership reassert themselves, rebuilding the pressure for a new round of reorganisation. Giving socialist firms "accounting autonomy", abolishing plan targets, and calling for competitive behaviour by simulated market mechanisms — always have a degree of artificiality. They go against the grain of the system. One could compare them to a game of chess where you play against yourself. They bear much the same relation to capitalist market competition as grand manoeuvers bear to war, — which is not to denigrate manoeuvers nor to praise war: just to note that they have different consequences and involve different sanctions.

If this diagnosis is right, we should expect to find some of the following symptoms: rewards do not directly depend on *results* (winning a battle, holding a bridgehead), but rather on *reports* (the umpire's findings about the simulated battle). There is an extra degree of freedom about the presentation of "facts": it is better for example to call the glass half-full than half-empty. Monitoring, sampling, supervising, controlling, assume ever larger proportions. Hierarchy and rank have naturally a greater weight in a report-based than in a result-based reward system. Pleasing a hierarchical superior and pleasing a customer do not have the same relative values in a state-owned economic system as in a private firm; though any hierarchical superior is no doubt pleased if his subordinate pleases a customer, the agency problem makes the feedback from customer to superior much fainter in the state-owned system. By the same token, through the length and breadth of the hierarchy, there are fewer surprises, fewer broken careers, greater security of tenure and much less random, unpredictable mobility. Suboptimal efficiency is accompanied by a certain cosiness, by stable expectations and moderate exertions.

3. PUBLIC AND PRIVATE GOODS.

In market exchange, a good is obtained by surrendering its equivalent. Benefit and cost are tightly linked. In public provision, a group, a community or society as a whole, bears the cost, charging it out among some or all of its members in some overt or covert fashion. Some or all members benefit. There is still a link between aggregate cost and benefit. However, for any individual member of the public, there is no link whatever between *his* contribution to the public good and the benefit *he personally* derives from it. This is so for one of two possible reasons. Either the technical-logistical nature of the good is such that it is "non-excludable": if it is produced at all, no member of the community can be excluded from its enjoyment even if he contributed nothing to producing it. National defence is such a good, and so is public order, knowledge, a language all speak, clean air, public hygiene, signposts, parks, and monuments. Or else the good is "excludable" and could be sold for profit on a market, but a community decides (or the political authority decides on its behalf) to provide it publicly instead. Education is a prominent example; instead of letting each parent buy schooling for his child privately, education is freely offered (in fact, compulsorily imposed upon all) and paid for collectively. The share of the cost borne by each member of the public has no relation at all to his having children to educate.

In a half-way house goods are sold in market exchange, but at a fraction of their cost of reproduction. The missing fraction is provided publicly, for example by a state subsidy. An individual's enjoyment of such a good is weakly linked to his contribution, for he pays something for each unit he consumes, but less than its cost, *i.e.*, the good is made partly public. Thus the publicness of goods is not absolute, but a matter of degree.

Needless to say, the production of public goods is, incidentally, also an instrument of social policy. The state can redistribute incomes basically in two ways. The one, overt and fairly precise in operation, is to tax some people and give the money to others. The merit of such transfers is that both the amounts and the identity of the beneficiaries are relatively visible. State and public opinion both can have a clear idea of who gets what. The beneficiaries dispose of the money as seems best to them — whether such consumer sovereignty is a good or a bad thing is a contested question and I will do no more than note it here. The other, more covert way to redistribute is to provide public (or half-public) goods out of general revenue. With this method, who pays for what and who derives how much net benefit is at best a matter of guess-work, at worst a question that cannot ever be answered, even in principle. The tax-and-transfer method is consonant with responsibility and accountability, the public goods method with solidarity and a communitarian spirit.

However, let me clarify a possible misunderstanding. Redistribution is a political act, applied to modify a distribution emerging from economic exchanges. If the political authority is simultaneously the owner of all the means of production and the employer of all labour, it *ipso facto* determines the distribution. It sounds absurd to say that it seeks to redistribute one way what it has distributed in another way; if it considers that the distribution needs to be corrected, why has it brought it about in the first place? In other words, since a socialist state has a price policy and a wage policy, it ought not to need a social policy.

Yet, even in a completely socialized economy, final prices and incomes are not purely a matter of political will; the state may still need a social policy, if only to undo with its left hand what its right hand has done. On the other hand, if its price-wage policy really contains all its social policy, it does so because and to the extent that it is a policy of producing and pricing public or partly public goods, subsidizing or giving away some — which is precisely the point I am labouring.

An axiom distinguishing the self-image of the capitalist from the self-image of the socialist system is that in the first, goods are produced in expectation of profitable exchange, in the second in response to a collectively reached definition of need. Public goods are an alien element in the capitalist system; its Platonic ideal is a pure market order. Production for private profit is likewise *systemfremd* to socialism; if a Platonic ideal of it existed, all goods in it would be public, in obedience to the rule: "from each according to his ability, to each according to his need". In strict logic, under pure, Platonic capitalism all human cooperation would spring either from affective motives or from the quest for profit; with everything (including law and order) bought and sold as a private good, there would be no public authority, for people would leave nothing for it to decide. Under pure socialism, all human cooperation would be directed to commonly agreed tasks, there would be no rationing by the purse, all goods would be provided publicly, hence all production decisions would, by definition, be collective political decisions.

It is no great discovery that real-life, real-time systems are impure; nor is it a surprising finding that in their erratic progress through time they preserve some atavistic traces of their systemic essence. Both systems display a confusing mixed pattern of unevenly taxed and cross-subsidized flows of goods and services, some more public, others more private. Nevertheless, "privateness" is more characteristic of capitalism, "publicness" of socialism. It is a modest achievement to have saved at least this much from our initial axiom. Such as it is, it will help us to some equally modest deductions. It is not a moral judgment, but an analytic implication of the nature of publicness that the greater the share of public goods in the national product, the greater is the part of coercion and the smaller is that of personal choice in the allocation of resources. Coercion to contribute my work or my money to the public provision of a good which I can enjoy whether or not I contribute, can always be construed as flowing from my and everybody else's willing consent, for we all know that without coercion, too few of us would contribute. The idea of the social contract is based squarely on this construction. Hence it is not a rhetorical statement, but a deduction from the essential link between socialism and the publicness of goods, that while the livelihood of capitalist man, his work and pay, his housing, his daily consumption are contingent on various private contracts he is a party to, socialist man's livelihood is primarily a matter of the social contract.

Once again, by another route, we obtain the result that in socialism, the political and the economic spheres are identical, while in capitalism they are separate though overlapping.

Socialist man is, of course, no less honest and conscientious than capitalist man — some would say he is more so. Nor is he less anxious to provide for his family and for old age. Nevertheless, his incentives being basically different, he lives his life differently. Much of what he absolutely needs is public or semi-public; rents are low, public transport is nearly free, while certain simple foodstuffs and selected "merit goods" are underpriced relative to their factor cost. Since there are no miracles, and everything must be paid for one way or another, "private goods" are correspondingly more expensive, many of them prohibitively so: in terms of money, when they can be freely bought; in terms of queueing and influence, when they cannot. Since much of a person's subsistence is provided publicly or quasi-publicly, while goods entering into discretionary consumption are scarce or disproportionately dear, there is a double reason for a totally different balance between work, leisure and consumption under socialism than under capitalism. Some of those who find the socialist balance unacceptable, may manage to plant one foot in the "grey" or "second" economy, getting "private goods" for discretionary, capitalist-style consumption, often at the cost of great strain and overwork. In this light, the oft-repeated joke that at the socialist place of work, "we pretend to work and they pretend to pay us", ceases to be hostile irony, and becomes a theorem of serious intent in the economics of public goods.

A social contract on such terms, incorporating modest material expectations as the price of taking it easy, offering high predictability and security, little competitive stress and little overt conflict, hierarchical rule, and limited responsibility, more order, and less freedom of expression, might not be to everyone's taste; but neither is its converse: what we might call the capitalist contract. Both involve various trade-offs, more of this for less of that, and while I make no secret of my personal view on the matter, I readily admit the possibility of legitimate argument on which tradeoffs are more favourable to whom. The central purpose of this essay was to trace their systemic roots: why certain conditions and tendencies are inherent in capitalist or socialist societies as long as they remain capitalist or socialist.

In conclusion, I reserve the self-indulgent privilege to note that, while both systems are what they are, each is also trying, or pretending, to be what the other is. Capitalism strives to be "caring", welfarist and "social", and socialism has, from time to time, ambitions to be efficient, technically progressive, and able to bring material abundance. Some of these costly ambitions are almost certainly condemned to fail; others succeed to the extent that they spoil the ability of the system to do what it was designed to do. It is heresy, but perhaps not absurd, to say that the quality of life in either system might, in the long run, turn out to be less frustrating if both were more resigned to be true to themselves.

ELEMENTS IN THE QUALITY OF LIFE

José M.R. Delgado

The excellent paper by A. de Jasay states that private versus public ownership, and their related controls, are important differences between capitalism and socialism, concluding with the remark that each system is "trying or pretending to be what the other is."

The aims of both socialist and capitalist societies are to improve their quality of life, specially in health, education, productivity and individual satisfaction. Their philosophies, procedures and results, however, are rather different. What is worse, their mutual misunderstanding and mistrust are magnified by presently uncontrolled atomic proliferation.

In my opinion, the *biological unity* of all human beings, including their drives, motivations and satisfactions, should be explored in depth to provide realistic bases for universal understanding and cooperation. Practical solutions should be sought to resolve the ideological and political sources of human conflict which are, largely, antibiological, and, as creations of culture, are, to a great extent, artificial.

According to Lenin, socialism should be a network of *civilized cooperation,* and Gorbachev's present efforts to achieve *"perestroika"* are based on plans to restructure the Soviet system to make it more efficient and competitive.

At the same time, Eurocapitalist countries are breaking down territorial and economic boundaries, reversing state controls of industry, and popularizing business. Millions of ordinary citizens are investing in the stock market for the first time, and are thus participating in the industrial development of many lands. The British government has sold almost 40% of its industrial assets to over 9 million private shareholders. The leading French investment bank, Paribas, which had 150,000 shareholders before it was nationalized in 1981, is today back in the private sector with over 3 million owners.

The economic level of people and their countries is assessed by calculating the gross national product, the production of steel, the *per capita* income, number of automobiles and extent of public transportation, and the number of household appliances. Telephone books are proof of national wealth. While in highly industrialized cities many books are needed to list all the phones in use, in some countries with millions of inhabitants, there is only a slim volume. Recent developments in microelectronics, computers, information theory, and scientific knowledge in general, have introduced new elements that contain few raw materials and use very little energy.

Unfortunately most rankings of the quality of life are based only on material aspects of productivity, with little consideration of the values that actually enhance human life. A prerequisite element for the improvement of living standards is brain power. It must be focussed on the creative, not the destructive use, of technologies, for the benefit of mankind. The quality of life is reflected in the availability of health services, educational opportunities, and other indications of community concern. Individual happiness cannot be measured in machines but in the relative freedom to structure one's own life: to choose where and how to live. In the present world, few people are able to obtain a high score on this kind of a scale.

Modern mass media, bearing the technical, intellectual and artistic experience of mankind, will inevitably affect the most remote and underdeveloped corners of our planet. This global impact must be realized with the help of the most industrialized countries, which can provide the communications hardware-which will improve dramatically the economic and social welfare of people. At the same time, in order to reverse the trend toward greater inequality in the levels of life experienced by the poor and rich countries, managerial and technical strengths must also be introduced. International terrorism demonstrates that we have no alternative but a massive, collective effort to solve present injustices and construct a world where a high quality life can be enjoyed by all — not a world in which the "haves" live in fear, and the "have nots" exist without hope.

We need futuristic planning to surmount the limitations of socialist and capitalist economies. We also need viable solutions to ancient and present conflicts. Modern neurophysiological and psychological knowledge should potentiate individual brains and lead to the creation of a "world brain." The human brain is not a dictatorial *director* of individual behavior, but rather a *reactive mechanism* to the information provided by sensory inputs. In a similar way, the "world brain" should be a reactive entity, with each member aware of his original bias and with the group aware of its dependence on the functions of individual brains.

The key to human potential is an organ we all share: the brain. Brains are similar in all healthy newborn human babies — in black, white, and yellow races; in socialist and capitalist countries; in rich and poor families. All of us are born with immature brains, ready to receive stimuli from their sensory environment, but initially unable to understand, select, or reject incoming information. Our brains are structured by the nourishment and training they are given. Genetic inheritance makes possible the appearance of cerebral structures, but their functional and material development are determined by the quality and quantity of sensory stimuli received, and the adequacy of the food supplied during growth. It is the social environment — not personal preference — which determines the ideological framework of the individual mind. Cultural conditioning, ideological indoctrination, and education in general will modify the anatomy, physiology and biochemistry of our neurons. The experience of each individual leaves material traces stored in his intracerebral memory.

In a recent article, Alexander King, President of the Club of Rome, stressed the need for "new ethical guidelines and moral values on which individuals and governments can operate," based on significant advances in the mind-brain-behavior complex. That science may provide a background of understanding of human conditions, promoting the values needed for survival and for human development. The neurosciences should deal with the nature of man, the meaning of consciousness, and the quality of life, which is, to a great extent, a relative value dependent on personal standards which reflect cultural indoctrination.

With the intelligent organization of our resources by leaders who are both efficient and ethical; by overriding national interests with international cooperation, our goal to improve the quality of life for all mankind may be realized. This goal involves the use of our natural environment with a human purpose: it must serve us. The possibility is unique in history because it depends on the appearance on earth of the only organ capable of awareness, superior intelligence, and future planning. The brain we were given was not invented by man: it is a product of natural evolution. We are only beginning to learn to use this source of power. The goals for mankind should be determined by the collective mind of the species, superseding limited and shortsighted political ideologies.

COMMENTARY ON A. DE JASAY'S PAPER

Károly Ákos

De Jasay has singled out three variable characteristics of importance in conditioning people's life regarding both socio-economic systems in order to show that they take different shapes and intensities in those systems. In both systems there are private and public forms of ownership. Under capitalism, private ownership is predominating; under socialism, the public form. It is consistent with the capitalist system for certain prior charges to be publicly owned, but it is alien to it for the equity, *i.e.*, the right to the residual income left after prior charges, to belong to the political authority. Under socialism, the equity of productive enterprises is publicly owned. Control under socialism belongs to the political authority; under capitalism, to a separate subset of persons. The extreme type of the people who decide what is to be done with the equity in the future is, under capitalism, the stock market speculator; under socialism, the civil servant. The first type is moved by hopes for greater gains and fears of greater loss than is the case with the second type. The implications for the quality of life seem unmistakable.

The comparison of the two social organizations describes them as linear versus triangular systems. Capitalism is triangular with capital, labour, and the state at the three angles. Accordingly, in politics a balance-of-power prevails with a modicum of impartiality on the side of the state. The socialist organisation eliminates the triangularity, creating linearity, as the universal owner-employer is, at the same time, the political authority, too. The triangularity can be advantageous, *e.g.* for environmental protection.

The whole style of life is characterized by certain divergencies as shown with regard to the *agency problem* and *public and private goods,* too. Both systems may even try or pretend to be what the other is. Capitalism strives to be "caring", welfarist, and "social", and socialism has, from time to time, ambitions to be efficient, technically progressive, and able to bring about material abundance.

A fine analyst, the author made us richer with a number of insights about the influence of both economies on the quality of life. At the same, time it seems his implicit opinion is that economics is the sole determinant of the quality of life. I cannot resist the incitement to speak here about certain human biological relations which, strangely enough, remain invisible through conceptual blindness. For the sake of brevity I shall illustrate my point by only one example.

As an introduction, let us remember that there is a quite common but rather neglected disease: cerebral palsy, an affliction beginning in infancy. In the United States for each million inhabitants, there are about ten thousand cerebral palsy children, of whom a quarter are serious cases. What this means will be shown by an example.

The subject of my example is the case of Merle, a West-German girl. As it happened, her mother wrote a letter to me on February 13, 1985. Merle was at that time 20 months old. As a spastic tetraplegic from the age of five months, she received the prescribed usual physiotherapy (Vojta, Bobath). Her condition and her mother's worries can clearly be seen in the following question quoted from the letter. "Can you see some way of help for Merle by which she could learn to sit, to stand, to walk?" At that time Merle was helpless and apathetic, without a satisfactory quality of life, obviously, while fully provided by her mother with her necessities, and by one of the most modern capitalist state health services against her disease. The professional prognosis about her recovery was hopeless.

Merle is now nearly four years old. She is a lively child with a strong will. She can, with a great indefatigability, walk a kilometer ("without exaggeration" — her mother wrote in a letter of August 14, 1987), can ascend the stairs, *etc*. She can sit alone at a table on a common chair while eating and playing. She well understands, as other children of her age, what is told to her but can clearly speak only some words as yet. She helps her mother much while dressing. A cursory glance at her may convince everybody about the high quality of her life. Her change affected her mother's mood, of course: her daughter became a source of happiness, she wrote in a letter.

Merle's change is due to a specific condition which, surprisingly is nearly invisible. She was not cured with any medicine; in fact, no specialist participated in her treatment. Even the physiotherapy which met aversion from Merle, has been, at my suggestion, stopped, in spite of the opposition of the district physician. The specific condition generating Merle's change was the mother's altered behavior. It may seem that this statement is incredible.

My first suggestion for the mother was to come with Merle to Budapest and visit the Petô Institute for an extended time, as the Petô-method can be very effectively used against cerebral palsy. But a child under three years cannot be treated without her mother. However, Merle's mother having two other young children to look after, could not follow my advice. As we, my wife and I, wished to help them, having no other possibility, we came and told and showed the mother how to deal with her baby. (Let it be mentioned here that we are not members of the Petô Institute. I was a friend of the late Dr. Petô, and studied his method and its progression for twenty years. Still it took more than a decade after his death, in 1967, before my wife and I found the theoretical explanation for the marvelous results of his method.)

Shortly after our first instructions given to Merle's mother, we were pleased to learn that Merle improved perceptibly: the apathetic state stopped. So our instruction relative to the attained development continued, mostly by correspondence. We even wrote a pamphlet for mothers of cerebral palsy babies when a second mother and child joined them. Also, at rare occasions, we met Merle and her mother personally, when they visited the Petô

Institute for two or three weeks some hours per day to get practical impressions.

The mother's behavior alteration can be described succinctly as follows. She learned how a baby with grave cerebral palsy could be activated by her mother to certain play with her if the mother restricted symptoms of the disease. On the other hand, the mother should deal with her baby much as mothers in general do with their normal babies. However, a mother of a normal baby is not aware of the sense of play. At first the baby is motivated for activity, and then his movements are channeled by the mother, thus increasing cooperation with her. This is done spontaneously by the mother and therefore it is thought to be intrinsic to the baby's development. Still, the mother of a cerebral palsy baby needs to get special instructions for dealing with her child in the above sense, and, in particular, concerning his symptoms.

The case of Merle was the first occasion for us to understand how amazing it is that a mother of a cerebral palsy baby is able to follow such instructions and apply them in practice proficiently.

Theoretically, it appears that when the mother is playing with her baby, or is nursing it, an "intercerebral field" between the two brains functions. It is formed by the "cooperative educational two-way relationship" between the mother and the baby, and its changes transform the physiological cerebral functions of the child. Thus the "anthropogenic cooperation" of the mother with her baby are, in fact, an inductive psychogenesis. The mother attains this effect not only unintentionally while she is playing with and nursing her baby, but by unconsciously following that guidance coming from the child's behavior. The importance, even the existence, of this guidance became noticeable only by the healing of cerebral palsy. Without the baby's directive influence on its mother, or the insufficiency of this, the rise of the performance level of the baby slows down or stops. The lack of guidance by the baby to the mother is a result of its movement disorders caused by brain damage. This brain damage is held by general medical opinion to be the *direct* cause of the cerebral palsy. However, it is its *indirect* cause, depriving the child's mother from the guidance she needs for her anthropogenic cooperation. Under normal conditions, the baby helps the mother to understand and solve his problems, and to increase his cooperation with his mother. As he learns, in their cooperative educational two-way relationship, to give increasing help toward the solution of his own problems, he is moving toward selfsufficiency. A mother of a cerebral palsy baby on the other hand, must and can be instructed to motivate her child to play with her adequately and to follow her baby's initially incomplete guidance, as Merle's case first showed. She is able, thus, to enhance the child's cooperation. As a part of this development, the symptoms of cerebral palsy will diminish, and, finally stop permanently. And here my example ends.

I wished to show that the mother's anthropogenic cooperation, so important for her child's quality of life, usually remains invisible. This seems to be paradigmatic, as anthropogenic cooperation operates among human beings until death. I might finish my discussion here. However, the case of Merle provided another lesson too.

We expected people would be pleased to hear that mothers could effectively curb cerebral palsy, a hateful calamity of mankind. It not only brings tragedy for millions of families, but burdens the state health services with very great expenses. And now we had in the mother-centered application of the Petô method, a nearly cost free solution of the problem, the traditional institutional solution of which would inevitably be limited to a small number of patients. However, in capitalist West-Germany, Merle's mother had to overcome the resistance of bureaucrats and specialists sometimes fighting against her with psychological terror. When she wished to share her experiences with other mothers of cerebral palsy babies for their benefit, *e.g.*, in a letter intended to be published in a journal for parents, she was hampered by a professor of special education. Thus only three other German mothers have so far gone along with her succesfully. Also, in socialist Hungary, the director of the overcrowded Petô Institute will not take steps to promote the mother-centered unlimited form of the Petô method, although she knows about their marvelous early results. Hence, in respect to the quality of life, not only the invisibility of relevant human biological relations should be taken into consideration, but also that active resistance which may arise from bureaucratic, monopolistic tendencies, from the misconceived defence of particular interests, and so.

ECONOMIC COOPERATION AND INTEGRATION OF EUROPE

Dr. Andrzej Werner

Since East-West cooperation is supposed to build European bridges, an *integration of Europe* and its short- and long-term progress will here be reviewed. We will examine briefly East-West trade record and its true business potential, as well as the capability of both the market and socialist economies to adapt to each other prior to their merger in a pan-European set-up.

In this respect, the post-war period has not brought much interdependence between East and West. Although, after a boost by *détente* and by easy Western credits in the 1970's, the trade of the Soviet Union and the six Socialist Central European countries[1] with Western Europe[2] grew very rapidly, the final outcome cannot be seen as a return to normalcy. The level of seventy billion dollars in intra-European trade in 1980, and about sixty billion dollars throughout the 1980s, did not mean a volume which is characteristic for neighbourly relations of industrial nations. It remains a small fraction of world trade. Even worse is the case of economic cooperation, which constitutes less than five percent of East-West transactions. Altogether it makes economic integration between Eastern and Western Europe still a topic for a very distant future.

1. REINTEGRATION OF EUROPE

Coming to the idea of "international economic integration", it is worth noting that, in the sense of linking up separate economies into arrangements of a broader scope, this idea has but a very brief history. The term "integration" was applied initially only to company mergers ("horizontal integration", "vertical integration"). It was not until after World War II, in connection with the appearance of the "Little Europe" of the six West European countries, that this term was first applied to programmes and processes of bringing closer and unifying economies on a trans-national plane.[3]

The very idea and the terms coined in this connection are by now well covered by various definitions and described in the literature.[4] This obviously did not help in tackling the subject, and actually hindered discussions. As someone noted, the very "attempt to bring a semblance of order to the fathomless chaos brought to the understanding of international economic cooperation by the myriad institutional concepts would call for a separate study".[5] Lacking a generally accepted definition, we shall rely on the approach taken by Wilhelm Röpke, one of the forerunners of the idea of European economic *rapprochement*.

According to Röpke, international economic integration means a state of affairs which allows for developing trade relations between various economies in an equally unrestrained and profitable way as "within the national economy".[6] Hence between the individual countries there should be a close community of markets and prices, turning them into a larger, natural entity. As the very minimum this, obviously enough, calls for a multilateral mode of conducting international trade within the zone, and free convertibility between currencies of the participant states.

As Röpke underlined, "If anything deserves the term of international economic integration, then certainly it was the pre-1914 world economy".[7] At that time, European economic cooperation was also marked by a high degree of openness to the outside world. All the countries themselves had close interlinks with the world economy.

Still, immediately following World War I, and particularly at the time of the Great Depression, there was a reversal of the earlier tendency to foster the free flow of goods, capital, resources and people. In effect the 1930s marked the final disintegration of the European and world economy.[8] Hence the current need for and aspirations toward European integration must actually come down to its *reintegration*. Hence the effort, above all, calls for eliminating the *causes* which led to disintegration, an element we do not always care to admit.

It is not out of nostalgia that we relate this historical experience. Prior to 1914 we also saw resort to military means for solving various trade and economic conflicts. In fact, one would be hard pressed to call the world of that day and the overall state of intra-European relations as *"une belle époque"*. Still, we look back to those days just realising that, unlike the present, both before 1914 and after, up to 1933, Europe found itself capable after every war of resuming normal trade and fostering economic cooperation. Currently, even full normalisation is hard to attain, to say nothing of a reciprocal economic *rapprochement* of the two parts of Europe. The persisting divisions, and their very political and systemic nature, continue to prevent this.

Another lesson of those days up to 1933 should be the realisation that economic protectionism, state control, and nationalism are not only the enemy of free trade, but that economic tensions, the antagonistic blocs and their rivalries lead, in the end, to military belligerence. The fact that contemporary Europe has so far successfully avoided another "civil war" was possible, as we know, only at the cost of constant friction, costly armaments and the development of nuclear weapons — all of which are hardly tolerable. Accepting that, peaceful coexistence should contribute to more than just tempering mutual hostilities. it should lead also to probing the roots of the present divisions. Here, we face another hard question: how these roots and divisions should be treated and addressed? How can their adverse effects be prevented altogether, or, at least, minimised?

2. Economic Divisions

While on the subject of causes underlying the present divisions, we have to remember that but a few years were needed after World War II for the anti-Nazi coalition to disintegrate for good. The old divisions concerning Germany were replaced with new ones, by their nature still more fundamental and conflicting. The border dividing the East from the West runs along the Elbe River and it splits the continent in two also on the economic plane. In this area one may note, also, the most fundamental political and organizational changes.

On the *western* side: the Marshall Plan and OEEC founded their reciprocal relations on the principle of liberalising trade — with the European Communities serving as a nucleus for broader economic and political integration. Furthermore, this "Little Europe" has firmly anchored the western part of Germany with the West. The Federal Republic had been subjected to a process of decartelisation and economic deconcentration. It had also shaken off its pre-war totalitarian features linked with the Nazi regime; in effect, West Germany became like the rest of the neighbouring democracies.

On the *eastern* side: following the take-over of power by the Communists in eight central and south-eastern European countries, an entirely new economic system was introduced there, with the paramount role in the entire economy played by the Communist Party and the State. In effect, in the eastern part of Europe the play of market forces was replaced by very rigid central planning, itemised production quotas and targets operated by a hierarchical management applying centralised allocation of production means, capital equipment and financial resources. In this, very much Soviet type of system, sometimes called the "command economy", business motivation and decision-making processes are much different, and much more entangled in bureaucracy, than is the case with western countries. The calculation of costs is entirely different. A different meaning is assigned, and a different role played by economic benefit, with the social function taking precedence over profits, and regulation and subsidies over selfsustaining growth.[9]

Even in the area of foreign trade, the price system is different. A government monopoly on trade, tight controls over imports and exports, the non-convertibility of currencies and their central allocation, make for having the domestic market prices bear only a very loose and very indirect connection with world market prices. The tools of trade policy differ, with a clear preponderance of protectionism and non-economic instruments. With such tightly insulated and closed markets — and, in the sense of classical economics, one would have to call them "non-markets" — there is no need for resorting to quantitative restrictions, duties, or other instruments of market economies.

Even the economic links with the Soviet Union and the other Eastern Bloc countries are but institutional in nature.

> While at times the term "common market of the socialist countries" has been used, it is — as we noted — no more than a metaphor, especially when applied to the international links established to-date, where the "institution" of the international market mechanism is practically non-existent and national markets are isolated from each other.[10]

This does not change the fact that these countries politically and administratively orient themselves for trade and economic cooperation mainly among themselves. From the moment the socialist camp was formed, the substantive and institutional bonds of its member states, particularly with the Soviet Union, were of an integrating character, though for the first two decades, 1948–1968, even the very term "economic integration" was political anathema.

Divergencies in systems and deep economic divisions which came to the fore, starting with the close of the 1940s, between socialist and capitalist Europe have become further cemented by conflicting ideologies and openly hostile political programmes. As was noted earlier, both sides claimed superiority of their systems. The East predicted the inevitable collapse of capitalism and the victory of socialism. The West "to make the world safer for democracy" has launched containment policies with overtones hinting at the "roll-back of Communism". So it came as no surprise that, along with the start of the Cold War, intra-European trade in 1949 dropped by half to less than $1 billion. A slow recovery started only with the "thaw" of 1955.

While it did mean a steady increase in the trade volume along with some liberalisation, another ten years were needed for the first transactions in economic cooperation to manifest themselves. The first harbingers came in the latter half of the 1960s, or, more specifically, at the turn of that decade, when the first government-level long-range framework agreements were negotiated in the area of industrial, scientific, and technological cooperation. Next, already at the time of *détente,* a full thirty years after the war, there was some further trade liberalisation. The West also considerably curtailed its strategic export controls carried out through COCOM.

Yet the most important element, which in the end was decisive for the real boom registered at the time in intra-European trade, were Western credit facilities. When the "Helsinki spirit" permeated through to financial relations, and Western banks and governments started to advance considerable sums to the socialist countries, the purchases of the latter in Western Europe climbed from some $5 billion in annual volume in 1970 to more than $30 billion by 1980, a 6-fold increase. Western countries for the first time in years had a surplus in their trade with Eastern Europe.[11]

TABLE 1 (1958–1980)

Trade of the Socialist East with Western Europe (in current prices in billion of U.S. dollars)						
EXPORTS:	1958	1960	1965	1970	1975	1980
CMEA[6]	0.8	1.0	1.7	3.0	8.1	15.8
USSR	0.6	0.9	1.1	2.2	7.3	21.8
TOTAL	1.4	1.9	2.8	5.2	15.4	37.6
IMPORTS:						
CMEA[6]	0.7	1.0	1.7	3.1	11.6	16.4
USSR	0.4	0.7	0.7	2.0	8.2	14.4
TOTAL	1.1	1.7	2.4	5.1	19.8	30.8
Grand Total:						
TURNOVER	2.5	3.6	5.2	10.3	35.2	68.4

Source: Own calculations on the basis of *Monthly Statistics of Foreign Trade,* Series A, OECD, Paris.

Growing imports by Western Europe were also held back by the market situation and growing prices for the primary products and food produce exported by the East, and particularly the fuel market following the two oil shocks. In effect, exports from the socialist countries to the West grew seven-fold, exceeding $37 billion. Despite such a dynamic expansion of reciprocal economic relations, the divisions present between the two parts of Europe have not been overcome.

Intra-European trade, though significant for both groups of partners, and particularly important for the socialist countries, which desire to import much more, remains on an unsatisfactorily low level in relation to the volume of world trade, the more so when one considers the geographic proximity and the considerable share of both parts of Europe in world GDP. Suffice it to recall that, in 1986, the CMEA countries represented only 4.2 per cent of EEC exports, and 3.9 per cent of EEC imports.

TABLE 2 (1981–1986)

Trade of the Socialist East with Western Europe (in current prices in billions of U.S. dollars)						
EXPORTS:	1981	1982	1983	1984	1985	1986
CMEA [6]	12.9	12.1	11.7	13.2	13.2	14.6
USSR	22.0	22.9	22.4	23.6	21.0	17.4
TOTAL	34.9	35.0	34.1	36.8	34.2	32.0
IMPORTS:						
CMEA [6]	13.7	10.7	9.9	10.1	11.1	13.3
USSR	13.7	13.6	15.3	13.8	13.8	14.4
TOTAL	27.4	24.3	25.2	23.9	24.9	27.7
Grand Total:						
TURNOVER	62.3	59.3	59.3	60.7	59.1	59.7

Source: Own calculations on the basis of *Monthly Statistics of Foreign Trade*, Series A, OECD, Paris.

The European socialist countries have but a marginally higher share in EFTA trade. Even though their relations with the neutral countries are frequently cited as a model of good-neighbour East-

West cooperation, the Soviet Union plus the European socialist countries participated in only 7.6 per cent of EFTA exports, and in 6.1 per cent of EFTA imports (figures for 1986). The share of transactions of longer range cooperation, again, remains negligible. It is estimated to account for barely 3 to 4 per cent of overrall East-West trade.[12] Given all this, it would still be difficult to claim any degree of economic *rapprochement* between the two parts of Europe.

As it turned out, the 1970s boom, though undoubtedly very important for the development of mutual relations, failed to secure the necessary stability. Immediately following the events in Afghanistan of 1979 and in Poland of 1981, a market curtailment took place in economic relations. As part of its policy of economic sanctions, the West withdrew numerous commercial and financial facilities. In turn the East charged the United States — above all — of waging an economic war, and called for erecting an edifice of international economic security. This turnaround was affected by the worsening overall economic conditions in Europe and elswhere, coupled with substantial cuts of many hard-currency imports by the East, due to its entanglement in heavy foreign borrowings which now had to be serviced.

Today, from the perspective of several years, one can observe another alarming development. Both parts of Europe have further begun to *drift away* from each other. The Western countries are involved with restructuring their economies to effect more technological change, raise the share represented by services in the GDP and in overall employment, and increase the share of sophisticated new industries, such as electronics, highly advanced computers, genetic engineering, *etc*. Their Eastern counterparts, on the other hand, still remain largely inward-looking and heavily focused on the so called Sector A; capital equipment and heavy industries, to the exclusion of consumer goods and services. They go on with developing their extremely energy-consuming and material intensive industries.[13] Moreover, in East-West trade, the CMEA countries increasingly tend to do business not with their West European neighbours but with overseas countries.

3. Pressures for Change

Of course, all this contrasts with the hopes raised by the 1970s *détente*, when both goverment leaders and the media harped on broad normalisation and meaningful change. This led people to the idea that the post-war barriers would be dismantled, and Europe at last would return to normalcy. Nonetheless, the barriers did not come down. Despite the human contacts — which continue — Europe remains divided, and is bound to remain abnormal and potentially explosive.

Although there are still some people who speak of convergence, of an eastward or westward tilt, for the realists the likeliest scenario is that nothing much will have changed by the year 2000 and even during the early decades of the next century. These, however, are not the prospects that present and future generations of Europeans wish to be reconciled with for the next 40 years. The peoples of Europe have never come to terms with the existing divisions and the ensuing hardships affecting them in so many ways for so long.

It is also a certainty that overwhelming might has not solved the problems of Europe either. It seems incapable of ever solving them in the future, though power and coercion have been used as the main instruments for policing international and regional stability. Although for pessimists the quest for change continue to be the art of the impossible, the people of Europe feel that it must go on.

Given the search for peaceful, *non*-military solutions suitable to present day Europe, a natural choice seems to be East-West trade and cooperation. These, it is said, bring people together, and could lay the material foundations for European *rapprochement* and regional security. There is also a conviction about great inherent reserves in the area of economic cooperation. Some go so far as to suggest revitalising the Rapacki Plan for denuclearisation and disarmament in Central Europe, coupled with a more assertive pursuit of economic interfaces between the two halves of Europe. This, it is said, could prove a better way for easing tensions between NATO and the Warsaw Pact than trying to deal with military confrontation using the traditional, yet very difficult, process of arms control. In this context, various forms of joint creative financing schemes have been suggested, with some even talking of a Western type of Marshall Plan for Eastern Europe.

More daring ideas have also been advanced. Since the Soviet allies in Europe seem now to have a much wider leeway in shaping their own economic security, it has been suggested that the West should switch from an Atlantic Alliance to a Pan-European Entente, to assure peace and jobs and that

> by cutting the Gordian knots of their separate political and economic limitations, both CMEA and EEC might be able to overcome their separate limitations through a more perfect West and East European economic union and political alliance.[14]

Hence, it is suggested, any further integration of the twelve EEC countries should cross the Elbe River and embrace the East European members of CMEA to form — as a start — a pan-European trading bloc, independent of either superpower.

4. Grand Designs

It is difficult to object to new visions. Indeed, whatever else can be done to undo Europe's post-war divisions should be investigated. What role could East-West trade and economic cooperation play in this? What other non-economic arrangements must be made? On the other hand, such daring ideas appear to lack political realism and seem to call for too much too soon. One should consider more closely what kind of political and system changes could be vested in the East through new openings in intra-European business while the political atmosphere is conducive to this.

In that respect, the post-war record is quite straight. The West found itself unable to quarantine the East economically or to check its economic growth, although it did succeed in delaying specific elements of that growth. The same held true for the development of weapons systems. The East can be denied access to certain technologies, but it cannot be prevented, above all in the case of Soviet

Union, from acquiring or matching such know-how in the not-so-distant future.[15]

Furthermore, the last 40 years have clearly shown that political concessions would not be traded by the East, nor could the West's economic leverage bring about any significant political or system changes in the Eastern part of Europe. Never has a situation developed where the USSR would give precedence to economic advantages before its strategic or political interests, including in its relations with Western Europe. It would be naive to seek any analogies with the Tsar's economic or trade policy of pre-revolutionary days. There is no doubt that any sort of "Alaska deal", or the sell-out of any sphere of influence, must be categorically ruled out. Moreover, Soviet autarchy is sufficiently well rooted to thwart attempts at forcing a collapse of the Soviet system through economic actions.

To these sober conclusions the Trilateral Commission added another one: "that the extension of economic relations with the East will not lead any of the CMEA countries into a political alignment with the West."[16] For the Soviet Union and for its six fellow-members in the Comecon, it is an iron principle to make sure that their own trade constitutes 60 per cent of their overall turnover, with the remaining trade relations spread out geographically and kept down to a safe level, never to exceed 40 per cent of the total.

Similar concern over undue reliance on any single source of supply or marketing outlet was shown by the West when it came to the Natural Gas Agreement with the Soviet Union a few years ago. It may seem a paradox, but there are many facts to indicate that efforts to bring the East and the West closer to each other are anything but rooted in business advantages. Certainly, the economic crises of the socialist countries are being overcome (if and when they are) mainly within the bounds of their own national economies. When these countries do decide to resort to foreign help, they address themselves for assistance to the Soviet Union or fellow-members in the CMEA. The reasons for such a course of action are not entirely political, either. It is just that much simpler to trade with these countries, as they pose lower volume requirements and quality standards. Moreover, any cooperative arrangements or other measures aimed at the economic integration of those countries come into being as a result of political decisions and very detailed inter-governmental agreements. The interests of a specific national enterprise matter little in such cases.

Now let us have a closer look on the potential of the European Economic Community. There is no doubt that the EEC played an important — perhaps decisive — role in creating peace in Europe, especially in its western part. Its member states which in the past have frequently gone to war with each other, have now for many years become oriented towards very close cooperation, and cooperation not limited to the economic sphere, at that. Their reciprocal trade represents almost half of their overall trade, thus laying solid foundations for the economic interdependence of one country with another, and a global interdependence of the Community as a whole. This tempers any persisting differences, and leads to further unification of the member countries. Does this mean, however, that a similar integration programme may be incorporated into pan-European relations? Certainly not, although trade and economic ties between the East and the West should be much closer than they are now.

The relations maintained by the socialist countries with the EEC and the EEC Commission in Brussels are nothing new. Still, one must bear in mind that until Helsinki, *i.e.*, up to 1975, the East had denied even *de facto* recognition to the EEC. The author can still remember the time when, in the early 1960s, he along with members of other delegations from the socialist countries, had to leave the United Nations debates on sugar and wheat in Geneva whenever EEC Commission representatives were present. Still, it is not routine for the CMEA countries to have bilateral commercial treaties with the EEC. Hence, for any CMEA country, full membership or even a looser association with the EEC are out of the question. Any EEC efforts directed to this end would be considered in the East as unfriendly gestures, trespassing on vital interests of the Socialist Commonwealth.

However, let us assume the impossible — in the foreseeable

future — that the political climate in Europe has finally changed so much that it has become sufficiently peaceful and good-neighbourly for institutional relations between socialist Central Europe and the EEC for cooperation to stop being a political anathema. Would it then be possible for the EEC to admit new members from the East into the Community? One could really doubt that.

You could point out the many stumbling blocks to enlargement of the EEC which stem from differences in the levels of economic development between the industrial North and Greece, Spain, Portugal, or Turkey. When one would consider the CMEA countries, further economic factors would inhibit access to the Common Market. In addition to inconvertibility and payment problems of the CMEA members, one could cite, *e.g.,* their trade protectionism, the monopolistic structure of their economy and its omnipresent statism, all on a scope unprecedented in modern times. But the decisive factor preventing both sides from considering the possible marriage of any socialist country with the EEC would be the antagonistic differences — political, systemic and ideological — which have split Europe into capitalist and socialist halves. The differences by themselves prevent the possibility of transforming the Common Market of Twelve into a pan-European Trading block. Of course the same applies to possible expansion of the CMEA.

Anyway, quite recently at a reception in Bonn in September of 1987, Erich Honecker reminded the other guests that they should nurture no doubts that capitalism and socialism were and shall remain to each other "as fire and water".[17] That leaves us with what business is usual in the divided Europe.

5. Prospects for East-West Trade

Many still believe that intra-European trade has a great untapped potential. They think that should the political and economic barriers be removed, trade and economic cooperation between both parts of Europe would develop very dynamically. In fact, things look very different. The incompatibility of the two economic systems, not to mention other economic and trade factors, keep, and will keep, the two parts of Europe well apart.

Undoubtedly, the geographic proximity, well-developed communications, and other existing elements of the economic infrastructure, such as the networks of banks, insurance companies, *etc.*, could facilitate economic cooperation and the easing of each other's shortfalls. These are to be found both in the branch structure of industries of the East and of the West. It should be kept in mind that the East, especially the USSR, has more raw materials and fuels than the West European countries. It is also an irrefutable fact that the markets of socialist countries suffer from an excess demand for many goods and services, and that their economies urgently require a profound restructuring.

No doubt, the continuing technological gap between the CMEA countries and the West represents a substantial potential for Western business, now and in the years ahead. Nonetheless, there are several problems inherent even in this. Apart from the concern that technology transfers can contribute to bolstering Soviet and Warsaw Pact military capability, there are several economic and systemic constraints. The single most significant one remains the inability of the East to produce enough export surpluses to pay for its imports. And this brings us, again, to the systemic heart of the matter of why East-West trade has once again reached a low point, and cannot enjoy a normal development.

One should then ask whether the Eastern debt and payments difficulties are caused by international politics or Western protectionism? Or do they stem from the structural inability of the Soviet-type economies to produce enough goods and services to be marketed home and abroad? The latter seems to be the answer.

Economic shortages that plague the Eastern countries cause both a great demand for imports and a lack of exportable goods, a situation which, in itself, cannot generate much trade unless new easy foreign credits are forthcoming.[18]

Certainly, there are trade and economic barriers faced by Eastern exporters. Certainly, the Common Agricultural Policy, protection schemes for ailing EEC industries, and the EEC trade preferences for developing countries weigh heavily on opportunities for Eastern exporters. But this, in itself, does not explain why the CMEA share in EEC imports has been steadily shrinking: from an insignificant 4.2 per cent in 1983 to 3.2 per cent three years later. The same situation can be observed in EEC exports.[19] The share of Soviet and East European markets declined from 3.1 per cent in 1983 to a paltry 2.5 per cent by 1986. If trade barriers were the main reason behind this trend, then intra-German trade — conducted duty-free and partly subsidized — would have reached a much higher volume. In reality things look different. In the 1980's, the share of the Federal Republic of Germany in the total foreign trade turnover of the German Democratic Republic oscillated between 8.5 per cent and 12 per cent, while the share of the GDR in West German trade was always less than 2 per cent. On top of that, a significant part (30%) of the GDR's exports go to West Berlin.

The trade successes of the so-called NICs (Newly Industrializing Countries such as Taiwan and South Korea) are another proof that it is not trade barriers, but overall economic performance which is behind the East's export failure in Western markets. The NICs — which after the Second World War started from a generally lower level of development than the CMEA countries — had been developing so rapidly that already by 1963 their *manufactured* exports to the OECD as a whole were, in terms of market share, almost equal to the share of the socialist countries (1.8 % *vs.* 1.6 %) However, over the years the share of the NICs has steadily climbed to reach 8.6 per cent, while the CMEA has recorded a *drop* to a negligible 1.4 per cent.[20] Things could not have turned out otherwise, taking into account the fact that, in addition to the economies of shortages, the CMEA countries have so far failed to turn from inward-looking and extensive economies to the outward-looking with an intensive growth. As a result, the commodity pattern of their exports to the West has remained unchanged for years. Instead of exporting highly processed, sophisticated manufacture of goods and services, they export fuels: oil, gas, coal. The latter, along with other primary and agricultural products earn between $3/5$ and $2/3$ of the East's total hard currency revenues. One could add that the total *per capita* exports of the CMEA countries in 1980's merely reached the level of between $350 (USSR, Poland) and $1,300–1,600 (GDR and

Bulgaria), while at that same time the *per capita* exports of West European countries were at the level of $3,000–$6,000.

All this indicates that Western credits and voluminous imports in the 1970s did not bring much change to the East. "Imports for Exports" and other ambitious investment programmes of the Eastern countries did not produce the anticipated trade surpluses, so feared by some in the West. As grains, fuels, and an assortment of consumer goods used up a great part of the earnings, trade in technologically advanced products with the West remained at a much lower level than had been expected. In general, the rate of absorption of foreign technologies by the East remains low. Imported technology cannot be easily diffused throughout the economy.[21] Furthermore, Eastern enterprises have limited abilities to match the productivity levels attained in the West using the same technologies. Hence, not much can be done from outside to bring fundamental performance and export improvements over there. The brunt of this task falls on the East Europeans themselves — to carry through economic and political reforms in their countries. They have to first succeed with *"perestroika"* before pan-European cooperation can expand, and reintegration of Europe can become a fact.

6. CONCLUSION

All this does not mean that, in the meantime, the efforts to promote business and intra-European cooperation are to be slowed down. Both the East and the West should foster all possible actions on all possible levels — by private business, governments, and international organizations. Special attention should be turned to liberalizing trade and, above all, to financial facilities which can ease the debt burden faced by the East. Joint ventures and other arrangements for conducting business on CMEA markets should be actively probed.

Apart from government and business initiatives, multilateral approaches should also be considered. The existing international organizations, such as GATT, OECD, and the UN Economic Commission for Europe have been set up specifically to encourage expanded trade relations. Other opportunities for East-West cooperation could come as a spin-off from EEC-CMEA dialogue. Further meaningful assistance could be offered by international financial agencies, such as the IMF and the World Bank, to those of the CMEA countries that are advancing their economic *perestroika*.

Economic reforms, creating a real market in the socialist countries, will take considerable time, probably years. Further, the modernization and reconstruction of European economies will not be easy for the East nor the West. Social and political tensions could ensue as a dangerous "offspring". It would be in the common European interest to ease economic frictions and prevent them from effectively distorting the international climate.

One area, for certain, calls for *urgent* action now: namely pan-European protection of the environment — on a scale much broader than the one being discussed now. Economic cooperation in this vital field could well serve as a stimulus and model for pan-European undertakings in other fields of mutual interest.

NOTES

1. For the purpose of this presentation the terms "East" and "Eastern Europe" are used to denote seven members of CMEA, the Council for Mutual Economic Assistance (also known as the Comecon): the Soviet Union plus six countries of Central and Southern Europe: Bulgaria, Czechoslovakia, the German Democratic Republic (GDR), Hungary, Poland and Romania. The remaining CMEA members, notably Mongolia, Cuba, Yugoslavia, are not covered by this term.

   As the Soviet Union is the dominant country on all counts in Socialist Europe, it is right to note that its GDP is estimated to be about 2.5 times the size of the six CMEA members of Eastern Europe taken together. Poland represents about $\frac{1}{3}$ of Eastern Europe's GDP and about the same proportion of its population.

2. The term "West" is normally equated with the industrial countries of Western Europe, North America plus Japan — members all of the OECD, the Organization for Economic

Cooperation and Development. In this paper we refer to "Western Europe" meaning all the European countries of the EEC and EFTA, regardless of their geographical location, given that the main division of our continent runs along "capitalist" and "socialist" lines.

3. Jan Tinbergen explained in the foreword to his *International Economic Integration* (Amsterdam: Elsevier 1954) that its first edition in 1945 was entitled "International Economic Cooperation".
4. See: Fritz Machlup: *A History of Thought in Economic Integration*, London and Basingstoke: The Macmillan Press 1977.
5. Andrzej Wasilkowski: *Prawne i ekonomiczne pojecia integracji miedzynarodowej* (Legal and Economic Concepts of International Integration) in: Studia Prawnicze PAN, 1969, Volume 23, p. 53.
6. Wilhelm Röpke: *"International Order and Economic Integration"* Dordrecht: Reiser Publ. Co. 1959, p. 225.
7. Wilhelm Röpke: "Integration und Desintegration der internationalen Wirtschaft", in: Erwin von Beckerath, ed.: *Wirtschaftsfragen der freien Welt*, Frankfurt: Fritz Knapp 1957, p. 494.
8. Hence the first book by W. Röpke was entitled: "International Economic Desintegration" (Edinburgh: Hodge 1942). Other authors also refrained from writing on "integration". See, *e.g.*: Moritz J. Bonn: *The Crumbling of Empire: The Disintegration of World Economy*, London: Allen and Unwin 1938.
9. See: Milton Friedman: *Market or Plan? An Exposition of the Case for the Market*, London: CRCE 1984.
10. Marian Guzek: *Miedzynarodowa integracja gospodarcza w socjaliźmie* (International Economic Integration in Socialism) Warszawa: Panstwowe Wydawnictwa Ekonomiczne 1971, p. 55.
11. Data used throughout in this paper come from what are believed to be reliable sources, mostly from Western statistics. However, no attempt has been made to attach footnotes indi-

cating the sources or data adjustments, since the figures are meant only to aid in general analysis of major developments and prospects.
12. Antoni Makac: *Handel Wschód-Zachód. Miejsce i szanse Polski* (East-West Trade. Poland's Place and Chances), Warszawa: Wydawnictwo Ministerstwa Obrony Narodowej 1986, p. 99.
13. See: Jan Winiecki: *Economic Prospects — East and West. A View from the East,* London: CRCE 1987.
14. Andre Gunder Frank: *The European Challenge. From Atlantic Alliance to Pan-European Entente for Peace and Jobs,* Nottingham: Spokesman 1983, p. 84.
15. See: *The Economist's* comment on the latest Kongsberg-Toshiba sales to the Soviet Union: "Come on, COCOM" (July 31, 1987), pp. 18–19.
16. Robert V. Roosa, Michiya Matsukawa, Armin Gutowski: *East-West Trade at a Crossroads: Economic Relations with the Soviet Union and Eastern Europe,* The Trilateral Report: 24, New York: New York University Press 1982, p. 5.
17. See: Martin E. Suskind's report in *Süddeutsche Zeitung* (September 9, 1987), p. 1.
18. See: János Kornai: *Economics of Shortage,* Amsterdam - New York — Oxford: North-Holland Publ. Co. 1980.
19. See: George N. Yannopoulos: "EC External Commercial Policies and East-West Trade in Europe", *Journal of Common Market Studies* 1985, Volume 1, pp. 23–27.
20. *The OECD Observer* 1984, Volume 128, p. 13.
21. Z. Fallenbuchl: *East-West Technology Transfer. Study of Poland 1971–1980,* Paris: OECD 1983 — or earlier: R. Amann; J.M. Cooper; R.W Davies — eds.: *The Technological Level of Soviet Industry,* New Haven: Yale University Press 1977.

COMMENTS ON PAPER BY DR. WERNER

A. de Jasay

I just want to give you my own interpretation of Dr. Werner's paper. To me it is two papers, but he is too much a diplomat to send in two papers; he has made them into one. I will try to separate them out. One is what I would call holywater. It is the sort of thing that you read repeatedly in the Washington Post. "Peace speak." "East west *détente.*" "Kissingerism". "We have to cooperate, and trade; trade is good." The other paper is not at all like this. It is not wishy-washy. It's scholarly. I think it is a first class paper. I congratulate him on this intellectually reputable enterprise, the acute diagnosis. Let me very quickly demonstrate what I mean. For a start we have statements that the first time there was any real rise in East-West trade was when the West gave money to the East to buy goods with. Then we have the further statement: the exports of the West to the East grew to from something to $50 million. I'm not looking at the cause, I'm just looking at accounts that remained in balance. The two sides of the account rose to the same level. Well, if trade stayed in balance, where did the money go? During this period, the indebtedness of what we call the socialist countries has increased from the order of zero to the order of $100 billion, give and take a billion here and there, and this is odd!

I go to the second statement I am querying. We learn that the West found itself unable to quarantine the East economically or to check its economic growth. But did it have a good enough go? And, again, where did the money go? Who gave the money to whom? This is very odd.

Now let's come back to what I call the wishy washy paper, the "peace speak." Economic integration could lay the material foundations for European *rapprochement*. But I don't think you believe this. Any further integration of the EEC countries should cross the Elba and embrace East European members. Well, we all very well know why this is just not on. It is not a matter of not enough *rapprochement,* not enough *détente*. This was just one example to characterize what I call "peace speak" and "*détente*."

Now let's return to the other paper, which is strong meat. That is very very good stuff. The real questions and the answers to them are not in the economic sphere, says Dr. Werner. Absolutely right! Is there anything better suited to cooperation in other areas? Is the economic area promising? He says not. I think he's proved it. It is very well done, and I wish more people could have asked these questions and provided an acute diagnosis without the sort of illusion-mongering which you get at the East European desks of the United States State Department. East-west trade will supposedly even out our differences and will lead to *détente* and peace. It will create vested interests. Kissinger would say: let us create vested interests in East-West trade. And then the Russians will be hooked on trade and they won't let go. As Dr. Werner realises, there is no question that this is ludicrous. The likely scenario is that nothing would have changed. Nothing would have changed into the next millenium! Never has a situation developed where the USSR would give precedence to economic interests. Absolutely right! Can I add something if I may? The reason is not that they are self-denying. The reason is that you have a system where, again, the incidence of benefit and sacrifice doesn't fall on the same people. When I am the commanding officer of a troop I can say: Go and die! and the troop would have done so. But I would not have gone and died. I would have to stay back in the command post. And this is exactly the situation in which command economies have such a magnificent stance, saying they would do this and not accept that. "We will starve." But the commanders would not starve; the people would!

That is why it is naive to state that the economic interests of Russia would lead it to do such and such. No! Only the global interests of Russia would lead it to do such and such, within which the economic is a component part. But they are not like us. They can take any sacrifice, because they can always shift the effects of the sacrifice to people lower down with no voice in the decision-making.

PROSPECTS OF EUROPEAN INTEGRATION BLOCKS

Professor Ivan Maksimović

As is known, European economic and political integration rests upon — and is at the same time divided between — two gigantic institutionalized blocks: the European Economic Community, (EEC), and COMECON (Soviet *ekonomičeskoi vzaimopomšči*), the Council for mutual Economic Aid. Both blocks, *i.e.*, institutions, are basically large economic and political integrations encompassing the largest part of the European territory, population, and economic potential. (Comecon also comprises some overseas countries as well.) Both large integrated communities result from long historical and economic processes and laws (merger of markets, concentration and centralization of capital, services, goods and production) with the aim of increasing national and European competition, efficiency, and development. They also result from the operation of conscious, teleological factors: political, ideological, cultural, and valuational, with the aim being to preserve and further expand these communities' systems of production — one capitalist; the other socialist — to strengthen the blocks of integrated countries, and to use integration as an instrument of political and ideological fights between the two world systems.

Today they are very strong and powerful integrated economic and political blocks which set their imprint on European life end processes as a whole, and, in a good part, on the world's as well.

The EEC came into existence as an integrated whole by the end of the 1950s, nowadays merging almost all West European countries into a uniform European market. In 1981 Greece was included, and soon, probably, Turkey will be as well. Having over 350 million inhabitants, an average *per capita* social product in the community amounting to over 10,000 dollars, and a proportion of the world trade and monetary reserves amounting to 37 percent (in 1981), the EEC is no doubt one of the most powerful world state communities. Founded on the basis of the Rome Treaty in 1957 with the aim of achieving a better unity of the countries of Western Europe, of forming their common market as well as of lessening the postwar blockade, customs, and other obstacles in commodity exchange, the EEC has gradually grown into a monolithic, homogeneous, and unique integrated community. Making efforts, in particular, to make as integrated as possible the agrarian, social, and regional policy of member countries and to finance their development, the EEC has established numerous financial and other institutions for pursuing this policy (the European Agricultural Fund, the European Investment Bank, *etc.*). They also formed the European Monetary Union with its ECU as a common currency of the European monetary system. In its recent phase of development, the EEC has taken on the grandiose task of absorbing the new historical wave of the world's technologization, the new information-technological revolution in the next 10 to 15 years, as well as to formulate up to 1992 the EEC's uniform economic policy, thus transforming itself into a completely integrated and supranational economic-political community.

As against the EEC there is COMECON, another powerful European community (in part a world community, as it also comprises overseas members Vietnam, Cuba, and Mongolia). Initially conceived as a political block, more than an economic integration, and based upon the principle of "proletarian internationalism" (since 1968), COMECON has gradually acquired the characteristics of an economic integration as well. Ranging from a coordination of the member countries' plans and the bilateral principle of cooperation, COMECON has evolved into an organization of multilateral cooperation in some strategic and essential spheres of development, such as: energetics, nuclear energy plants, interconnecting electric energy systems, joint investment in the sphere of chemical industry, oil pipelines, and, in recent time, in the production of food and raw material, as well. On this basis COMECON not only increasingly unites the same or similar political and economic systems, but also merges their national economies into one integrated whole, thus making their productive and energy inputs variedly dependent. So, although smaller than the EEC by the value of financial investment and its proportion in the world's and European trade, the planned integration of COMECON as an existing economic force, and even more, as a spatial, geopolitical, and economic potential, represents, no doubt, one of the most significant integrations of Europe and the contemporary world.

As for Europe's future and the World's as well, one of the most important questions should certainly be posed. If we bear in mind the impact of economic forces of integration, the convergence of different systems, and the expansion of a uniform market, we should ask ourselves whether these two powerful political and economic integrations, the EEC and COMECON, will come together and gradually transform themselves into a uniform European economic, if not also political area with a uniform market, by the end of this millennium, or in the first century of the third millennium, or will they continue to clash more and more as polarized and autarchic wholes under the influence of convergent economic and political and cultural-historical forces?

Of course, this question cannot be answered precisely. But a sort of answer arises from listing and comparing negative and positive trends which might help in creating a uniform European economic integration and a uniform European market.

When considering the major *negative* trends opposing further integration both *within* the EEC and COMECON, and *between* them, one certainly should bear in mind significant differences among individual state communities with regard to the economic and natural wealth they dispose of, the achieved technological and economic development, the development of science, and numerous cultural-historical differences. All of them affect various political interests and ideological consciousness of the members of these integrations, and essential differences in the economic systems, even within the same integrated communities. Also there are different types of ownership relations and of markets, state interventions, economic instruments (foreign exchange, trading, credit) through which interests of individual nations and of their political ideologies are achieved. Particular mention should also be made of external factors (the other capitalist nations: above all, the United States of America and Japan, as well as of developing countries, the "non-aligned" world, which can operate as a disintegrative factor in terms of their interests as against the further integration of specific European interests).

When considering *positive* trends, the objective economic laws (competition, concentration and centralization of capital, and internationalization of production and turnover) offer hope for an unavoidable further integration process within and between European integration wholes. In view of the new scientific-technological-economic revolution, these trends call for broad international and even world frameworks for their further regular development. On the other hand, there are also significant institutional, non-economic, and military forces. For although the division of Europe, military insecurity, and a new role and significance of the state have affected stimulatively the first European integration processes, above all from the point of view of autarchy and economic-political polarization between large political pacts after the Second World War, (the Atlantic Pact, the Warsaw Pact) they have nevertheless given birth to a series of economic programmes and institutions (the Organization for European Economic Cooperation), the OECD, the European Monetary Union, the European Coal and Steel Community, EFTA, *etc.),* which figured as a negation of autarchy and helped the expansion of European economic integration. And COMECON too, is more or less a model of development evolving from autarchic-political to a more economic one.

On the other hand, the possibility of a nuclear war threatening not only Europe's total destruction, but also that of the whole of humanity — offers nowadays no alternative except disarmament and peace. In this sense, the military factor, now, represents an integrating and uniting, rather than autarchic and disintegrating force, and increases the prospects for an overall European integration.

So if we separate and analyse the numerous positive and negative factors leading towards the further and more profound process of European economic and political integration towards European universalism, the need for a uniform policy and market, and the merger of existing opponent integrations to make a homogeneous whole — it is clear that a process of the operation of forces with divergent and opposite impact is here what matters. In our opinion, many decades are still needed, and a significant step further into the Third Millennium, in order that conditions be reached for a fuller European homogenization. The economic and political systems the existing powerful integrations represent, should approach significantly, and this should be understood: that one is to expect the economic and technological factors to prevail over political and cultural differences, which are rather of a lasting character resisting unity and changes. In this sense we share both scepticism and optimism expressed in Dr. Andrzej Werner's lucid introductory paper.

THE ECOLOGY FACTOR: COMMON CONCERN FOR A SHARED ENVIRONMENT

Nansen A. Behar

The continent of Europe, which is the place of meeting and interaction of the old and new civilization, is threatened by an ecological disaster. The past thirty years, called by scholars and politicians years of a revolution in science and technology, have entailed greater environmental pollution than the preceding two hundred years of industrial development. The uncontrolled development of technology, not matched to the balance of Nature, consumption not matched to real human needs, and the militarization of the economy, have, in a great number of European countries resulted in the exacerbation of the ecological crisis.

More than in any other region in the world, in the Old Continent the ecology factor has international dimensions. Here it is difficult to differentiate between the national and the regional (and even continental) dimensions of the ecological crisis. A multitude of independent states coexist on a relatively small territory, and their biospheric systems are closely interdependent. For instance, the European rivers (the Danube, the Rhine, and others) cross the territories of several states, and the water pollution travels from one country to another without any national frontier restrictions. The common seas are also polluted: the North Sea, the Baltic Sea, the Black Sea, and the Mediterranean region. The "acid rains" cross from one territory to another. The international character of the ecological crisis in Europe calls especially urgently for international cooperation in this sphere.

All phenomena of this nature should be subjected to a thorough scientific analysis: not an analysis *post factum,* but preliminary unbiased studies of the potential consequences of any possible excesses. Scientists from different countries must learn how to work together. International cooperation is indispensable on all matters concerning the stability of ecological conditions on Earth.

THE ENVIRONMENT AND THE FUTURE OF EUROPE

The ecology factors are increasingly becoming restrictive factors and adverse conditions for social and economic progress in Europe. The quality of the basic media — the air, the land, and water — where man develops his economic, social, cultural and other activities; is deteriorating. According to calculations of the United Nations Statistics Institute, Europe is the continent of the lowest rate of birth compared to the other continents. If that situation persists in the future, due to worsened ecological conditions, after the year 2000 a zero or negative population growth might be expected in the European continent. Naturally, other factors, too, exert an influence on the demographic situation, but the ecology factor is an essential one. Europe is vulnerable to manifestations of the global ecological crisis, while contributing quite a bit towards its exacerbation. A striking example of that interdependence is the concentration of noxious substances in the atmosphere of Europe. According to UNEP findings[1], the atmospheric concentration of several gases is increasing in Europe. The level of carbon dioxide, the most important factor creating the "greenhouse effect", is expected to rise by 30 per cent in the next 50 years. This build-up of gases is likely to increase the Earth's surface temperature by between 1.5 and 4.5 degrees C by the year 2030. In the Northern latitudes the winters will be shorter and wetter, the summers longer and drier than they are now. These changes could have a major but unpredictable effect on agriculture and the natural ecosystems.

The oceans will warm up and the sea levels will rise by about one metre, which will bring disaster to millions of people living within several km of the coastline, especially in Europe. This forecast goes to show that there is an urgent need for international action to minimize the future "greenhouse effect" warming and its social aftereffects.

THE ECOLOGICAL CHALLENGE AND THE NEED OF INTERSTATE COOPERATION

The pollution of the natural environment during the last decade has been a phenomenon acquiring international dimensions on the European continent. This can be felt with particular force in such a relatively small European region as the Balkans, which experienced the first acid rains. The three Balkan countries bordering on the Danube (Yugoslavia, Romania, and Bulgaria) are affected by the high degree of pollution of that big European river. The atmosphere above the Balkan Peninsula has also been highly polluted in recent years. These processes, which have their social dimensions as well, have compelled the Balkan countries to consider the ecological problem in another aspect.

Due to the low intensity of a number of socio-economic processes in the world economy, during the earlier period the combination of elements which transforms the ecological problem into a global one was still lacking in the region. Since the 'sixties, as a result of the growth of the world's industrial potential, the advance of science and technology, and a definite change in the character of the economic ties among countries in the world, the ecological problem has assumed global proportions.

What is meant is the emergence of a completely new situation which, in its content, offers no analogy in world history. The ecological crisis now affects the health and development of man himself, and is becoming a social factor. *The need is emerging for transformations in the socio-economic structure that will make it possible to cope with the crisis in the relations between society and nature.* On the other hand, this problem develops by necessity into an international one, because no country is in a position to fully preserve its natural environment by itself unless the other countries (its neighbours, in particular) take coordinated action in the same direction.

A number of measures are being adopted in the industrial

states aimed at the centralized protection of the environment. This process is stimulated by such factors as the threat posed by the rise of social tensions connected with the worsening living conditions, particularly given intensified urbanization. National programmes are worked out and adopted, as well as programmes of the local authorities, which include measures to purify the environment, and to bring the economic apparatus in compliance with the established standards of "clean" production. Besides, there are two groups of means and methods of regulating the ecological processes in the developed capitalist countries:

(a) *indirect methods:* tax reductions, compensation loans, creation of a "market" for the purchase of "pollution rights", and other typically market-economy methods; and,
(b) *direct or administrative methods:* imposition of fines, bans on production, closing down of enterprises, direct subsidies, *etc.*

The direct measures taken by the state to preserve the environment predominate in the socialist countries. There is a growing awareness that short-term *post factum* acts cannot possibly solve the problems of the natural environment at the contemporary rates of economic development. The idea that a genuine equilibrium between production and nature, between economic growth and a clean environment, may be achieved only under conditions of a highly effective link-up between resources, production, and consumption is becoming dominant as a way of social thinking. It is necessary to create a social system containing within itself the incentives for the development of production processes that are ecologically harmless, and to determine optimum norms of consumption that rule out the squandering of natural resources (this being the other aspect of pollution).

Unlike the national level, where the protection of the environment involves the combined operation of state and social factors, *on an international level the state plays a more important part in the protection of the environment.* There are a number of international documents which appeal for greater attention and vigilance in relation to the state of the planet's ecosphere, with particular reference to the most dangerous factors of pollution. Parallel to that, it is necessary to determine also the main objects of protection. Such objects are: the world's oceans and seas, the gas composition of the atmosphere, the global climatic conditions, the thermal state of the natural environment, and others.

In addition to that, the interested parties in Europe may solve, through multilateral and bilateral programmes of cooperation, individual problems connected with the protection of the air and the water resources from pollution caused locally by the operation of industrial enterprises or by other polluting factors.

Some of the most important measures of an international character for resolving the ecological problems on a global level are taken by the UN and by its specialized agencies. The Stockholm Conference in 1972 adopted a plan for international cooperation in the conservation of the environment. The mechanism of this cooperation has been further improved through the specialized organizations of the UN. The United Nations Environment Programme (UNEP) was set up as an organization entrusted with coordinating international initiatives related to the environment. Individual aspects of this problem are tackled by the Economic and Social Council of the UN, by UNICEF, UNESCO, *etc*. In addition to the intergovernmental organizations, the problems of the environment are handled by a number of non-governmental international organizations as well.

Unfortunately, regional ecological cooperation in Europe, and especially in the Balkans, lags considerably behind the existing international structures. Despite the big strides taken by *détente* in the region, the social forces in the Balkan countries have not succeeded in overcoming certain barriers to the adoption of state decisions to build more effective mechanisms for solving the crisis aspects of ecology. There are numerous ecological ties and interdependencies between the individual geographic zones and belts, which largely account for the existence of a unified geographic and climatic complex. Besides, the transfer of undesirable ecological processes from one country to another essentially becomes a transfer of social tensions, since it implies damage inflicted not on the international but on the national quality of life. Bearing all that in mind, we believe that in the Balkans, it is expedient to set up, with the help of international organizations, a Regional Institute for Monitoring and Management of the Environment. Of course, its operation must be included in the system of the all-European ecological cooperation, because the ecological problems of the Balkans are an integral part of the all-European problems.

In Europe, deciding the ecological future of the European nations calls for interaction on three levels: global, regional, and national. It is only in this way that the motto of the parties of the "green": "Think globally, act locally", can yield actual results. Because if what is done in a country conforms to the regional ecological requirements, while the neighbouring country pollutes the elements of the environment which are international in nature (the air, water, *etc.*), the national efforts of the former are in vain. As a result what is "exported" is not only environmental pollution, but social tensions as well. In this sense "ecological sovereignty" is a fiction, and it differs in principle from the political sovereignty of the individual countries.

The regional treaties on environmental protection and the partial agreements along these lines contribute to the establishment of a future ecologically-balanced Europe. Regional solutions could be sought in such European subregions as Northern Europe (including the Baltic), Central Europe, France and Britain (in connection with the English Channel), the Iberian Peninsula, the Mediterranean region (where a number of international agreements have been reached in the ecological sphere), *etc*. Of course, the regional accords are but a step to the establishment of an all-European system of environmental control and measures for environmental protection.

ECOLOGY AND PEACE

The arms build-up influences Europe's balance of resources in two ways.

It does so directly, as a result of the consumption of vast material, labour, and other resources (some of which are limited) for military purposes. Insofar as the irrational utilization of resources is the other side of anthropogenic pollution, this process of resource depletion for military purposes deepens the ecological harms in the modern world.

Indirectly, it does so by diverting the material and financial means necessary for the solution of the ecological and resources crisis, and by undermining the international cooperation necessary for overcoming such crises.

The intensive military build-up, particularly in its qualitative aspect, deforms techno-scientific progress, and diverts its results further and further from real human (including ecological) needs. A relatively higher proportion of the qualified work force is employed in military production than in civilian production. The specialized nature of modern military production has led to the rise of certain features of employment in it which are related primarily to the brisk development of military technology.

The demand for qualified workers for the military industry is particularly high among certain professions, in particular electronics scientists and engineers, aviation engineers, instrument-making technologists, *etc.* Studies of the structure of employment in the developed countries have shown that these professions are unconditionally necessary for the technological build-up of a new industrial structure which would incorporate ecological criteria in its functioning (production-recycling, communicative, and other systems). Thus by attracting qualified specialists to itself offering them various privileges, the military sphere is hindering the achievement of harmonious proportions in the creation of material facilities for environmental protection, thus deforming the overall reproduction proportion.

Will the cutting of military programmes and military budgets really slow down techno-scientific development on a world scale? After all, the European community is counting on science and technology also in implementing a European monitoring and environmental protection system. The opposite question can also be asked: is not a society which has to rely mainly on the military to develop its techno-scientific potential doomed?

It is evident that partial or complete disarmament can create no less powerful stimuli through state finance (centralized in budgets) for the development of true techno-scientific progress. It is sufficient to mention such opportunities as space research (for peaceful purposes), the fight against modern diseases (heart disease, cancer, allergies, AIDS, *etc.*), the utilization of the world's oceans, and, particularly, the fight to cleanse and conserve the natural environment. These tasks require the latest technology and large investments, and cannot be solved by a private firm or institution without state assistance. This can become possible if the countries are freed from their crippling military budgets. One type of anti-humanitarian stimulation of techno-scientific progress must be replaced by another type of socially-guided scientific development corresponding to real human needs, And these needs are most closely related to "the house we live in": the natural environment.

Concerning resources, the fact that the modern military industry is one of the chief consumers of scarce materials leads logically to the conclusion that the slow-down of military production would be a natural way of alleviating the world raw materials problem and redressing the balance between resources and production.[2]

The situation which has emerged raises, on the one hand, the question of how to guarantee enough natural resources in the future, and how to prevent the exhaustion of all reserves of fertile land, drinking water and other natural resources, and the degradation of the natural ecosystems, resulting from expanding production; but on the other hand, the question of a further advancement of science and technology, of socio-economic progress, to help boost the output of raw materials.

The combination of two global problems — the problem of war and peace, and the ecological problem — make it, above all, necessary to seek general, supra-national solutions to these crises. This imperative is firmly opposed by the existing world military division of states in Europe and the confrontation in international relations. Ecological cooperation is a unique barometer of the state of international relations as a whole. At times of *détente* it is stepped up, while at times of greater mistrust and growing military expenditure it decreases. Neither should movement in the opposite direction be underestimated: international ecological cooperation, as this was underlined back at the Helsinki Conference in 1974, is one of the basic elements of the material basis of *détente*.

The mutual influence and interrelation between the two global problems of war and peace, and ecology, does in its own way influence the world's resources crisis. The struggle for a clean Earth is inextricably linked with the struggle for a peaceful Earth and aims at providing two aspects of human life, two inalienable rights: the right to live in peaceful, and in normal conditions. Every step towards disarmament will not only make easier the solution of the ecological problems, but will also free resources which are of exceptional importance to development. It is the duty of the world scientific community, and of the organized movements of environmentalists, to elucidate the complex links and relations between armaments, the ecology, and resources, to warn governments of the immediate dangers looming and to draw up plans for rational, ecologically-compliant conversion. The future of Europe depends on the solution of the essential global problems of our time: disarmament and ecology.

NOTES

1. UNEP Environment Brief No.1, The Changing Atmosphere, Nairobi, 1987, p.1–5.
2. An interesting study on "Minerals as a Factor in Strategic Policy and Action" has been made by Helge Hveem in Global Resources and International Conflict, ed. by A. Westing, Oxford University Press, 1986, p.56.

REFERENCES

Boserup, E. (1965) The Conditions of Agricultural Growth, Allen Unwin, London.

Capra, F. (1982) The Turning Point.

Dorcey, A.H.J. (1984) "Interdependence Between the Economy and the Environment: From Principle to Practice"

Background Paper OECD International Conference on Environment and Economics, Paris, 18–21 June 1984

Dubos, René (1980) The Wooing of Earth.

Earthscan (1984) Environment and Conflict: Links Between Ecological Decay, Environmental Bankruptcy and Political and Military Stability, IIED, London.

Frolov, I. (1982) Global Problems and the Future of Mankind. Progress Publ.Moscow.

Hill, A.V. (1960) The Ethical Dilemma of Science.

Mesarovic, M & Pestel, E. (1974) Mankind at the Turning Point, The Second Report to the Club of Rome.

Pelt, Jean Marie (1976) L'Homme Renature.

Simon, J. & Kahn, H. (1984) The Resourceful Earth.

Thirgood, J.V. (1981) Man and the Mediterranean Forest. (Academic Press, London, 1981).

White, L. (1967) The Historic Roots of Our Ecological Crisis, Science, 155, 1204–1207.

COMMENTS ON PAPER BY PROF. BEHAR

S. Andreski

I'm not normally restrained by politeness from criticising views with which I disagree but in this paper I find no grounds for disagreement. So I will only add a few remarks on other aspects of the problem.

In the first place, I would like to express my support for Professor Behar's view that this problem is more important than any other. Ideological differences pale into insignificance in the face of the danger of an ecological catastrophe, because what does it matter whether you have democracy or dictatorship if you cannot breathe the air, or if you are dying of cancer? This does not, of course, mean that the political differences are unimportant, but they presuppose the survival of mankind.

If we compare the record of East European governments and societies with that of the West, we find that there are great sinners on both sides. However the record of the East European systems is worse, largely in consequence of the lesser efficiency of the economy. For instance, in terms of energy used per unit of GNP, France ranks the best whilst Hungary is the worst in Europe. It is, incidentally, strange that the collectivist economy which is most market oriented, is also the worst sinner on this score.

There are certain aspects of ideologies on both sides which are very harmful. They have a common element: the stress on purely material welfare. In Marxism there is all this talk about materialism, the material structure or basis, and so on: in fact and idolization of the purely economic. In the West, a similar idolization of the economic goes under the name of monetarism. There is a core of truth in monetarism as an economic theory: namely, that if a government runs constantly into a deficit, then there will be an inflation. But with Mrs Thatcher's government, monetarism has become a kind of cult, the main dogma of which is that nothing matters that cannot be expressed in money terms. This kind of narrow-minded accountant's mentality leads to a neglect of long term economic issues such as the ecological. For this reason, the British government is among the worst sinners on this score. In European discussions of remedies, the greatest opposition usually comes from Britain, with the help of Spanish and Italian delegates, whereas the Scandinavians and the Germans have a much better record.

In Western Europe we are buying our comforts now at the expense of future generations. The East Europeans have not attained a comfortable existence by this method: they are ruining the environment for future generations, but for no benefits to themselves. Whereas the latter attitude is sheer folly, the first is certainly unethical. One of the reasons for its prevalence is that most of the decision-makers are old men who seem to be guided by the saying "Why should I worry about future generations, what have they done for me?". So we have a moral problem here: a question of a moral imperative.

It is certainly completely false to imagine, as many of the Greens do, that making the means of production the property of the state is the cure for ecological evils. Eastern Europe is the proof. In the West, nationalized industries are among the worst polluters, as for example the Central Electricity Board in Britain, whose experts resort to all kinds of subterfuges in order to conceal its responsibility.

It is sad that many scientists allow themselves simply to be hired to spread half-truths (if not complete untruths), using all kinds of spurious arguments. The ploy is to confuse "not proven to be the case" with "proven not to be the case", using "not proven to be the case" as if it were "proven not to be the case".

Nobody would confuse the two arguments in dealing with his own affairs. Everybody assumes that the lack of conclusive proof should induce one to act on the side of caution. If someone has doubts about the steering in his car, he will not accept an assurance, "Oh go on. Don't worry. It hasn't been proven it will go wrong". "No." he will say, "I want to be certain that it will not fail". In contrast, when it is the question of whether ozone is going to disappear from the stratosphere, the supposedly hard-nosed scientists advocate doing nothing until we have conclusive proof, hiding their imprudence behind a spurious interpretation of the scientific method.

If we compare the Eastern and Western political systems, we see that their strong and weak points are different. One of the weaknesses of the systems based on general elections is that the politicians want to buy votes with cheap promises of a bigger pay packet. In this kind of situation it is very difficult to get general approval for any policy which serves only the long term interests of the electorate, let alone the interests of future generations. One could imagine that an authoritarian system might have an advantage in this respect because its rulers can compel people to make sacrifices for the sake of future generations. Unfortunately such rulers were in fact primarily concerned with building industrial power in order to have military power, and neglected the task of securing a decent environment for future generations.

In an authoritarian system, no independent groups can spring up and exert influence, as has happened in the West, usually in opposition to the attitude of governments. Unfortunately, the ecological movement got mixed up with some circles or individuals who bring it into disrepute: firstly, by politicising it unduly and trying to connect it with programmes which actually don't have anything to do with this issue; and secondly by being very unrealistic and self-contradictory.

To give a small but symptomatic example: I have attended some of their meetings, and the room was full of smoke! Many of them think they could ensure a good environment by dividing society into independent little communes. This may be excused as an understandable reaction to the crazy cult of the big, but nonetheless it is a chimera, because the little communes of old were constantly at war with one another. So you cannot ensure peace by dividing society into small groups, particularly as many environmental problems can only have a global solution. Even more absurd is the notion that it is possible to accommodate an infinite number of people within a finite space. It is tempting to disregard the fact that any adaptation must be costly. We have become so accustomed to wasting energy — to living in, generally, a very wasteful way — that it would be very painful to change our habits. My only disagreement with Professor Behar concerns his worry about a reduction of the population of Europe. I don't think it would be bad if the population were to be smaller, provided of course that the reduction of the European population were not nullified by an influx of immigrants from parts of the world where population explosions are still going on.

Perhaps the greatest contribution that Europe could make to peace would be to try to give a good example on ecological issues. Quarrels about polluting each other could become the most important source of conflicts. If pollution by one country could threatened another with disease or starvation, the latter could even go to war to stop it. There certainly is a great potential danger in this kind of ecological aggression, as well as in the consequences of the depletion of natural resources.

Turning against science (as some of the Greens do) offers no escape from environmental dangers. Even with a much smaller population than the present, a non-self-destructive economy will need much greater scientific knowledge than a system based on a drunkard wastrel's attitude to natural resources.

COMMENTS ON PROF. BEHAR'S PAPER

Vassilis Karasmanis

Firstly Prof. Behar seems to be worried about the low rate of population growth in Europe and attributes this (among other factors) mainly to "worsening ecological conditions". However, given that

a) we cannot have unlimited growth of population in a limited planet, and
b) that ecological problems are related to the growth of population, we should be happy, rather than anxious about the low rate of birth in Europe. Moreover, although demographers agree that better economic conditions in a country or a social group generally lead to a lower rate of population growth, it has not been proven whether, and in which direction, bad ecological conditions affect the rate of birth.

Prof. Behar rightly observes that "short-term *post factum* acts cannot solve the problems of the natural environment at the contemporary rates of economic development". We take measures only when an acute environmental problem appears, but we do not really try to create a different attitude towards the environment: an attitude of collaboration and harmony between man and nature, an attitude that would not allow the problem to arise at all. On the contrary, we behave as if we were masters of the earth, exploiting it and fighting with it without understanding that our intervention in nature, in the name of economic welfare, often creates other more difficult long-term problems.

We have therefore to ask ourselves: is it possible to pursue unlimited economic growth in a limited planet containing limited resources? If we answer "No", then we have to reconsider all our models of economic development, and our attitudes and values towards nature.

Our current models of economic development would seem to have no future. It cannot any more be taken for granted that the environment and its natural resources are "free goods". Our economic welfare and growth involves a great deal of damage to the environment, without any consideration for the future generations that would live on a devastated planet. In this way we have exhausted almost half of the petrol stock of the earth, in only forty years, while the earth "worked" for thousands and thousands of years to make it. Our models of technological and economic development, being linear, are at variance with the natural cycles of the earth. We have therefore to create a new social and economic order that would be in harmony with nature.

We should probably speak about a more or less stable economy, paying attention more to qualitative development than to quantitative growth. We need an economy of the useful, and not the useless, that takes care of our limited resources and relies on collaboration with nature and not domination over it, recycling, soft energy, alternative technologies, longer life of industrial products and a new peaceful orientation of our science and research, as Professor Behar pointed out.

However, such changes are interrelated with changes in our mentality, values, and attitudes regarding the relations between man and nature, and the relations between man and man. We need more "soft" than "hard" values: that is values relying on collaboration, harmony, and the development of our inner human abilities, instead of values that exhort violence, fighting, and domination. Without changing our "hard" attitudes and values, the result might be either a nuclear war (relations between man and man) or an ecological catastrophe (relations between man and nature).

Moreover we need an outlook which is holistic rather than fragmentary. That means interdisciplinary approaches to various social, economic, technological, and environmental problems. It means, also, that we have to give priority to the humanities and environmental sciences. The ideal would be to arrive at the unification of knowledge and values in one system, without one of them being dominated by the other — something that we find in Plato's philosophy.

I am afraid that Prof. Behar's concern for peace basically focuses on preventive measures aimed at deterring war. I would like to argue that peace is more a matter of the positive elaboration of a new mentality that can be achieved through better widespread education at all levels.

This leads me to my final point. In order to address the major ecological problems we have been considering, I want to claim that a crucial step should be not, as Prof. Behar seems to think, central state and interstate *planning,* but rather the preparation of a long-term, well-sustained ecological educational policy, a new period of enlightenment oriented to the new values and attitudes *towards* nature. These values ought to form a coherent system which does not allow conflicts and contradictions. Such a policy is, I believe, indispensable for the formation and enhancement of the new values and attitudes we are looking for.

Centralized state-planning is not only inadequate, but can also prove harmful for our purposes and is no substitute for the educational process that I am proposing. The alternative could be a new institutional framework for the economy, oriented towards decentralization, autonomy, and cooperation.

The antagonistic contemporary states may be unable to bring us out of the crisis. Decentralized, more self-sufficient economies, in harmony with the local environment, may be a better solution for the future. Aristotle demonstrated that if we want to have real democracy, *i.e.,* not only equality of rights, but also active participation of every citizen in political life, there is an upper limit to the possible size of the cities or states.

Nevertheless many — and sometimes more serious — problems are not local, but occur on a larger scale. So what is really needed are various levels of political institutions, from local to international, that would be able to confront the various environmental, social, and economic problems according to their respective extent.

EDUCATION FOR A COMMON FUTURE: CULTIVATING A PAN-EUROPEAN IDENTITY

Adelheid Babing

I work at Berlin Humboldt University, which has the honour to be named after the Humboldt brothers, who were two of Europe's greatest minds of their day.

Alexander and Wilhelm von Humboldt were not only brilliant scholars and advocates of humanitarianism, but they were also great believers in political understanding. Fulfilling governmental and academic assignments in various countries in Europe, Asia, and Latin America, they resolutely worked for the ideal of peaceful international cooperation to become a living reality.

No more than a few hundred yards from my university, you can see what may easily be called the Number One border in Europe at the Brandenburg Gate. And there are not a few people in Europe who rightly say that if we have peace in that area, there is hope for peace everywhere else in Europe. It is probably true to say that my country lies right in the heart of Europe, *i.e.*, at the place where the continent is most sensitive and most vulnerable. I live in an area where the two principal military blocs in the world today border on each other, and the two basic world systems of today act on each other in a most direct manner.

In the course of my life I have often found myself in situations of political tension, feeling concern for peace and fear for my own safety. You will all be aware of the problems that have arisen from the fact that there are two German states and that the city of Berlin is divided. Everybody who has to face, and cope with, these realities every day is bound to become particularly sensitive to the dangers that may be caused by conflict; and it will be easy to see that people there have a powerful motivation to find solutions to crises.

People in Europe, just like mankind as a whole, are now at the crossroads. We have to choose between jointly preserving peace or jointly perishing in a nuclear inferno. The continent has the world's largest military build-up, ready to plunge it into destruction. It may all too easily turn into a powder-keg exploding the whole of the world. We must take a look at the European situation, and conceive ideas for the future of the continent. In our day and age, however, we can do so only if we do not disregard the vital interests of mankind as a whole. We shall, therefore, have to remember that we are not only responsible for our own lives, but also — and mainly — for the lives of our children, grand-children and great-grandchildren. Yet we should not forget either that pan-European identity has, of course, particularities that distinguish it from, say, some pan-African, pan-Asian or pan-American identity.

The distinctive features of our continent, and the Occident generally, are revealed in art, culture, science, philosophy, religion and history. Yet the new issues and challenges of our day affect *every* country and *every* continent. They cover all fields and are, as we all know, social, economic, political, scientific and technological in nature. They are just as much related to the *common nature* of diseases and life-threatening social phenomena like drugs and terrorism as they are related to their *combatting* and *prevention*.

Any answers that may be found must serve to safeguard the social and natural conditions required if human civilization is to continue. This requires the international community to accept joint responsibilities and take joint action. And this, in turn, gives the political and moral quality of international relations top priority in human evaluation. The way in which the two basic, radically different social systems in the world today will be dealing with each other in the future is of crucial importance for the survival of mankind. In this nuclear and space age, problems, tensions, conflicts and crises can be resolved in only one way: by peaceful means. Controversies between the systems do not, however, *as such* pose a danger to peace. Peace will be really threatened only if plans are made to settle such controversies by military means. And since the use of military force would, in our day, inevitably lead to the destruction of all life on our planet, it is absolutely imperative that mutual guaranties and solutions be found that take account of the security and peace interests of *every* nation and are based on the idea of a security partnership.

Our Occidental continent, whose magic and attraction go as far back as the days when it was given its name in accordance with ancient Greek legend, can be preserved only if the world is preserved as a whole.

So, European security requires global security. Arms limitation, disarmament and security partnership are vital if comprehensive inter-governmental cooperation is to be achieved, both in Europe and the rest of the world.

The cooperation that this requires to be carried out among countries receives particular impetus from the high standards achieved in the course of the scientific and technological revolution. Yet the results from that revolution differ enormously from country to country. Cooperation between the two basic social systems is particularly important when it comes to using scientific and technological achievements for social progress. But cooperation is also indispensable if the achievements are to be protected from misapplication, *e.g.*, if criminal manipulation of genes and destruction of the environment is to be avoided. These matters must be regulated by common consent. The urgency of this is graphically demonstrated by the generally known recent disastrous consequences of scientific and technological progress, consequences that were due to negligence and a missing sense of responsibility. Let me also remind you of the enormous challenges that doctors are now jointly facing in combatting diseases, like AIDS, that threaten the whole of the world and require urgent containment if mankind is to survive.

OBJECTIVES OF AN EDUCATION IN LINE WITH THE NEW THINKING

In the present nuclear age, many new lines of thought have developed in philosophy and art. Quite a number of them are associated with negation. Many concepts have lost their life-affirming meaning and are no longer future-oriented. They express the helplessness that common sense is beset by at the thought of a possible nuclear confrontation. Present-day philosophical currents that preach such views are spreading resignation, anxiety and fear. They paralyze all favourable emotions, extinguish confidence, and stifle any belief in the future. They even kill human will-power. Education must never allow the rising generation to succumb to this kind of hopelessness. Throughout human history, education has been seeking to enable young people to live up to the needs of the future. In the nuclear age, when the question has to be decided of whether mankind is to survive or not, all life-affirming philosophies should be given pride of place.

Of primary importance among these concepts is the contribution that education has to make to the safeguarding of peace in the world. This is one of the goals that have to be jointly reached by either of the two basic social systems and by all social classes, and that require a large number of tasks to be fulfilled. It is one of the major objectives of education to instil the love of peace as an activating factor into mass consciousness. Whatever ideology and belief our contemporaries may adhere to, they will have to view the world in a different light and see themselves as world citizens.

The traditional rivalries among European nations and the animosities born of the use of force must be overcome. Everybody will have to shoulder the responsibility for either a flourishing life on our planet or the eerie radioactive silence following a nuclear war. After a war of this kind, nobody will be left to bring about reconciliation; there will be no thereafter. Who would be prepared to take the blame for not having prevented disaster? We women are said to be particularly adept in educating young people for peace. We know how to placate brawlers, defuse tension and make peace. This is certainly due to the fact that we are destined to pass life on. And this, in turn, is precisely why we women are so powerfully and passionately committed to providing a truly humanitarian kind of education.

Modern educational concepts should, I believe, be based on a number of common premises in all countries. And if we could set what may be called a European example to the world, we should be helping enormously towards establishing education for peace.

Education for a Common Future

This kind of education should first of all face the task of overcoming the kind of thinking that presents the use of force as the most suitable means of settling conflicts. Unfortunately, there have been all too many instances in European history when philosophies and ideas that fostered an alleged superiority of a certain nation and a certain way of life finally turned into sources of conflict and proved productive of confrontation and aggression.

If we now wish to take up the idea of educating young people for a pan-European identity, we can do so only on the basis of concepts that favour peaceful international understanding, neighbourly relations among countries and mutual respect, so that our continent may survive.

This includes education for patriotism. People who love and respect their own country will also be able to appreciate what other nations have created. An education that enables people to be kind to their own nation will also enable them to be kind to foreign nations

Europe has a large number of nations and nationalities, which differ enormously in national character, religion and way of life; and what is more, they all live in either the one or the other of the two radically different social systems that are in existence today. Yet what all their national cultures have in common — and this does not only apply to Europe — is a basic humanitarian concept, which finds expression in folk art, literature, paintings, and religious and philosophical schools.

Common humanitarian values — like humanitarianism, opposition to hatred, abhorrence of violence, readiness to help, sympathy, kindness, justice in the qualities of life, respect for the uniqueness of every individual, appreciation of individuality, and the recognition of everybody's right to live — reflect the humanitarian traditions of our national cultures, whose highest values we have to rely on when educating young people for a future common Europe. If education is to make young people uphold these values in the future, the situation that we find ourselves in today will require us to educate young people for a security partnership among states that have adopted either the one or the other of the two basic social systems.

This calls for education to be conceived at several levels; and it implies that education consists of rather complex processes. The levels are closely linked.

Today, education for peace means instilling into young people the capacity for advocating peaceful coexistence between the two basic social systems and the states that have adopted them. To begin with, this education requires providing technical knowledge concerning the issue of war and peace; concerning the facts of international political issues, the relations between them and the laws governing them; and concerning the reasons for, the contradictions in, and the possible solutions to, the world situation. To put it in a nutshell, it requires making people accept the idea that peaceful coexistence, disarmament, and an alliance of reason are viable propositions.

Yet in the first place this necessitates developing the skill of applying technical knowledge in practice. It means instilling into people the capacity for passing judgement, for drawing conclusions from their knowledge for their action, and for assessing their own practical experience in the light of that knowledge. There is no need, I think, for explaining the risks caused by any ignorance of the consequences that the use of belligerent means may have in our day and age. There is, however, one point that every educational concept that serves the interests of peace should pay heed to: that there are a lot of people in Europe who had some first-hand experience of war and the suffering that war brings in its wake. One of the things that we must seek to achieve is to make use of those people's experience in the education of young people. After all, there is a much larger number of people in Europe who were fortunate enough to grow up without any such horrifying memories. And this is precisely why education has to make young people work for peace without their knowing the horrors of war; and a war, if it broke out today, would put an end to the physical existence of these people. This means that young people have to be taught to believe in values that they have to acquire in ways other than those in which all the generations before them had to acquire them. And this gives education new tasks to fulfil.

If the young people of both today and the future are to be capable of using knowledge appropriately, they will have to be enabled to pursue humanitarian forms of behaviour with active tolerance and matter-of-factness. This mainly applies to the way in which they are to deal with those who hold political and religious beliefs that are different from their own. Tolerance requires people to respect views different from their own, consider such views as food for thought, and be flexible, understanding, and sympathetic in their reactions. Yet tolerance can be successful only if it is practised by absolutely everybody involved in any particular case.

An essential condition for the development of the capacity for tolerance is the capacity for *dialogue*. This question is now taking on a completely new significance because different school systems take very different views of education for dialogue. The question has taken on a new dimension as a result of the task that young people must be educated for peace. Only *via* dialogue and communication can new ways be found of working out joint solutions. What matters in this context is both the capacity for putting forward arguments, and the art of making masterly use of the word. Is this given enough attention in the educational systems in operation today?

Education for tolerance and dialogue is closely connected with the education for *conflict settlement*. In this paper I do not, however, wish to deal with all the opportunities offered for the purpose by educational sciences and social psychology, which have been looking into these matters for decades. It appears appropriate, though, to mention some of the problems that may arise.

If we believe that we can cope with future difficulties only if we accept the principle of peaceful coexistence, we should realize that the potential of any education in this spirit can be utilized in several different ways. We should, on the one hand, tell young people about the conflict sources and settlements of the past, presenting them in their historical contexts and explaining experience regarding successes and failures in this respect. And on the other hand, we should cite examples demonstrating what solutions have been found in international politics in *our* day and age, and make clear what alternative is the only possible one at the present time. We should in this way try to make young people gain rational insights and feel emotional bewilderment. Only in this manner can we motivate young people to take action that expresses and improves their own attitudes. Education must therefore present actional premises that refer to both young people's microsocial environment — their dealings with friends and their activities in learning groups — and their macro-social fields of activity, which will require them to engage in political solidarity, peace action, active membership in public organizations, *etc*. As is well-known, the experience gained through personal activity is indispensable for the development of the human personality, for a person's view of life, and for his value judgements. If there is a great deal of aggression in a person's everyday life — *e.g.*, in his family, among his friends and acquaintances, and in his working and educational environments — it will be difficult to enable him to conduct a businesslike constructive dialogue when conflicts have to be coped with. This shows what I can no more than hint at in this paper: that education is not only provided by the traditional educational institutions, but also comes from many other sectors of society. A very prominent part is played by the media. The media exercise a very considerable influence on everyday value judgements and also, of course, on politically and ideologically based views of life. This is why the contribution of the media to education should be in strict accord with an educational concept that is based on humanitarianism.

Education for the peaceful coexistence of nations means that the ability should be developed to consider, work for, and finally make, *compromises*. This can also require overcoming old modes of thinking. People will have to subordinate — and, if need be, limit or suppress — their own interests, if this allows finding mutually acceptable joint solutions. Compromises will never, of course, succeed in ironing out ideological differences, which will definitely persist. But we must in future be even more successful than we have been so far in giving fair recognition to positions that are diametrically opposed to our own, and in subjecting them to businesslike scrutiny.

To see compromises as successes rather than defeats means thinking along new lines and deriving result-oriented action from such thinking. This is a logical conclusion that can be drawn from the recognition of the existence of the two radically different social systems in the world today. Trying to find new ways and means of settling conflicts, we should assign a prominent place to compromise. Education in this spirit means developing a readiness for compromise, and telling young people that two parties that pursue different, maybe even opposite, aims can nevertheless work for joint goals. Well-balanced and harmonious relations can today be attained in the social field — and even more so in the political field — only if compromises can be thrashed out. Compromise is a new, but inevitable principle of political action in our day. If mutual relations are to remain intact despite conflicts and differences of interest, there will be no way around compromises.

Compromises may also involve showing subdued reaction to the desires, ideas and propositions of the other party, considering its special interests and concerns, and making efforts at finding levels at which businesslike communication is possible. The capacity for dialogue and compromise is also particularly important in view of the high standards reached in the advancing scientific and technological revolution. The way in which this revolution is being carried out will have an enormous bearing on the survival and progress of mankind.

This is why education faces the task of instilling into succeeding generations a *sense of responsibility* that takes account of the new dimensions appearing in many fields as a result of the progress made in science and technology. More and more people begin to realize that a person's responsibility for his own action will in future include his responsibility for the lives of *all* people. Let me just remind you of the many recent technological disasters that had immediate consequences for a large number of people. Neither must we forget the problems that may arise from any ill-considered, reckless use of sophisticated technology. Such problems will only serve to worsen the situation of mankind. Education for considering the consequences of one's own action well before the action is taken must now more than ever be part and parcel of any modern educational concept that does not want to fall behind the constant stream of technological innovations. Education for responsibility includes education for respect for life and nature, for the protection of plants and animals, and for the appreciation of beauty, generally, and of mankind's art treasures, in particular. This kind of education also requires helping young people to realize that the nature of our planet belongs to everybody and that the art treasures of one nation form part of the heritage of entire mankind.

Of similar importance is education for the responsibility for settling global issues like underdevelopment, starvation, drug addiction, and disease. These are problems that beset the whole of the world and can only be resolved if people accept joint responsibility and take joint action. If we wish to preserve the earth — the "blue planet" of the universe — which is frail and small, we shall have to overcome the age-old modes of thinking and acting that present violence and destruction as permissible. And we shall have to do so even if there are a number of people who regard this as illusory. Many people — people upholding a wide variety of ideologies and belonging to many different social classes — are already setting a fine example to us by demonstrating how all these problems can be resolved in the spirit indicated. And in this context there is a lot of exemplary humanitarianism around that may very well be used in education.

Education for the application of these sensible values, for their development and for the appreciation of their wisdom must be the concern of the whole of mankind at the threshold of the third millenium. Only in this way can mankind make use of the many benefits that it may reap from this, benefits on which Wilhelm von Humboldt had this to say:

> If there is an idea that has been becoming increasingly visible and valid in the course of history, if there is an idea that gives evidence of the frequently denied, and even more frequently misunderstood perfection of the human race, it is the idea of humanitarianism, the desire to break down the barriers that prejudice and all kinds of lopsided views have allowed to go up between people, fanning animosity, and to treat the whole of mankind — without regard for religion, nation and colour

— as one large fraternal tribe. This is the final, the supreme goal; it is the extension of man's existence. And both were planted in man by nature."

It is with this in mind that I should like to wish us all success in our efforts.

NOTES

Books

1. Ackermann, P.; Glashagen, W., *Friedenssicherung als pädagogisches Problem in beiden deutschen Staaten* (Stuttgart Ernst Klett, 1982)
2. Akademie der Pädagogischen Wissenschaften der DDR, *Pädagogik und Schule im Kapitalismus heute* (Berlin: Volk und Wissen Volkseigener Verlag, 1987)
3. Bast, R., *Friedenspädagogik* (Düsseldorf: Schwann, 1982)
4. Gromyko, A.; Lomejko, W., *Neues Denken im Atomzeitalter* (Leipzig, Jena, Berlin: Urania-Verlag, 1986)
5. Humboldt, W.v., *Gesammelte Schriften.* Herausgegeben von der Königlichen Preussischen Akademie der Wissenschaften Berlin, Band VI, 1.
6. Neubert, H., *Europa 1945–Europa 1985* (Berlin: Dietz Verlag Berlin, 1985)
7. Meissner, H.; Lohs, K.-H., *Frieden ohne Alternative* (Berlin: Akademie-Verlag Berlin, 1985)
8. Röhrs, H., *Friedenspädagogik* (Frankfurt am Main: Akademische Verlagsgesellschaft, 1970)
9. Schauerte, W., *Europäische Integration und Politische Bildung* (Bonn: Pädagogische Fakultät der Rheinischen Friedrich-Wilhelms-Universität, 1981)
10. Weidenfeld, W., *Die Identität Europas* (Bonn: Schriftenreihe der Bundeszentrale für politische Bildung, 1985)

PAN-EUROPEAN EDUCATION FOR PEACE AND THE FUTURE

Jean-Marc Gabaude

In the face of the threat of nuclear war and the risk of the destruction of humanity, the fundamental problem, of prime importance to each and every one of us, is to *build World Peace;* a form of peace which is not merely a precarious absence of war, but a positive mutual agreement for the development of individuals, of populations and cultures, and for *humanization.* Such a peace-objective calls for two kinds of conditions:

I   A generalization of socio-economical and political structures, of self-governing democratization and humanist socialism, and an increase in the part played by international authorities;

II Greater importance given to the function of education.

These two kinds of conditions have in common the fact that they underline the inseparability of peace and development. To give impetus to the complex development of the human being and to advance the causes of *democratization, socialism,* and *education*: to do all these is to work for peace.

The improvement of education is a powerful means for building up world peace and a common future. It means combining our efforts to this end in every country and in every continent. This is why we are advocating *pan-European* education for peace and the greatest future for Europe, which implies reforms both in the educational system and in the *mass media.* Such reforms would presuppose a concerted effort amongst European states and an agreement on the programme.

We are advocating a *pan-European* educational system. This should include an extension of the nursery school system. Indeed, preschool education stimulates children's sensori-motor, emotional, aesthetic, verbal and intellectual development, and facilitates their relating to others, notably by rendering any kind of aggression unnecessary. We know that the first six years have a determining influence on the rest of life. The nursery school is a place where the child learns to socialise and, at the same time, builds up a personality.

It would be necessary to make school attendance from *four* to *eighteen* compulsory. For the curriculum, it would be appropriate to provide an element of *pan-European citizenship studies,* imparting an idea of a peaceloving Europe, a Europe of *human Rights and the European citizen,* and imparting an understanding of points of convergence in legal systems, and the progress yet to be made. Similarly the history and geography curriculum should be *Europeanized.* An intercultural effort would also be welcome to provide an outline of the various literatures of Europe and of the reciprocity of influence and exchanges. We ask for this educational policy of *Europeanization* to be pursued at the tertiary level on the one hand and, on the other, through in-service training. All trained personnel and, *a fortiori,* the teaching body, should be trained with this end in mind. For primary and secondary school teachers, a minimum of five years in higher education is necessary.

At the same time it would be worthwhile to intensify student and pupil exchanges between European countries, language-learning visits, staying with families and in institutions, study trips, competitions, effective twinning schemes between towns, schools, colleges, universities, and so on. Furthermore, a *pan-European* University in each country, as well as numerous *pan-European* educational institutions, should be created along lines yet to be laid down.

In addition we want to see an agreement for the development of a new pedagogy, modernised and active, that is to say a pedagogy which fosters a sense of responsibility in the pupil, which encourages free expression, research, creativity and critical awareness, giving full importance to artistic and physical education. All this would, admittedly, presuppose adequate financing, but this could replace some part of the military allowance. Such an education would constitute a preparation for the role of citizen, in the fullest sense, in a democracy; and a preparation for the role of militant member of an integral peaceloving *pan-European* community.

Before tackling the related question of the educational duty of the *media*, it is worth underlining the philosophical principle common to modern pedagogy and *media* education. *Socialization* is a factor in *individualization*, and Society should become a means in the service of the individual person, the only *end in itself*.

Education is a long way from being reduced to the mere action of the educational system. It is also the pressure exerted by society as a whole, primarily by way of the *media*, on the being and behaviour of individuals. What is important is that all the countries of Europe should, progressively, without constraint and preferably by emulation, succeed in raising the cultural and informative level of the *media*, at the same time seeking to bring together the peoples and cultures of Europe. The *media* should facilitate the exchange of information and programmes between all the European countries through the free circulation of ideas, artistic productions and art events, cultural gatherings, critiques and declarations of counter-authorities, and so on. The audiovisual media should become the theatre of debate (economical, political, philosophical, ideological, aesthetic, *etc.*) on the scale of *Europeanism*, in order to come progressively to the constitution of a *pan-European* community thinking space. The communication and confrontation of points of view has an educational significance, and "mass-mediatization" is capable of inculcating a potential *pan-European* consciousness. Instead of simply reproducing existing values, the audiovisual media and the press should contribute to the establishment of *pan-European* values. Europe should become an educating society and an environment for both initial and continued education. We are banking on *Europeanization*. We are banking on East-West Cooperation and a *pan-European* Identity.

BIBLIOGRAPHY:

GABAUDE, J.M. (sous la direction de). *La pedagogie contemporaine*. Toulouse, Privat, 1972.

GABAUDE, J.M. *Philosophie de la scolarisation des années 1880 aux années 1980*. Toulouse: Publications de l'Université de Toulouse-le Mirail, 1987.

NOT, L. *Les pédagogies de la connaissance*. Toulouse: Privat, 1979.

WHICH HEART OF EUROPE?

Tamás Kozma

Professor Babing says that her country "lies right in the heart of Europe". And she is right, especially from the point of view of present international politics and the future of world peace. Let me follow her by saying that all Europeans have this "heart of Europe" feeling. All of us came here with the feeling that our native lands in one sense or an other — lie just in the heart of the Continent. A nineteenth century proverb — once common among the Hungarian nobility — can best illustrate this feeling. The slogan says that *"Extra Hungariam non est vita":* There is no life outside of Hungary. Modest noblemen used to add: *"Si est vita, non est vita:"* Certainly not the same life, if there is any. Let me assure you that many of us, Europeans, can quote parallels from our own national heritages.

But if any of us would be right, all of the others should certainly be wrong! If the Carpathians were really the centre of the Continent — as some geographers as well as others used to say — the Balkan countries would be counted as parts of the Near East, as they were called once upon a time by British travellers and foreign politicians. While, on the other hand, if the heart of Europe were really to lie in the Carpathians, Britain would under no circumstances be part of our Continent.

Statements like these are not more than the clear signs of ultra-national commitments backed by historico-geographical prejudices. All of us may agree with that. Somewhat more complicated is the quest for the roots of the prejudices. Why do we have this "heart of Europe" conviction, if we know intellectually that it comes from pure prejudices? Perhaps it is an expression of the belief that our own countries had made the sole important contribution to the heritage of Europe. Germans may rightly say that peace along both sides of their common border reduces political and military tensions in the whole Continent. From that assumption *they* are the political centre of Europe. Bulgarians and Macedonians may also be right saying that their motherlands lie in the centre, for they have reserved the original patterns of Christianity, and they were the ones who transmitted these to the Slavs, the largest family of the peoples of Europe. Mediterranians would have the right to state that they are the closest successors of the Roman Empire, and from that premise, *they* are the historical centre of Europe. The Baltic as well as the Atlantic societies could, however, point to their merchant activities which have modernized Europe — so they form the modernization centre of Europe. At the same time the Poles and Czechs would have an equal claim to say that not only do their territories lie in the geographical heart of the Continent, but they have also connected the East to the West by disseminating Roman Christianity among the "barbarians" of the Medieval Great Migrations. Why do not *they* form the centre of European survival and recreation? This "heart of Europe" conviction is not only common, but may also serve as an argument in foreign politics. Remember the Austro-Hungarian Empire of the nineteenth century, which declared it had the role of balancing Europe between Czarist Russia and Prussian Germany!

One root of this "heart of Europe" conviction goes back to our maps. Their designers always start from their own geographical standpoint, showing the distances between themselves and the next of their physical environment. The first well-known map of the Continent — the Islamic Book of Maps of the Xth century — shows the Mediterranean and the Gulf states as the middle of Eurasia. This came from the experiences of the Greek and Arab merchants who travelled precisely these areas. On the other hand, the Portolan Maps — the maps of the sailors of the twelfth-thirteenth centuries — mapped the seas more than the mainland, to show the safest ways from one harbour to another. The "heart of Europe" conviction has its economic and technical roots in those centuries.

But, it has roots also in public education. None of us, Europeans, can imagine an elementary school without a wall map of the Continent and our native lands. All of us would have the memory of the boring lessons during which we were watching not our teacher but those maps. Those wall maps have formed our geographical and historical views. A recent comparison of some European geography textbooks clearly shows that various books use different maps of Europe according to their countries of origin. Hungarian pupils can usually not answer the question whether Scandinavia or the other regions of Europe have larger interior geographical distances. Youths and adults in the Soviet Union regularly use the term "West" to refer to territories that lie to the West of the Ural Mountains, those mountains being right in the middle of their maps. The wall maps have made a great impact on our conviction that just we — and not others — lie in the "heart of Europe".

But schools give only the first impact. It is mass communication that provide us with up-to-date information. Let me remind you of the different maps of the Continent which you may meet on the screen, in the newspapers and advertisements, as well as during your travels. There is a consensus among geographers, historians, teachers and other specialists that our Continent starts at the Atlantic shore and ends at the foot of the Urals. Europeans always had a feeling that the British Isles belong to us too; while the British sometimes think the opposite. But anyhow, it is Europe as we commonly think of it and speak about it.

A geographical presentation of Eur-Asia, however, has other implications. It refers to the geographical fact that there are no physical border lines between the two continents. We can choose rivers like the Danube, Dnieper or Volga, or mountains like the Carpathians or the Urals as physical border lines; but they will be more of a convention than a reality. Further on, a geographical presentation of Eur-Asia may involve that Europe has no geographical identity itself, and can only be understood in relation to Asia.

The third type of presentations of Europe can be seen in several tourist offices, travel bureaus, stations, and timetables between, say, London and Vienna. It can also be watched on the evening news programs of several TV stations. This type shows Europe as if it had lost its Eastern part: as if Prague and Berlin, Dalmatia or the Black Sea were not parts of it. An extreme idea in itself, it has, of course, further implications in international politics.

Those information environments in which we, Europeans, live, do not necessarily suggest the common heritages and the common future of our Continent. While the "heart of Europe" conviction is widely accepted even today, the idea of a common future is more an intellectual creation than a popular belief.

There is no question that we should do something about this. The question, however, is whether we could do anything to turn the "heart of Europe" conviction into a pan-European identity. It is precisely this question that we may raise individually but can answer only collectively.

DISCUSSION ON BABING

Gordon Anderson

I think that I can agree with almost everything you said in your paper. Perhaps there are some things which were not said which lead to my comments or questions. I support education for peace, for dialogue, and for patriotism. However, I think most current peace education is considered by realists as politically naive, and can be taken advantage of. Therefore I think that peace education must also include respect for power, as well as respect for life and nature, and I think, in the foreseeable future, there is danger for political leaders, both East and West, of taking education to be soft or wishy-washy when it focusses on dialogue and cooperation, and I'm not sure if this will have the effect that you want. Does the education that you propose consider this element of power, which is a more masculine trait perhaps?

Evanghelos Moutsopoulos

I've heard all three of our panelists with great interest, and first I would like to ask a question of Prof. Babing before going on with my comments and personal proposals. I heard Mrs. Babing mention all social classes, perhaps instead of both classes. All social classes means something more pluralistic and I don't know whether this is referring to white-collar workers, blue-collar workers and so on, and if this means an abandoning of the basic conception of only two existing classes, a ruling and oppressing class and an oppressed class and if through this multiplication of classes that class struggle would come very soon to an end.

On the other side, I very much appreciated how Prof. Babing spoke about the division of Germany. We all hope that one day this division will be a bad dream, and I remember that, when I was recently in Berlin, there was some kind of unrest under my windows at the hotel. Young people asked to be allowed to join their brothers in West Berlin for a rock festival, and then I saw them being pushed by the police. The same thing occurred in West Berlin during the same day or so during the visit of Pres. Reagan. There were some young people demonstrating against that. And I could see on my television set each station depicting the situation on the other side. I think that this is mainly not a philosophical but an educational issue. I also think that the previous generation has been very guilty towards ours. But I wonder what are we doing ourselves for the next generation at the educational level. In this respect I'd like to congratulate Prof. Gabaude for his proposals. Prof. Gabaude conceives of further educational policy as a unification, a pan-European education as a merging of individual state educations. And I have such an example of what has occurred between France and West Germany, not only at the practical level but also at the ideological level, and I hope myself that very soon we'll have such a merging between educations of Greece and Turkey, at the ideological level too.

Now, as far as Prof. Kozma has said, and with respect to his own proposals, I would say I was very pleased to hear him say that we should urge our governments from below to change the attitude towards a very general restructuring of education in Europe. Well, he also pointed out that there is a problem, a linguistic problem. Today, in the EEC, we have eleven official languages. Well, the same thing occurs at a lesser level the UN and in UNESCO, with five official languages, and two working languages. I would go further in spite of the fact that personally my mother tongue is literally French, but I would prefer that we consider Esperanto as a common language. Esperanto has proved to be a very efficient language. It is very easy to learn. I speak it and I really think that it is very easy to learn within a month.

Vassilis Karasmanis

I have some questions mainly. Prof. Babing, speaks about patriotism. I would like to ask, how can you find the limits between patriotism and nationalism, especially when we have the German experience of the nationalism and the exaggeration of the German folk? That's one question.

Another question is that she speaks about education in all its highest humanitarian values and we have a set of really high values. The thing I want to ask is: do these values constitute a coherent set or not? This is very important for education. For example, take the notions of equality and freedom. Freedom in a society and translated also as economical freedom produces inequality. On the other hand, economic equality and policy sometimes limits freedom, so in this sense we need a set of values that must be coherent. That's a problem for an educational program. Another thing is that she speaks about the humanitarian tradition of Europe. There are some people who think that the whole problem of the world, the ecology, nuclear war, and others come from these traditions, especially from the anthropocentric notion that is very much at the center of this tradition. I don't like your opinion about this.

Another question is that among the values we have to teach young people, we have dialogue, tolerance, democracy, and so on. I think Professor Kozma said that only education in these matters without a change in the social and political structures is not enough. For example, in a country in which we don't have democracy or open dialogue, if we teach students these values, this means social revolt some years later, or the students will see these teachings as hypocrisy when they compare them with the social environment.

Another thing: such teaching, if it's not accompanied by general social changes, looks a little paternalistic towards the youth.

Alexander Shtromas

There are three problems to which I think the panel has not addressed itself. First of all, each country, whatever the nature of the country is, has a certain set of ideological values and orientations. I don't think that, in any of the countries we could see in Europe, the set of goals of education which was presented by Professor Babing could fully and ideally correspond with them. And here is the problem, how realistic would it be for the educationalists in all countries, East or West, to seek to implement those goals of education, and what compromises should be made or what pressures should be exercised in order to reach those goals? It is a political question.

The second problem which arises, in my view, is the problem of how realistic, in view of those circumstance, this education would be. How well prepared would the children be to face the world in which they enter if they are educated in some values which are not corresponding to the existing values of the societies in which they live? And thirdly, even if we ignore the first two problems, the real and most important question is how could we assess the readiness of educationalists themselves to instill such values into their pupils or students? There is a saying which says, addressing medical doctors, you cure yourself first. Shouldn't we say the teacher should teach himself first, then we could see how those results of the education of the teachers could be translated into the education of the pupils? So those are the three main problems which I find when reading Prof. Babing's paper.

Now, one dubious and controversial problem which was raised in Prof. Babing's paper has to do with education for patriotism and internationalism at one and the same time. I agree that, without love of one's own country and one's own people, one is unable to love mankind. I think internationalism, as preached by many schools of thought, is education for the love of people. At the same time, people live with biased preferences towards their families, their communities, and their nations. If we don't take into account those preferences of people, and instead ask them to love everybody equally, we will fall out with real life, and such an internationalism would be really anti-human. So that line of argument I accept fully. You could only understand the problems of other nations and sympathize with them, if you feel very deeply about the problems of your own nation, but that's not sufficient. You see, the problem here is to distinguish between patriotism and nationalism. Unlike many other people, I think patriotism is a notion which implies the love of one's own country and preaches the love of one's government. Nationalism, on the contrary, to me, is a love of one's nation, and implies disobedience, and maybe rebellion, against one's own government if it is not beneficial to the nation. In that sense, a German patriot, during the the last war would be, in my view, loyal to Hitler, whatever his doubts about the regime, out of patriotism, but a nationalist would seek to destroy Hitler, and seek the defeat of Germany in the war, for the benefit of the German nation. To me the people who were loyally fighting on Hitler's side were patriots, but those who were opposing him were German nationalists. That is the difference. If we talk about values, we should include all the values, including the love of one's own nation. We should divorce them from the value of loyalty to one's own government, which is connected to the notion of patriotism. And in that sense they should be better elaborated. And the final point, since the history of Europe is so full of conflict, so full of wars and cleavages, and there are prejudices among many European nations toward other European nations, how do we bridge those differences? And here I think the internationalist attitude could be applied with the result that if we really care for our nation, we also would like to beat out the sins of our nation. So the revision of historical values, of assessment of historical events, should take place in terms of repentance or revision: to say, well, that was wrong on our behalf, not necessarily on behalf of the other nation. And I think this also is totally contrary to patriotism in European countries, and could introduce them to internationalism, because we want, out of love for our nation, to see it be nurtured, but, in that sense, we have to denounce and renounce all the bad records of history our nation has pursued.

Ljubisav Rakic

My objection, and the same time a question for comments, is the following. You know we are faced today with a new heritage besides the old heritage which belonged to past history. We are faced with a new heritage which is developed on the basis of huge developments of science and technology. And maybe in this new heritage we could find more in common than in the old heritage, which too much divided us. If we look at history, especially European history, with hundreds of countries and states and sub-states, we could find many things that divide us, but when we come to the new heritage, the heritage of our time, of our civilization of the twentieth century, we find many things in common, especially, the development of science. With all the sciences, and the natural sciences in particular, we could find many things in common, which could put us on a common path to look for a European identity, at least in this part of education. And, of course, how could we find in the future a technical and technological education in balance with the humanities, when we have a lack of humanities in all levels of education? My proposal would be keep the balance between a very sophisticated scientific education and the humanities.

Raymond Tschumi

I do not believe in education in the sense of state education, or political education. I don't believe in its efficiency, or, perhaps, even in its relevancy. Some of the comments sound to me a little redolent of the League of Nations', not United Nations', but League of Nations', idealism. We should realize that we are not pan-European minded. We are very far from that. I would just give an anecdote from my own experience, not as an educator but as a father. My first son went to school, although he is French-speaking like me, in the German part of Switzerland. One day I asked him: what did the teacher tell you? And he said he talked about the Helvetians. Good, what did he say about the Helvetians? Well, he told me that the Helvetians were Germanic people. A few days later I met the teacher and I asked him: Did you say that the Helvetians were a Germanic people? And the teacher looked at me frightened and said, "What, is that not true?" Well, it proves that this is what he had learned.

Years later, exactly 14 years later, a daughter of mine went to school and in the third year, now they had a history book for the third year, it was 151 pages about Swiss history, the rather remote past. Of these 151 pages, 150 were devoted to the history of the German Swiss, you know their customs, the way they cooked meals, the way they fought between each other, and so on and so forth, and three-quarters of a page were devoted to the Helvetians, who were described as foreigners. Now this is an example of ethno-centrism in public, in state education. It's not for the whole population of Switzerland, only for one district in the canton of St. Gall.

Andrzej Werner

I would like just to add to the discussion by providing the information that between the Federal Republic of Germany and Poland there is some cooperation of reviewing and changing the textbooks, especially on history, and I think that we have already achieved some sort of understanding and progress in that area to eliminate the mutual prejudices and chauvinism on both sides. Maybe that model could be followed by other countries as well.

I would like to congratulate Prof. Babing for her paper and especially that she preaches so much for tolerance. That's great! And that she makes a good place for patriotism in pan-European identity. But what your paper lacks is a recognition of hatred. Why, why, have I been raised, after the Second World War, in hatred?

Stanislaw Andreski

I would like to make one suggestion concerning education for peace. I think we don't actually need to make people love all mankind, and I don't think that the preservation of peace now is based on that. It is based on enlightened self-interest. I think the reason why we have peace is that war has become so unprofitable, and thus I think that one of the important contributions to peace is trying to educate people in thinking rationally, not jumping to conclusions. Therefore I would say that purely intellectual education, teaching young people to think rationally, to evaluate consequences is, in itself, an education for peace.

THE EMERGENCE OF A WORLD CULTURE AND EUROPES'S FUTURE

Raymond Tschumi

1.1. WHAT IS WORLD CULTURE?

Air travel, chains of hotels, the mass media, and rock music may give the impression or illusion of an incipient, spreading world culture in one language: English. If more evidence outside of mass culture were required, one might allude to the universality of art and science. Under closer scrutiny, however, the nice phantasm will soon dissipate.

And yet one can hardly deny the need for a world culture, under present conditions, and for many reasons. In my essay I shall try to delineate the conditions and problems of a world culture and at the same time to argue that cultural isolation in Europe, splendid or not, must be overcome. This endeavour is all the more difficult because everyone belongs inside a particular culture which he claims to be the only one, the supreme one, the eternal or sacred or absolute one. Historical and comparative arguments will have weak effects on ethnocentric positions.

Established meanings and absolute values will have to be opposed, and this can be done successfully if one can show that the hierarchy of meanings and values is such that there are no ultimates, that the latest truth or value is likely to be supplanted, and that the change is not an aimless mechanism.

On the basis of scanty evidence, we may suppose that life would have been unbearable or meaningless to our first ancestors without their belief in magic. It is far more evident that for many people nowadays a vague notion of science has the last word, even if the kind of science they believe in is not of the kind that admits of values. Now, magic and scientism have little in common, except in their universal claims.

If meaning were not open, however valuable its contents, it would soon turn into a tyranny. As examples of arbitrary meaning, medieval institutions come to mind: heraldry, falconry, bestiaries, syllogisms, *etc*. But even if we have lost the grand hierarchy of medieval meanings, we are not short of hieratic ideologies today. Fixed meanings may allow for stable conditions, but they resent change, not to speak of progress, and end in destruction and war. This is the case of all *utopias,* which have in common the attainment of a certain desirable, permanent, and final level. They can at best serve as temporary incentives, but are bound to turn into straightjackets. Besides, no utopia can give birth to a democratic society, for even if a majority of people subscribe to its aims, these have to be imposed as soon as it achieves power. It turns necessarily into a decadent dictatorship which will never take account of the will of its future victims. *Open* meanings suppose confidence in others, including future people — the very basis of democracy — and they even suppose the love of others — the very basis of ethics.

1.2 THE DIVISION OF EUROPE

So far we have advanced very little in our search for the conditions of a world culture. Before we proceed, however, we ought to briefly consider the present situation in Europe, where the division in two blocks — East and West — since the end of World War II, does violence to centuries of linked development and to the common heritage shared by the arbitrarily divided parts. At least culturally, the border between the two parts cannot be recognized by anyone caring for the future.

The dangers of opposing two absolute world views are obvious. On the one hand a materialistic, on the other hand a kind of free market ideology, by raising rival claims, are being provincialized; and high technology, mass communications, and space exploration via satellites, instead of opening borders, exasperate differences.

The future of Europe — if Europe has a future — depends not only on the free exchange of cultural goods across borders, but even more on a renewed creativity in all fields. No one can create in a closed system. In order to enter new ground, a scientist must not only have all the relevant information at his disposal, but also feel personally urged, without external compulsion. Similar remarks apply to the arts: even if an artist shocks his contemporaries — the more advanced he is the more challenging — the more he takes account of the widest possible tradition, the greater his originality. Now if the heritage is divided through and through, nothing of value can be added to it, except more broken pieces.

1.3. Universal versus standard culture

A culture that would not debate with Krishna whether to act or not, or that would not wait for the next story of the *Thousand and One Nights,* could only move backward. A world culture that would ignore the masterpieces of universal literature would soon fall back into provincial seclusion. The printed book in any language remains the depository of what is most valuable and permanent.

This universality, however, dies out as soon as it ceases to be incarnated by groups or individuals. One might even dare to say that there are only individual cultures communing in an ideal universality. This extreme statement would of course underestimate such historical categories of culture as judaic, alexandrian, islamic, or celtic. But the fusion of past or dead, especially oral, cultures in an all-encompassing written one, would not retrieve them from disaffection and oblivion.

Some aged representatives of extinct oral cultures are living monuments. The present abounds in such examples of cultural seclusion and extinction. No world culture can grow on such waste. Steps must urgently be taken to remedy this loss, not by a conservative attitude, but by a tolerant and pluralistic one.

2. Conditions for a world culture

2.1. Freedom of expression and of research

Freedom of expression and free research belong to these conditions. Lip-service is paid to both, but neither is respected.

Free research means that the scientist is free to choose his field, his method and above all his aims. Most research is conducted under state or industrial supervision; as a result the scientist is under compulsion to investigate what he is not interested in, according to methods which he disapproves of and, what is worse, in view of planned anonymous aims which he cannot subscribe to or which destroy his authentic experiences. This is clearly the case of military research, but is also true of one of the apparently most peaceful and useful kinds of research, when chemistry is in the service of agricultural production. There is no better example of the circularity of industrial research than the case of those insecticides which kill the wrong insects and birds, poison water and cause chemical industry to bring antidotes to the market of scientific farming.

The dangers of this *circulus vitiosus* are so obvious that common people are frightened with the apocalyptic vision of world destruction followed by a return to cave dwelling, a nightmare exploited by science fiction.

Instead of a return to cave dwellings, there is a better solution, namely an appeal to the conscience of scientists. But here the difficulty lies in their belief that there is no such thing as a conscience, at least no such object worth studying. Max Weber's view,[1] according to which science is *"wertfrei"* "value-free", still applies, in spite of many physicists appealing to moral values. What sounded like a liberation (*"die Wissenschaft ist wertfrei"* — "science is value-free") must now be interpreted as decadent irresponsibility.

There is an unprecedented split in our scientific culture, inasmuch as its whole development has been so thoroughly abstracted from the rest of culture, including moral and aesthetic values, that any appeal to moral values in our time is bound to sound hypocritical, for either as a scientist you find no authoritative recognition of values as such, or you feel responsible as a citizen, but as such you stand in conflict with your scientific education.

2.2 REUNION OF THE TWO CULTURES

Culture is plagued with other and more severe splits and dilemmas, all of which represent different cases of restraints on free thinking. The split of the two cultures is well known since C. P.

Snow and F. R. Leavis[2] proved antagonistic and irreconcilable. The ideological and commercial restraints on the freedom of writing are other cases to the point. I should like to emphasize only one aspect of the struggle. In universities, especially among sociologists, the diehard positivistic view of conditioned writing is prevalent. This means that the writer is seen exclusively as a mouthpiece for general social trends. The unwritten law that applies in his case is that the more general, representative and inclusive he is, the greater. Anyone asking for a criticism of the writer as such would derogate from the canon, and it hardly occurs to anyone that the writer might influence society, in other words that he might be an author in the real sense of the term!

2.3. END OF REDUCTIONISM

All the restraints on free thinking have something to do with what is generally called "reductionism".

Basically, this word denotes a tendency to apply exclusively quantitative criteria to knowledge and action. Already in the eighteenth century, David Hume urged us to burn all books that had nothing to do with functions and quantities.[3] Still underlying much scientific, academic, and philosophical endeavour is the belief in the possibility and desirability of translating physics into simple numerical relations, biology into physics, psychology into biology, ethics into conditioning, and language into symbolic logic. The lure of the ultimate, simple, and quantitative formula, lies at the end of the road.

2.4. ETHICS

The most pernicious effect of this tendency consists in denying all traditional *values,* aesthetic and ethical alike. Words like "virtue" or "beauty" have lost their currency. There is such a loss of transcendental dimensions in our lives that we are prone to revert to superstitions. Religious fundamentalism and esoteric, exotic, or astrological lore seem to compensate for the emptiness in our lives.

A rehabilitation of *ethics* could perhaps offer another compensation, but all the traditions leading to an ethical view of human life seem to be abandoned. In the second century AC, Plutarch could not only apply moral criteria to his lives, but propose at the same time an ethical view of history. This is what Jean-Jacques Rousseau,[4] for whom virtue was no empty word, admired so much in Plutarch. We may still read Plutarch[5] with profit, but we have lost his moral bearings. He could rely on the whole development of Greek philosophy and especially on the strong ethical bent of stoicism. Contemporary biographers and historians are judged according to scientific criteria, and tend to ignore possible ethical references or judgements.

It is probably impossible for any single philosopher to reinvent ethics after all his colleagues have ceased to raise ethics to the importance of logic. Besides, there is no such thing as scientific ethics, at least if, by science, we mean a discipline that deals in objects and quantities.

The normative transfer which makes ethics possible cannot be operated in our time without reference to specifically human values. I do not mean here that we should restore the platonic cult of permanent, transcendental ideas like 'goodness', or in medieval Christian values like the 'cardinal virtues'. Ethical values are specifically human in that they find their origin and their end in human culture: that is, in man's ability to create something that does not exist in nature. With the risk of oversimplifying, we must take account of the necessary opposition of the terms or concepts of nature and culture, however vague and undefinable they may be. This opposition conditions the otherwise vague division between the natural sciences and the humanities. If the humanities appear today in a defensive or lost position, this is arguably because they have ceased to proclaim, assume and maintain the belief in irreducible human freedom. This loss of belief is obviously due to a pressure on the part of the natural sciences, to a difficulty in operating a normative transfer, and, finally, to the lack of scientific foundation for any assumption of human freedom. A symptom of this disbelief is Ayer's definition of freedom, in a famous essay, as "elbowroom".[6] That philosophers should approve of such a definition, even without cynicism or malignity, demonstrates how far we are from the sheer possibility of a solid ethics.

3. THE HISTORICAL SETTING

3.1. EUROPE IS ABROAD

When Cicero studied on the island of Rhodos, he had to make a speech in Greek in order to demonstrate his rhetorical abilities. His listeners congratulated him, all of them except one, an orator whose name, according to Plutarch, was Apollo Molon, who kept silent and, when asked why he looked so sad, replied that the young Cicero had learned from his Greek masters and excelled in their own language to the point of surpassing their art, but he, Molon, was sad to know that Cicero would soon practise in Rome, so that with him the last thing the Romans had left in Greece, eloquence, would leave Greece.

This classical anecdote may serve as a model of the relation between European and world culture in the present century, if we suppose that, after assuming a leadership some five centuries ago, European culture is now being transferred to other, new places. Europe is abroad, according to the sad prophets, and their lamentations in the desert spread a sense of being relinquished of all the good spirits. Vulgarity occupies the front scene, and the best minds leave for the new worlds. Where are the geniuses in poetry, painting, music, dancing, sculpture, architecture, science and engineering? The very notion of 'genius' and of 'masterpiece' belong to dusty documents, according to the heralds of postmodernism. It is not so much Europe that is outdated than the solid modern world in which Europe played a leading part, historically from the Renaissance to the end of the past century.

3.2. THE MODERN PERIOD

What is coming to an end with the modern era is a practical and mental attitude underlying activities and thoughts. Basically, the modern temperament approached the world, or what it came to call "reality", with the unprejudiced and challenging daring which gave rise to the great discoveries and inventions underlining these five centuries. As to the literary and artistic masterpieces of the period, one may venture to attribute to them the same qualities of daring inventiveness. The examples would be too many. Now, as each attitude stirs up the corresponding objects, this daring inventiveness was the human challenge to a world which was still imbued with magic, on which the spell of a theological hierarchy had just been cast, and which was gradually emptied of its spirits and demons to become sheer reality, a kind of solid material reference.

Long term historical changes are not changes in technology, but *changes in consciousness*. It is not the world that changed in the modern period, but the eyes that looked at it. What changed the world (without its being transformed into anything else than what it had always been) is, paradoxically, that it disappeared or dissolved by the end of the last century. Historically, one may discern two phases: the initial phase in which a new, scientific vision invented and clarified such notions as 'object', 'reality', 'matter', 'mechanism', 'force', *etc.*, and the final phase in which these clear views of the world became confused. If we realize how far we are from Herbert Spencer's clear and simple view of the world as the sum of matter and energy, then we can perhaps guess how many conceptions have changed since the nineteenth century, for it is as difficult to know how our neighbours feel as it is to know how the so-called primates must have felt.

The world that came to an end a generation or two ago had a solid frame, at first theological, then scientific, and it would be wrong to despise the beliefs that solidified that frame, for our beliefs are far more uncertain.

3.3. POSTMODERNISM

What we have learned from the dissolution of a solid frame is the consciousness of being involved in whatever objects we create. In other words, we have lost the innocence of a period that strove to get rid of original sin, to the point of denying the validity of ethical thinking. At the end of the second millenium we are the heirs of an amoral and antiaesthetic turn of mind, insofar as we have not yet tried to face a new situation with resolute courage.

It is true that both the ethical and aesthetic assumptions were based on a firm belief in a unique God that had created a good world in which man, free to disobey, was redeemed by a Saviour. This is the grand conception of Milton's *Paradise Lost*.[7] Ethical and aesthetic values, however, are not necessarily tributary to monotheistic views, and it may even be argued that Christian ethics originated in platonic ideas, what is good and what is just referring to an absolute ideal, but no less real justness and goodness. Though a return to platonic essences can hardly be advocated with any chance of success, a reminder of their former strength and influence is perhaps useful at this point.

Not only theology, but also science is of much relevance in the present debate. No science can offer the foundations of any value, especially since Max Weber attached to its name the ominous and significant but misleading epithet of *"wertfrei"* ("value-free"). And yet there is no scientific activity that does not raise moral questions.

4. THE FUTURE: PROBLEMS AND HYPOTHESES

4.1. THE FRUITS OF EXPERIENCE

The whole problem may be set in terms of experience. Any experience raises questions beyond itself and beyond the person involved in it. Our very cultural situation forces us to grow conscious of our shortcomings, of our ignorance and of our involvement. There are fewer possibilities of evading our responsibilities, of delegating punishment to a jealous God, and of assuming that reality can be known and explained. Thus every individual action and thought entails a reflexion on its sense. The meaning of life is no longer given first or fixed by ecclesiastical authorities, but results directly from our actions.

In this perspective, values are the fruit of experience, and meaning harvests the seed of our actions. Individual experience thus entails limitless consequences far beyond individual foresight, but not beyond individual responsibility. Scientific and artistic experiments are not discharged of the responsibility in which the main condition of hope for a world culture must be seen.

4.2. THE FUTURE LIES BEHIND

The long-term cultural situation of the future appears thus, retrospectively, as opposed to the one that obtained at the turning point between the pagan and Christian worlds, when great ideas could move people, and endow their life with a value and a meaning. The philosophers of our situation are not idealists, but existentialists. The scientists no longer try to show God in his creatures, and the poets no longer try to justify the ways of God to man. Our future is not before us, but behind us in the sense that it increasingly depends on what we do, and on what responsibility we assume.

4.3. Europe as a Phoenix

It is obvious that the deep changes which already determine the future originated in Europe, but at the same time these changes occasion a large amount of self-destruction. Moreover, the other parts of the world seem to be in a favourable position since they have less to destroy and should be less afraid of innovation. And yet it is difficult to know, on the eve of a new period, who is going to take the initiative in long-term and far ranging steerings.

The decisive element is, of course, the birth of a new, critical consciousness, and of the corresponding creative attitude, and here no one can say where the first signs can be detected. Examples of a critical or destructive sense abound everywhere, especially in the arts. The parodistic trend in films, in literature and in the visual arts is not only pugnacious but also successful, a surprising phenomenon if we consider how unpopular irony is at other periods.

4.4. Self reflexion

The movement of self-reflexion in the arts is perhaps more constructive. It manifests itself, in particular, in so-called "metafiction", an offspring of the *"nouveau roman"* (new novel) and of the structuralism of the sixties and seventies. Self-reflexion is also in vigour in such "metadisciplines" as the history and philosophy of the sciences, where, instead of 'progress', Kuhn[8] introduces the notion of 'changes in paradigms'.

4.5. Self-destruction

Self-reflexion, as it is practised, may be self-destructive, in so far as the very structures which it detects have a tendency to dissolve under close analysis, in accordance with a largely unexplored dialectics. Basically, self-reflexion, as it is practised, is destructive of the most important of its constitutive elements: the self. It is superfluous, at this point, to report the announcement made by Jean Paul Sartre of the death of God and the one, made by Foucault, of man's death.

If man is dead, and structures have no subjective center, then there is no person, and the very notion of self becomes meaningless. This corrosive reflexion entails further consequences. There are contemporary authors — I know some of them — who deny that they have anything to do with the composition of their work: that the work — a mixture of autobiography, poetic fragments, self-criticism and parody — composed itself, so that if an author emerges at all out of this novel without a plot, without characters, without a theme, and without authorial comment or narrative sequence, then the author emerges out of the many empty spaces as a shrill voice, a sad laughter or as the very distance between his self-projections and the person of the writer, whose life is irrelevant.

4.6. ANTI-CLASSICISM

As a subsidiary remark, one might add here that, contrary to the classical novel, metafiction is characterized by an allcovering projection of a subject who only occasionally becomes a self, and, still more rarely, an author. And metafiction is not alone in this, since similar types of self-projection became apparent in other forms of artistic expression, especially in painting, during the second half of the last century. The classical novel and drama are characterized, on the contrary, by the discretion of the author, who hides behind his characters in order to fully manifest their feelings and motivations. In this case, the plot develops out of the same motivations, betrays hidden motives, or challenges the characters. Even if there is a hero or a protagonist, the play or the novel sets several characters in the foreground and the author is nowhere to be seen, but there is an author, even a kind of sublimated, omniscient entity who, from the start, knows the issue of the tragedy, and who will reveal the truth of the characters in such a way that, when the play is over, the spectators will feel the satisfaction of understanding, at last, what moved the characters.

4.7. THE INVENTIVE READERS

Here I must apologize for this digression and return, if the verb is adequate, to the future, where the clear and orderly composition of a work of art is missing and where, ironically, the self that projects itself everywhere assumes no authorial responsibility, and thus leaves readers and spectators alike with a thirst for motivation, for justification, and for explanation. Apparently the right response to such disorder is a knowing, self-deprecating laughter: a good sign after all, if we remember that hardly any audience in the past ever liked to be thus insulted, or, at least, reminded of its shortcomings, instead of being flattered. Some will ascribe this humiliation to the collective masochism associated with a decadent European culture. Others will, rather, interpret the new aggressive fashion as a call for creativity on the part of the anonymous readers, listeners, and spectators. The empty spaces, the missing plots and the absent characters have to be filled by someone who is not the author, and this call flatters the readers' ingenuity. If you are left without a ready-made explanation, then you have to invent one, and if you do not find any, at least you enjoy the superiority of your sour knowledge. You will not throw tomatoes or rotten eggs at the actors because you feel they are honest.

The situation of painting is just as critical. A concrete painting by, say, Tapies, may be interpreted as a material wall or, contrarily, as an expression of mystical longing. The concreteness of the surface provokes a reaction through which the self is engulfed in nothingness. There is no new "ism" that does not produce its acknowledged critics, whose language is reputed to be all the more authoritative because it is confused and abstruse.

4.8. AIMLESS AUTOMATION

No doubt the ambiguous and antithetic character of contemporary art, compared to the monolithic and semantically consistent aspects of former works of art, denotes a disorientation which contrasts with the opening of the modern period, symbolized by the compass and the first crossing of the Atlantic Ocean in six weeks — a performance that was not surpassed for more than half a century! The aimlessness of much present activity is overtaken only by the vision of a computerized automatic civilization where no one would remember what are the goals of production and who steers the whole machinery, if anyone does. In this respect the enormous output of science fiction exemplifies the conflicting situations in which apparently perfect, highly developed societies find themselves when power and the occupation of new natural or artificial planets are at stake. For such conflicts, there is no other explanation than the old conventional dichotomy of the good ones and the bad ones, with the corresponding fake ethics and the monstrous love between human beings and robots.

Since we have touched the question of automation, we may consider at this point not the effects of automation, which are being closely examined, but the more important and rather blurred problem of its aims and ends. As an example of these problems we should mention the control of the genetic code and, more generally, the so-called biological revolution. The question does not consist in asking which species is better adapted, but which new species can be manipulated to fulfill planned production. The question is so acute among futurologists that some of them already seriously consider how to replace organic bodies like the human body by electronically-minded beings whose inorganic body would better tolerate space conditions.

4.9. THE MECHANIZATION OF CULTURE

This is only one example of the kind of research which, passively supported all over the world, hides its ultimate end: the mechanization of culture, and the end of man. Against this destruction in the name of science, the humanities and a last recourse to laws and ethics are too weak. In order to face the innumerable challenges of the twenty-first century, more positive and creative goals must be aimed at than the transformation of the human species into a thinking machine in order to invade and exploit outer space. Among these challenges, those raised by technological innovations may be enumerated: fertility control, control by drugs, laming weapons, controlled thermonuclear reactions, urban concentration, progressive automation in trade and industry, genetic manipulation, change of climate, space exploration, *etc.* Each of these innovations, needless to say, adds its own problems to the existing ones, thus calling for a world wide ethical solution. As we have seen, there is no such solution in sight as long as the antihumanistic trend prevails. Now, the humanities were not the privilege of Europe, nor of any particular culture. By throwing all traditions overboard, the new technologies can only increase the sense of frustration, emptiness, boredom, and vain distraction which seizes the disoccupied and aimless masses. How can you persuade anyone that his life has a meaning if you do not *trust him to lead his life in his own way?* This is the central cultural question beyond all religious, social, psychological, scientific, and political considerations.

One of the important questions of the future: the aims — rather the impact — of technological innovations, is thus left without an answer. Anyone who would like to have a positive aim in sight would have to reconcile innovation with tradition and submit future achievements to traditional value judgements.

Unfortunately, the specialists who are deemed to be competent in technological matters are selected according to criteria strictly relevant to their special field, thus building the present without foundations in the past.

A striking example of this lack of continuity and foresight is the way atomic energy plants are built and run before the problem of waste disposal has been solved, not to mention security problems. But a better, if less spectacular, example is the hasty machine translation programs announced since the fifties. In a feverish Cold War competition, both the Americans and the Russians announced that they had invented a translating machine. The results were disappointing, and they are still disappointing today, even with the help of computers. One of the lessons that can be drawn from these examples is that advanced technology produces machines which are built before anybody knows what purpose they serve. The question asked is not what tools can be used, but, given the tools, what can I do? The tool is the master.

5. THE ASSETS

5.1. INNOVATION

This situation must be reversed if a world culture is to replace technological war. *Innovation* is a good thing if it does not consist in producing machines and weapons aimlessly, under false pretexts like "deterrence" or "to increase economic power". The last two decades have seen the birth of a strong movement of public opinion all over the world against the predominantly economic viewpoint of the post World War II period. 'Environment' is no longer an empty word, and gains an urgent priority. The aim of preserving and improving the environment is now recognized by millions of people across all borders as superior to economic power. This is new, this is positive, and this modestly contributes to the emergence of a world culture where each individual would be conscious of belonging, together with all others, to something much bigger than his immediate social horizon. What is still more important is to realize that the achievement of peace between nations and between man and nature should not be left in the hands of politicians, technocrats, or ideologists, but lies in the decision of a free individual who is open-minded or responsible enough to be trusted by democratic institutions.

5.2. INDIVIDUAL CONSCIENCE

Here lies, in my opinion, the mainspring of world culture: there is no progress and no future that is not based on the individual conscience, a notion that is relatively new and far from being recognized or established. It is new in Europe because those who were first in proclaiming the rights of an individual conscience, the Protestants,[9] fell back, later, to an institutionalized observance of rules. In fact no one so far, not even the existentialists, ever recognized the possibilities of a society of truly independent persons. These possibilities are so tremendous that philosophers, theologians, and, above all, politicians, shrink back from their implications. And yet the thought of a common individual who assumes a vast responsibility always finds popular support. It is true, however, that this figure usually takes the shape of a national hero, and that this kind of identification often contributes to national fanaticism. People identify with heroes in proportion as they delegate responsibility to authorities.

The idea of an individual conscience is revolutionary because, to be realized, it requires the individual to assume full responsibility, at least for what he does, without identifying with readymade models, obeying rules, or conforming to institutions. Even if the advent of this individual is not for tomorrow it may be considered as inevitable that, the urge (reactionary people would say the 'temptation') being strong enough to challenge totalitarian inertia, the individual of the future will not only be inclined to take advantage of his possibilities, but will readily assume the corresponding responsibility. This process will take much time and many little steps, but no better future is in sight, as we all hope.

6. CONCLUSION

6.1. THE SOULLESS SPECIES

After five centuries of uncritical scientific development, a new era has started in which new aims and ends will have to be found in full consciousness of human possibilities and limitations. The initial momentum of this new consciousness should be the realization that cultural history is not the history of civilizations with their arts, religions, tools, and techniques, but, more fundamentally, a succession of steps crossing new thresholds of consciousness, each time with new aims in view.

Prehistoric human fossils lie millions of years behind us and, after over one century of research, we still approach them from one single viewpoint: evolution. It is not impossible to conceive how a certain development, the one that leads to the discovery of the evolution of species, against the undisputed belief in a God-created world, may, in its turn, resist a new critical and dynamic viewpoint. If, indeed, traces of lost species are left, the consciousness of their evolution is on the move, but consciousness cannot move passively, according to rules or laws. Its creativity is difficult to admit without adopting a critical attitude to five centuries of scientific development.

Now, the cultural world is still steeped in frames of the nineteenth century. Humanity is still viewed in categories of species, from a viewpoint that proclaims its objectivity and lays aside what is original or individual. Our world is framed by a geometry that provides no holes for the soul.

6.2. Critical moves

The advent of an individual conscience as the nucleus and origin of a world culture is resisted from many sides, but progresses in a way that has nothing in common with mechanistic, automatic, dialectic, or deterministic processes: once a new threshold of consciousness has been crossed, it happens that everything *is* different. Some will object that everything only *looks* different, but their objection belongs to an uncritical period when the division and separation of the subject from the object was an unquestioned ontological dogma.

However desirable objectivity may still be, we have learnt to be critical of this dogma, well knowing that the ultimately decisive components of objects are steeped in and proceed from an active consciousness of which we are barely aware.

6.3. The active consciousness

Culture as a whole in its developments from its earliest forms of expression, exemplifies the progress of consciousness from its primitive manifestations in the shapes of fetishes, monsters, and giants, to gods, ideas and essences; from a belief in magic, to a consistent theology; from the contemplation of a God-created world, to the exploration of a material universe; from magic, religious, and realistic conceptions of art, to a critical view of images.

And there is no end of discoveries, no final message, no ultimate stage, no absolute truth, as long as human consciousness is alive and active, but there is a common goal and a convergence of all individual consciences in proportion as they assume their share of responsibility. Great religions had local origins. World culture emerges from the ruins of Europe, but its origins lie in as many individuals as are ready to open their hearts and minds.

NOTES

1. Max Weber, "Der Sinn der Wertfreiheit", in: *Logos,* Bd. VII, 49-88, or: in Kröner Verlag Stuttgart, 1968, 263–311.
2. See: Graves, Nora Calhoun, *The two cultures theory in C.P. Snow's novels* (Hattiesburg, U.P. of Mississipi, 1976)
3. David Hume, *Enquiries concerning human understanding and concerning the principles of Morals* (Oxford, Clarendon Press, 1974): "When we run over libraries, persuaded of these principles, what havoc must we make? If we take in our hand any volume: of divinity or school metaphysics, for instance; let us ask, *Does it contain any abstract reasoning concerning quantity or number?* No. *Does it contain any experimental reasoning concerning matter of fact and existence?* No. Commit it then to the flames: for it can contain nothing but sophistry and illusion." (XII, III, 165)
4. *The Confessions of Jean-Jacques Rousseau* (tr. Maurice Leloir, Norwood editions, 1984)
5. Plutarch, *Parallel Lives* (11 volumes Loeb Classical Library, Harvard University Press, no date).
6. Alfred Ayer, "Freedom and Necessity", Polemic, 1964; reprinted in: *Philosophical Essays,* London, Macmillan, 1954.
7. John Milton, *Paradise Lost* (ed. Alastair Folwer. London, Longman, 1968).
8. T.S. Kuhn, *The structure of scientific revolutions* (Chicago, 1962, 1970).
9. Raymond Tschumi, *La crise culturelle* Lausanne, L'Age d'Homme, 1983, 150–153; Jean Delumeau, *Naissance et affirmation de la Réforme,* Paris, PUF, 1965, 275.

DISCUSSION ON TSCHUMI

Prof. Radnitzky

"The scientist is under compulsion to investigate what he is not interested in according to methods which he disapproves of." I think to unravel the confusion on this page one needs certain distinctions. First the distinction between the concept of basic science and applied science. Basic science is usually defined as projects with possible gains in terms of new knowledge. In applied science you have a practical problem and you think that scientific research may give you the knowledge you need in order to solve the practical problem. The distinction is relevant for methodology, because the method is the same in both cases. But it is essential and indispensible for science policy making because the argument which justifies the expenditures of resources in one or the other are completely different. In applied science, the case is very unproblematic. If you want to reach an aim, you must also want the means, and lesser means have certain consequences, and so on. But in the case of purely basic research, the justification of the use of other peoples' money is by far more problematic. As in some applied science, the problem selection comes from outside. This is in the nature of applied science. In pure science, by definition, the scientists select the problems themselves, and usually, in most countries, the state or a foundation set a budgetary frame and leave it to the scientific community to make the selection. Hence to regard this as a compulsion is a misunderstanding of the situation. Second, the assertion with respect to method I find ludicrous. It confuses several moments from research itself to the evaluation of the results of the application of resulting technologies. We must distinguish between, first, selection of problems or projects and, second, the process of research. The process of research is autonomous, and here the thesis that science is value-free applies, for any intervention in the process of research is counterproductive. Even in that Solzhenitzen example in which the scientists are working in the Gulag, they must remain free to judge the quality of their product. Hence in this case science is autonomous, and this is a part of a thesis that science is value-free.

Then we have a third phase: a creative search for possible technological relevance, and the implementation of these inventions into a technology. Then we have a fourth phase, the implementation of the technology, and fifth, the discovery of the effects of the application of this technology, with some of them intended, some of them unintended, unexpected or unwanted. And lastly we have an evaluation of the results of the application of the technology in practice from some extra-scientific viewpoint: an ethical viewpoint, for instance. These phases, it appears to me, have been confused in what he said about the use of chemistry in agriculture.

And then the difficulty with the thesis of Max Weber. I will not go into an exegesis of Max Weber's *"Wissenschaft ist wertfrei,"* the thesis that science is value-free. What can the thesis mean? To unravel its meaning, you must have a concept of science. The statements of science must have testable consequences. This is a prime earmark of science. And then science is viewed as a continuation of common sense enquiry. We have created systematicity. But the key feature is the testable consequences. This is what distinguishes science, and this is what is meant by saying it is value-free. It means, if science is conceived of in this way, that it is logically impossible that it can contain genuine value statements or norms. From this it follows that science alone cannot solve any ethical problems or any practical problems by itself. This is part of the message of the paper, but to attack Weber's *"Wissenschaft ist wertfrei"* is to commit a self-contradiction. It runs counter to the spirit of the paper, with which I am in sympathy.

And then, of course, I have great difficulty with such sentences, for instance, as those which translate physics into simple numerical relationships. What can this mean? Physics is a discipline, a theoretical physics, mathematical physics, experimental physics, what can it mean? Or does it refer to a physical theory. But a formula with a mathematical interpretation is not a physical formula. It is not a physical theory. It becomes a physical theory and formula only if it has an empirical interpretation and, thus, has a physical interpretation. So I find that I cannot understand this part of the text.

Alexander Shtromas

Well, I would like to start where Professor Radnitzky has finished, the *"wertfrei"* thesis of Weber. It is much more complex than that in Weber's perception. Weber does not really advocate simply that science is value-free. What he does advocate is that the choice of the subject for study is based on your values, based on your biases, based on your interests in the world, specific to you and your particular world view, but when you have chosen the subject, your own bias, your own value judgments really drive you to study it in a value-free way in order to establish the truth — and thus either confirm or revise your own position on the subject of your interest. In that sense, Weber does not deny the value approach and, of course, only truth could really and properly serve the values you hold. If it doesn't, then the values are not values, they are phoney symbols and prejudices. So I think that part of the paper, I agree with Prof. Radnitzky, should be thought over before it could be properly formulated.

But really what I wanted to speak about is something else. And that is that nobody who spoke, it seems to me, has paid attention to a phenomenon which is not the unity and plurality which was always very beautifully and nicely emphasized by Professor Beck and by the paper-giver himself, but there is something else, which is a unity itself, and that is world culture. You see, to me world culture is today an integral phenomenon. Shakespeare wrote in the English language, and Goethe in the German language, but they both firmly belong to the culture of the world and are incorporated and integrated in every national culture as inextricable elements. An impetus to German romanticism was given actually by Shakespeare; Herder introduced Shakespeare into German culture and really made it a part of that culture, and it developed its own force which, later spread to Russia, and elsewhere. What I'm trying to say here is the following: there is a phenomenon which is the integral world culture. There is a stratum in world society, we can call it the intelligentsia, which is the carrier of that world culture. When you listen to Professor Damnjanović in this conference, you would never say he is really only a Yugoslav: he is not. His frame of reference is German philosophy: Heidegger, and others. What he writes in his own language refers to something written in many other languages. Ideas like spirit, travel free, and travel wherever they want. So there is an identifiable phenomenon that is world culture, an integral entity, and there is an integral stratum which becomes a world class and that is the class of the intelligentsia, the carrier of those values and of those cultural achievements.

Having said that, I would like also to stress that it is pecular that cultural sorts of trends, integrated trends, travel usually in a much more rapid way from the west to the east than from the east to the west. I think the Anglo-saxon nations probably are culturally more isolated than other nations. Just to give you an example, I was lecturing my students on the political implications of Kierkegaard's existentialist philosophy, and explaining to them that the model Kierkegaard uses is the transition from the aesthetical to the ethical level of life in Goethe's *Faust*. I saw that my students didn't follow me. My assumption was that every more or less literate person knew about Goethe, but then I stopped and I asked my students why they were so puzzled. They said: "Do you refer, Sir, to Christopher Marlowe's Dr. Faustus?" "No," I said, "to Goethe's Faustus". "And who was Goethe?" Well, that couldn't be possible in any continental European country. No student in the last year of university education would make such a mistake. However, I think you could detect how English culture influenced French; French culture influenced German; German, Russian; Russian, Korean and Japanese. This process is still in the making. The thesis I would like the panel to address, is the question not of simple plurality in unity, but the phenomenon of forming world culture as the basis for future world society, and the place of the intelligentsia as the carrier of world cultural information of that world society.

Gordon Anderson

I appreciate your support for creativity and your criticism of reductionism, but I, too, had some problems with definitions and your terms. I think, as you probably indicate in your paper, values come from consciousness and consciousness comes from shared experience. I'm not sure if a value can be a value if it does not have some absolute aspect to it. It's a question from my study of Troeltsch, who talks about absolutes in a way that I don't think you're talking about them. And it seems to me that universal values as opposed to particular values might be what you're concerned about, because the absolutizing of a value can be very dangerous, especially if it impinges on other particular values and denies some universal values further realization. I think this is the problem of the modern era, which you point out. But I believe we have a shared experience, we have a world culture and from that we have a consciousness from which, perhaps, we can derive and spell out some particular universal values. From the world of biology, we have the need of food and oxygen which are values which, I think, we can agree upon. And, generally from sociology, family might be a value. On a more theoretical level, maybe some of your values of peace, openness, a better future, love of others, creativity, freedom to do research, a critical consciousness, global responsibility, *etc.*, these are all values, I think of the post-modern world era and products of our common experience. But there is also a problem if we push one of these universal values to the exclusion of other universal values. If you push freedom or openness and exclude other values that we commonly share, you also run into the same problem of reductionism that we had in the modern era if any are pushed dogmatically. So I think that the answer is to hold these values together in creative tension, and that without them you do have the isolatedness that you find in modern society. Perhaps one advantage the socialist societies have is that they do have values that try to hold the system together. We might argue that they aren't universally valid values, they might be partial, but they do give meaning and some cohesion to socialist societies as opposed to the West.

Raymond Tschumi

Golaszewska develops mainly the theme of the division of Europe, and this is rather a complement to what I said. Yes, the theme of Plato's ideal republic too, is an example. It's a very complex example, in fact, because, on the one hand, it may fall into the category of a mere utopia, but, on the other hand, it remains a kind of permanent model. As to Professor Beck, he makes complementary, mainly ontological remarks, and his east-west division turns into a polarity between East and West of East, understood as Asia, and West as the West that was born after the battle of Salamis in 500 BC. I can only agree with this view of making a synthesis. He's not the first, he follows a very deep and solid tradition, this notion of order in plurality. But this is not an aspect that I developed in my paper. I'm glad of this supplement. Prof. Radnitsky contends with some of my statements about science, which I admit are rather rudimentary. This is due to the fact that my paper is mainly, at present, about the arts, rather than about science. As I told you, I am busy with a book entitled "The Genesis of Expression". He makes a distinction, which is undeniable, between pure science and applied science, and all the various phases. I couldn't do that with so much precision. This specification of phases is very, very interesting, and so is the creative surge for the implementation of technology. I can only approve of all that, of course. As to what he and Professor Stromos said about Max Weber, I think there is a certain irritation in my paper because Max Weber has been turned into kind of a sacred cow. I quoted him and I want to be a little bullet-proof. I quote the passages. Due to this, I read all the allusions to *wertfreiheit* in his works. You know, they went through many versions. It's very difficult to get to the original. It's very much a matter of interpretation. I don't think, as you do Professor Shtromas, that we can say one it is thing and not something else. I mean, the term has been misinterpreted to the point of being applied to certain practices in the concentration camps, which were considered as scientific, and that these were examples of *wertfreiheit*.

As to your remarks about culture as a whole, I can only agree with these, although they cannot be proved. You gave absolutely unmistakable examples of cultural similarities and the way culture cannot be the monopoly of any people in any historical period, as well. This was a basic hypothesis of my first book, *A Theory of Culture*, but it remains a hypothesis. I believe I've found applications which seem to confirm this hypothesis. As to Professor Anderson, you emphasize the fact that I have another hypothesis, a risky point, that values come from consciousness.

If you define culture you kill culture. Culture is undefinible because it has no limit, it has no end. If you define it as Tyler did in the nineteenth century, in 1869, culture is everything man-made: in three words, oh it's very handy, it's very pocketable. But it leads to misconceptions, especially in sociology, and you end by declaring that a chamber pot is culture, and you make these distinctions between elite culture, Marxian culture, and so forth. These things do exist, but, again, division is the devil in all that, and I quite agree with Prof. Anderson that one should hold values in a creative tension, as he said.

Heinrich Beck

World culture is fundamentally a unity, and a unity in mutual acknowledgement, mutual respect, and universal value; it is the acknowledgement of another being as a value in itself. But I think that this mutual acknowledgement includes also, and necessarily, partnership and mutual completion in the different cultures, which must come together to form one world, one culture. World culture is not possible, I think, as a monotonous thing. World culture must include tensions, creative tensions, oppositions, not a uniform unity. It's necessary to reflect on the internal essence of world culture as complements of opposites, cohesions of human nature. I think that different cultures coming together in one world culture cannot act only in one direction but must integrate themselves. It is possible to see a certain parallelism to chemistry. There is an essential difference between only a mixture of hydrogen and oxygen and water, and a real integration of these to water. Water shows other qualities, new features than the mere mixture, and, similarly world culture inevitably cannot be only a mixture of different cultures, but must have an analogy to a chemical integration of different cultures, a new quality. I think mankind is about to take a new creative step in the evolution to a new type of human being, a fuller human being who integrates the positive aspects of Western culture and Eastern cultures, the positive aspects: more open, more communicative, more human. Mankind only can overcome when he changes intrinsically. In order to be able to survive, he must change in his essence, and this is a great chance for making that change. There is no alternative. There is no other possibility for survival but to change in the direction of a new human being. But it's also possible that the mother, in the moment of birth, by the mother I mean all of mankind now — in the moment of birth goes to death. It's also possible, but we have reason, I think, for a rational hope, for it is better to survive.

Chairman Damnjanović

I agree with the idea of Dr. Beck, and I would like to add that the philosophical climate in our time provides the art to recognize the other, his otherness, in his difference and in equality in the sense of the ancient Greek voice and, nowadays, in the sense of a cosmic voice.

THE ROLE OF EUROPE IN CREATING A PEACEFUL WORLD ORDER

Alexander Shtromas

The global East-West confrontation, which splits Europe into two opposed and seemingly irreconcilable parts, can hardly be understood in terms of clashing national interests. There is no serious conflict between the Western and Russian authentic national interests in any significant area. Russia has no territorial disputes with any of the Western powers, is not involved with the West in any trade wars or other competitive economic pursuits, and, as far as "influence zones" are concerned, these were delineated by the post-war settlement to Russia's more-than-full satisfaction and have never been seriously challenged by the West since.

The present East-West confrontation is indeed rooted, not in the conflict of national interests of whatever kind, but in the irreconcilable differences between the USSR and the West in their respective conceptions of the common foundation for a universal world order, which is to say that the substance of this confrontation is, in essence, ideological and global, and, as such does, not allow for compromise or lasting settlement.

The USSR, seeking to establish a congenial communist world order, is committed to the expansion of the Soviet-type communist system, whereas the West resists such attempts on the part of the USSR, aspiring — though without formulating this as its policy objective — for the replacement of the Soviet system in Russia by another system which, being more congenial to the West's own system, would stop threatening the basic security and stability of the West through engineering its communist transformation. To sum it up, one could say that, in the present East-West confrontation, the main issue at stake is on what universal foundations —

communist-totalitarian or liberal-pluralistic, and these are incompatible — the future world order is going to be based.

The contention about the ultimate goal of the USSR's policy being the establishment of a communist world order is treated by most analysts of international relations with a certain scepticism and disbelief. These analysts prefer to see current Soviet policy merely as Czarist policy in new guise in response to permanent Russian national interests, thus mechanically projecting old concepts onto new circumstances and, as a result, failing to incorporate the lessons of the twentieth century concerning national power. The mechanical projection of Czarist Russia onto the USSR is wrong, however, not only because of such general considerations, but also because it is inconsistent with the plain facts. From the eighteenth century onwards (more precisely, after the conclusion of the Nystad Treaty in 1721), Czarist Russia was a normal member of the European community of nations which, as every other member of that community, when driven by her authentic national interests and objectives, was able to establish genuine alliances with, as well as engage in wars and other conflicts against her counterparts in that community.

Before the Bolsheviks seized power in Russia in 1917, there was no such thing in the world as an East-West confrontation in the context of which we all now happen to exist. Whenever there were conflicts between Russia and some other European powers, these centered around peripheral matters (such as distribution of "zones of influence" or colonial possessions) and never challenged, either on the part of Russia or her adversaries and allies, the existence or the traditional order of any of the powers involved, with the one exception of the Napoleonic wars which were, again, ideological in nature.

Throughout its history, Czarist Russia was never involved in any conflict at all with the USA. Before 1917 these main political adversaries of the present day always maintained a perfectly friendly and cooperative relationship, exemplified by the USA's unequivocal support of Russia in the Crimean War, and Russia's consequent (in 1868) voluntary concession to the USA of Alaska and other North American territories (disguised as a sale for the merely symbolic price of 7.5 million gold dollars). After the collapse in 1871 of the French "Second Empire", a perfectly friendly relationship was established on permanent grounds, also, between Czarist Russia and France, and, as a result of the deal struck by Disraeli and Gorchakov at the Berlin Congress in 1878, all the major conflict-fostering problems between Czarist Russia and Britain, the main competitors for colonial possessions in Central Asia, were successfully resolved, too. In all conflicts between the Central and Allied Powers, Russia was always on the side of the latter, *i.e.* the USA, Britain and France, considering these nations to be her genuine and permanent allies, not, as in the case of the USSR during World War II, enemies turned into temporary allies of convenience.

In view of these facts, could, then, the anti-Western policy of the USSR be seriously interpreted as a mere continuation of international policies of Czarist Russia? Apparently not, but to scholars who are virtual prisoners of a "pragmatic" political philosophy which strictly prohibits the assessments of international political endeavours in terms other than expedient power interests, territorial gains, national security deals, economic gains, strategic advantages, and the like, no other interpretation is practically available, and they have to stick to it, however inconsistent with the facts such an interpretation may be. To admit and explain the actual drastic discontinuity between Czarist Russia's and the USSR's international politics, one has to be able to overcome the narrow horizon of the empiricist dogma, and realize that the USSR is not a mere nation-state, which Czarist Russia certainly was, but a communist clique-state, identifying itself not with any particular nation *(e.g.,* Russia), but with a globally-conceived ideological cause and, accordingly, with the proponents of that cause, organized in sectarian groups within every single nation and proliferated around the globe.

The USSR is doomed to pursue its anti-Western policies, as these policies are best suited for safely keeping in power and preserving the privileges of the Soviet ruling elite.

Today this is, indeed, the main driving motivation behind Soviet policy. However, the way in which the Soviet ruling elite

— an elite whose only claim to power is based on their being the "high priesthood" of the Bolshevik ideology of Marxism-Leninism — can preserve its position and privileges is by removing subversive examples, and by strengthening the myth that the system is unassailable and on the route of inevitable total victory, thus disheartening potential opposition. Stranded with their Marxist-Leninist identity, the Soviet rulers cannot successfully perform such tasks without relentlessly and with utmost determination seeking to establish a communist world order.

For the whole non-communist world is, for the Soviets, nothing else but such a "subversive example" which "must be removed"; and without proving the Soviet system's ability successfully to proceed with such a "removal", the Soviets can hardly strengthen the myth that the system is unassailable.

The most salient among such "subversive examples", representing a lethal challenge to the Soviet ruling elite, is, of course, untamed Western Europe flourishing just on the other side of the boundary of the Soviet realm of rule, and setting for the people inhabiting that realm a practical model for an economically, socially, and spiritually superior way of life, which, if unsuppressed, would sooner or later carry the subjects of the Soviet-Party state to follow suit. Hence, in order to preserve its power continuously, the Soviet ruling elite must not simply maintain the USSR's communist identity, but remain committed to communist expansion on the same scale as was the case in the heyday of the Bolsheviks' genuine communist zeal. Although Third World countries are more convenient targets for exercising communist expansion with impunity, they represent only the byproduct of the relentless Soviet expansionist drive, the main objective of which has always been and always will remain: communist Europe.

These inherent communist-ideological interests and objectives of the USSR are at variance with, and in direct opposition to the authentic national interests and objectives of Russia. Communist expansion gives Russia no economic advantage. On the contrary, it imposes upon her an increasingly unsustainable burden of expenditure which never stops growing since, in addition to the costs of expansion itself, Russia also has to bear the cost of maintaining in solvent condition the dwindling socialist economies of the ever-expanding number of her client-states. The strategic advantages with which communist expansionism is supposed to provide Russia are also more than problematic. Even if assuming that Russia sees her national goal in world domination and for this purpose needs to get a strategic advantage over the West, such an advantage bought at a price that high is bound, in the long run, to turn into a major strategic disadvantage. The problem here is that the nations of Soviet client-states are far from being thankful for Russia's care. On the contrary, in the course of getting the experience of the socialist way of life, even those of them which previously bore no prejudice against Russia are becoming her most implacable potential enemies, ready to join forces with the West against the USSR at the first available opportunity. Since with every expansionist success Soviet policing capacity wears thinner, while Western resolve to contain the USSR grows stronger, such an opportunity may eventually present itself in not too distant a future, spelling the demise of the USSR and, in the long run, the breakdown of the Soviet Empire altogether. The Soviet Union stands no chance of winning a prolonged confrontation with the West on any grounds — political, economic or military — but by pursuing an active anti-Western policy of communist expansionism, it risks to lose even those gains which, in a different situation, the West would never even have thought of challenging.

Hence, in order to ensure her long-term security and render her position of a dominant regional and world power immutably stable, Russia badly needs to establish and foster most carefully a truly cooperative and harmonious relationship with the West. For that sake Russia, would have to stop sponsoring communist movements and *régimes* around the world and, ultimately, renounce communism as the foundation of her policies altogether. There is nothing for Russia to lose from such a radical move, and everything to gain. This move, in other words, would be in the interests of the West as much as it would be in Russia's own national interests.

In the climate created by Russia's renunciation of communism and the ensuing East-West reconciliation, the fact that the presently Soviet-ruled non-Russian nations would regain the right of freely choosing and shaping their socio-political and economic systems, thus becoming entirely sovereign or genuinely autonomous, would by no means impair any true Russian national interests either. Under the new peaceful circumstances, without Western anti-Russian or Soviet-led anti-Western camps, Russia's closest neighbours would remain naturally bound to Russia, as Latin America is naturally bound to the USA, with the remaining mutual tensions and suspicions gradually receding and being superseded by mutual interests in economic exchanges and regional cooperation. Furthermore, only in cooperation with the West can Russia ever aspire effectively and promptly to overcome her inherent economic backwardness and thus reliably sustain her status as world-power. Large-scale Western technological assistance is only one necessary condition for Russia's fulfilment of that goal. Another one is Western provision of generous credits enabling Russia to import immediately and on a massive scale the widest range of Western high-quality consumer goods which have to be made available to the Russians in order to induce them to work conscientiously and try hard to earn good money. There are simply not enough locally-produced goods to go around, and their quality and assortment are insufficient to create the necessary incentives.

It follows from the above that while a world order universally based on liberal-pluralistic foundations and Russia's cooperation with the West would be lethal to the "USSR", its establishment is in the best national interests of "Russia", providing her with the only real hope for peace, security, economic progress and, ultimately, prosperity, which is to say that a new post-Soviet Russia, albeit not yet necessarily a liberal democracy, would do her utmost to put the artificial East-West confrontation to a definite end.

I believe that for the settlement between Russia and the West to be mutually satisfactory and fully acceptable to the West, it should be drawn up along the following lines:

1 Russia's total withdrawal from Africa and Central and Latin America;
2 Russia's withdrawal of support from, and full break with, the communist and related parties and movements throughout the

non-communist world, providing reliable guarantees of Russia's non-interference in the internal affairs of other countries;
3   The re-unification of Germany and conclusion with the new democratic government of a united Germany of the long-awaited peace treaty, guaranteeing national security and other long-term interests of all parties involved, thus establishing the foundations of a universally acceptable European order;
4   Western guarantees of non-interference with Russia's national interests in Central and Eastern Europe, the Caucasus, Central Asia, Mongolia, and China, that should be given in exchange of Russia's granting the right of self-determination to all nations presently living in the Soviet realm of rule, including the present union republics of the USSR in these areas, and involving, as a prerequisite, the unconditional withdrawal of Russian troops from wherever they are stationed outside Russia's borders.

A settlement along these lines, by having transformed East-West rivalry into partnership, would no doubt, be able to lay the necessary foundations for the evolution of a new peaceful and cooperative world order.

Under the conditions of East-West reconciliation, whatever conflicts of interest among nations still remain would be relatively insignificant when contrasted with the commonalities of interest that demand cooperative solutions. Indeed, most of the major problems the modern world faces cannot be adequately, and to any nation's full satisfaction, resolved by institutions of autarchic national sovereignty acting either separately or even collectively through various international agencies which have no sovereign rights.

There are two kinds of such problems: First there are those with which institutions of national sovereignty do not deal at all, as these problems are outside their scope, and international agencies, if and when they deal with them, cannot do so effectively. Among such problems the following should at least be mentioned: prevention of armed conflicts, authoritative international conflict-settlement, and peacekeeping generally: supervision over, and enforcement of international agreements and treaties, *e.g.*, those on human rights; world ocean and the international seabed, outer space, international territories, and other similar issues which are treated by international law at present as unmanaged areas of "equal opportunity" for all nations. Second are those problems with which the institutions of national sovereignty, along with the existing weak international agencies, try to deal but are unable to do so in a satisfactory manner, as they are either regional or global in their scope. Among such problems, the following are important: economic aid and development, and the whole task of bridging the so-called North-South divide generally; protection of the natural environment and solution of other problems related to human ecology; protection against famine, epidemic diseases, natural calamities, and similar disasters; development, management, and regulation of safety in the fields of nuclear, solar, and laser energy; regulation and management of demographic problems, *e.g.*, rational use of manpower resources; coordination of and supervision over some globally vital areas of scientific research.

The necessity of properly tackling these problems in the collective interest of all nations requires the creation of appropriate supra-national bodies of global regional authority that, together, would provide the foundation for a global commonwealth. In the disproportionately developed and highly interdependent twenty-first century's world, the establishment of a global commonwealth on such foundations, while to some extent reducing national sovereignty and instituting on an overriding level areas important to the sovereignty of mankind as a whole, would enhance the security and prosperity of each nation so substantially that the partial loss of national sovereignty would not count for much, provided it applied equally to all nations.

A few problems would however, remain even then. Because of the existing correlation of forces, a genuine settlement of East-West relations may automatically produce a world jointly dominated by the USA and Russia, the two most powerful nations on both sides of the present East-West divide, before the institutions embodying the global commonwealth would materialize. The Russo-American condominium over the rest of the world, thus naturally and momentously evolved, would be very difficult to change or even modify, as both superpowers could be expected to be extremely proud of, and satisfied with, their new role. Not only would they, thus, become the unchallenged masters of their respective geopolitical environments but, by having acquired in addition also the *unprecedented* capacity of jointly imposing and enforcing settlements of local conflicts wherever they occur, they would also gladly and without hesitation assume the functions of the policeman of the world. Initially, the world under a Russo-American condominium may indeed become a more peaceful and secure place, but in the long run this condominium would be bound to engender deep disaffection among all other nations. Resenting the loss of their previous freedom of action on the international scene, and driven by a sense of inferiority with regard to the two "big brothers", these nations would try to do their utmost to undermine the Russo-American condominium, thus plunging the world, maybe, into an even bigger chaos of constant cleavage, strife, and war than before, when all parties to local conflicts were able to use to their particular advantage the conflicting interests of the superpowers.

On the whole, a truly peaceful and harmonious world order is impossible without a fair distribution of national sovereignty among all nations of the world, as the problems besetting our planet at present clearly demonstrate. Only very few among the 180 or so sovereign nation-states are ethnically homogeneous political territorial entities, among which some *(e.g.,* the members of the Soviet bloc) are sovereign only nominally, and some are the result of artificial divisions of previously homogeneous nations *(e.g.,* the East and West Germanies, and North and South Koreas). Bearing in mind that our planet is inhabited by about 1800 different nations, it is only natural that the majority of the extant so-called nation-states are multi-national entities with, in most cases, only one of the co-habiting nations, and in some even none of them at all (as in many African states), being the real carrier of national sovereignty. There are at present about 1600 known national movements of stateless nations struggling for a sovereign, or at least truly autonomous, status. None of these movements show any signs of receding or reconciling with their nations' dependent *status quo*. On the contrary, all are steadily growing in strength, and constantly intensifying their struggle. One could conclude from this with a certain assurance that these national movements will not relent until their goal is achieved, unless the nation on whose behalf the struggle is conducted were, meanwhile, dispersed or otherwise annihilated by its ethnically alien rulers.

The Hungarian revolution of 1956; the attempt in 1967–1970 at creating the Ibo nation-state, Biafra, and the splitting of Nigeria on ethnic-territorial grounds; the actual splitting of Pakistan and creation in 1972 of the new state of the Muslim part of the Bengali nation, Bangladesh; the continuous struggle for a sovereign nation-state by the Palestinian Arabs, the Sri-Lankan Tamils, or the Timore people in Indonesia, are just highlights of the ongoing world-wide process of reconstruction of the present system of nation-states along genuinely ethnical lines which, now in more, now in less conspicuous forms, continues unabated.

No system of world order, whether the East-West confrontation continues or not, can be just and, as a consequence, reliably peaceful and stable without the present nation-states having undergone the process of fission (first of all in such openly multi-national settings as the USSR and Yugoslavia, but also, perhaps, South Africa, Nigeria, Czechoslovakia, Spain, Belgium, Canada, *etc.*), fusion (in the cases of Germany and Korea), and reshufflement. For example, in order for the Kurds to establish their nation-state, they would have to amalgamate Kurdish territories, taking them from Iran, Syria, Iraq, Turkey, and the Caucasian republics of the USSR; similar territorial reshufflements between Ethiopia and Somalia are necessary for solving the Ogaden problem; the same applies to the USSR and Iran housing the Azeris; or Pakistan, Iran, Afghanistan, Punjab in India, and the USSR, housing the Baluchis; as well of course, to most African states, inclusive of South Africa.

The Russo-American condominium over the world, while not being able to solve any of these problems (it could only temporarily suppress them by enforcing "for the sake of peace" the *status quo*) would, by reducing quite significantly the independence of all the sovereign nations, only greatly exacerbate them. The example of Europe could demonstrate how. The Russo-American global settlement would inevitably reduce to a minimum the American commitment to Western Europe. As a result, Russia, by the sheer logic of geopolitics, would become the sole dominant European power. Russia may substantially reduce its grip on Eastern Europe, but it would at the same time extend its prevalent influence over the European continent as a whole, East and West alike. Hence, "finlandization" may become the equal fate of all European nations, irrespective of what their geopolitical situation in the present world is.

At the same time Europe is in a uniquely strong position to ensure its full independence from both America and Russia, and thus also to prevent the possibility of a Russo-American condominium over the rest of the world from ever being translated into political reality. For this Western Europe should evolve its unity much beyond the present arrangement of economic convenience, as represented by the EEC, and become a single political entity speaking on the international stage with one voice and possessing a united military force. Neither the USA nor Russia would be able to push around such a united Europe, which would thus become a superpower in its own right.

A thus-enhanced Western European unity would hardly be, however, a sufficient guarantee for Europe to be able properly to assert itself against strong joint Russo-American pressure or to make its voice, when it is raised in opposition to the joint voice of the USA and Russia, effectively heeded. To put itself really on a par with a Russo-American alliance, Europe would have to become the champion and protector of the rights and interests of the non-West European nations, too, enlisting thus their support for European causes. To united Western Europe this role of spokesman for the rights and interests of so many nations would come naturally and easily, as acting on behalf of the specific and collective interests of a multiplicity of nations is exactly the European community's basic substance and cause.

To protect its nations from all sorts of eventualities (such as "finlandization" or joint superpower manipulation), and to be able to assure for them, under the conditions of East-West reconciliation, adequate independence and freedom, Western Europe must consolidate and build up much further its unity here and now. It should, without procrastination and delay, develop new, and endow with more power the extant, all-European political institutions; establish, first within NATO and subsequently independently of it, a joint European military command; and intensify all aspects of European relations with the USA, seeking to become indispensable to vital American interests under all circumstances.

It is in the pursuit of these objectives that Western Europe may become sufficiently united and strong to be able to withstand the Russo-American alliance and properly to defend from a joint Russo-American dictate its own nations, as well as the nations of the rest of Europe and the world at large. It is thus through the agency of a united Western Europe that the principle of fair distribution of national sovereignty may be practically and irreversibly implemented into the newly emerging universal world order, assuring its lasting peacefulness and developing harmony.

If a global Commonwealth is to become a viable and stable institution, it has to adopt as a criterion for a state's membership the assurance by that state of national freedom alongside all other democratic rights. The demand to surrender some elements of national sovereignty to institutions representing the sovereignty of mankind as a whole can be justifiably made only if this demand equally applies to all the nations of the world or, in other words — if the sovereignty of mankind is established on the basis of a fair distribution of national sovereignty and, conversely, equality of its limitations with regard to all nations.

To sum it up, the following may be stated:

1. As long as the USSR is a communist clique-state, the East-West confrontation is bound to continue unabated, making the establishment of a stably peaceful world order impossible.
2. The replacement in the USSR of the present *régime* by a Russian national government of whatever description and kind is the prerequisite for bringing the purely ideologically-motivated East-West confrontation to an end and laying the foundation stone of a stably peaceful world order.

3. A stably peaceful world order may properly develop and consolidate under the conditions of a fair distribution of national sovereignty among all the nations of the world.
4. The stably peaceful world order, thus developed and consolidated, would be able to evolve a global commonwealth: a complex of institutions embodying the sovereignty of mankind as a whole and thus endowed with the necessary authority effectively to deal with supra-national issues, which increasingly acquire an overriding significance for the survival of mankind.

COMMENTS ON DR. SHTROMAS'S PAPER

Tadeusz Golaszewski

One can distinguish two different coherent layers in Dr. Shtromas's paper: one of critical political knowledge, the other of utopia. His conception of three social, political, cultural, and economic powers, the USA, the USSR, and Europe, which are regarded as three national-state-territorial blocs, has precisely an utopian character. The idea of Europe's confederation has different aspects today. But a great difficulty consists in delineating the borders of Europe, due to the fact that the greater part of the USSR itself lies in Europe. I would only add to Dr. Shtromas's remarks the postulate of total freedom as far as the option concerning the attachment to one of the blocs goes, not to mention the cooperation and relationships of the states, which is so difficult nowadays. Also the division of Europe into East and Western should be settled — provided we accept such a division — not in a mechanical manner, that is, territorial decisions, but taking into consideration the genuine sense of belonging to a special type of culture and civilisation.

As a professor of pedagogy, I am not going to enter into Dr Shtromas's political and logical line, but I shall refer to the general theoretical problems. From the point of view of my discipline, I think — and I hope that this viewpoint is common to all of us — it is necessary to introduce, the sooner the better, an education for universal, stable and just peace based on total freedom.

So we can ask whether we have in mind a *pax europea* for all the world, or rather a *pax secundum europam* — peace according to Europe. Certainly it would be only an apparent solution of the problem if Europeans considered peace in the world as conditioned by Europe's hegemony: military, political, economic and cultural. It seems, however, that there are some phenomena and facts which entitle us to consider Europe as the cultural point in the establishing of peace, and to impose upon it a duty to act in this direction.

The heritage of European culture implies an idea that peacetime should be much more appreciated than war, which always implies disaster and destruction, sometimes on a world scale. Europe can be seen as an enormous treasury of ideas and works which were always attractive for most people, as they still are; moreover, they are more and more appreciated by all mankind who are aware of their uniqueness and value. Although the fascination with European culture brought about certain threats for various regional cultures — the existence of the universal values and universal culture as well — it gives rise to real and versatile intentional integration, fundamentally favourable to world peace.

An account of various historical experiences inclines the Europeans to speak loudly for peace, to demand it. Unfortunately, in most cases they were not such praiseworthy experiences. Europe distinguishes itself not so much by little military disputes, but above all by great imperialistic, powerful, plundering expeditions. Even the Napoleonic wars, connected with the ideas of the Great French Revolution, revealed the tendency to powerful invasions. These negative European experiences, especially those connected with the last two World Wars, are a stimulus to undertake actions for world peace which appeal to an imagination much stronger than the European "fight for peace". Yet, the tendencies for peace are known from antiquity to the present: from the *Pax Romana* to the League of Nations and the Helsinki Agreement.

The great intellectual potential represented by the scientific centres of Europe, as well as the common level of education and the decisive interest in the humanities, open a particular way of success in action for world peace undertaken by the Europeans.

Therefore, it is likely that European thinkers can fulfil the proper analyses of the state of things concerning the problems of peace, and can submit some program promising effectiveness and the possibility of peace being realised.

Finally, because circumstances point to Europe being an important leader in a fight for world peace, we can also mention the fact that for a long time it has played the role of a centre where crucial interests concerning the economy and politics, as well as culture, converge, and is thus a special object of cultural interest to all regional cultures in the world.

It seems that Europe, because of the very difficult political and economic situation in which it found itself after the Second World War, can hardly achieve anything in our times. Instead of obligatory decisions and decisive actions for peace, Europe can first of all propose theoretical considerations, elaborate declarations, organise international meetings and congresses, manifestations, and protests against war. All this is an attempt to organise the great, universal movement for peace. When it does not exist, terroristic groups, paradoxically declaring their will to peace, arise.

Therefore, it seems that it would be useful if Europe played in this matter a more responsible and decisive role. Even if it were only a function of a theoretician, an expert, a consultant, it should be treated more seriously, not as an abstract activity. It is important that practice, realisation of the postulates and programs, should follow theories.

On a universal scale, the tendencies for peace seem to increase. For forty years we have had peacetime in Europe, in spite of some temporary tensions and minor incidents. However, because of increasing military budgets all over the world and in Europe, too, the ancient motto is believed: *si vis pacem, para bellum*. We can suppose, however, with a cautious optimism, that in the twenty-first century the universal armistice will be achieved. And perhaps Europe will be the first continent which will be able to fulfil that ancient dream of mankind. May it not prove that real world peace comes too late: when our planet starts to cool, to die.

Footnotes:
In order not to be satisfied with the optimistic, utopian prognostication of universal world peace, I should point out some dangers, the weak sides of the movement for peace, as well as the conditions restraining the program in this sphere.

One can note the typical humanistic properties of the European style of life, *e.g.,* an inclination to express pompous slogans and a predominance of words over action. While even most lofty words do not initiate any activity, these words and the values which are represented by them, enter the world treasury of culture as monuments of good will.

In the words we use, especially in Europe, we can recognize some interior contradictions in the civilization of our time. The most fundamental include, for example, the following:

First, the aspiration for a rational and univocal specifying of goals in actions for the "fight" for peace — and, at the same time, the very term 'peace' — is ambiguous. Especially the ambiguity connected with hypocrisy is dangerous in this matter. The concept of world 'peace' should be completed by indicating what kind of peace is involved: *e.g.,* one that is just, securing freedom. Meanwhile in most cases 'peace' means "peace for us", peace according to us. Even the Nazis declared a handred years' peace, but it would be essentially totalitarian peace.

Second, rationalism opposes irrationalism more or less actively. So, the quite evident, rationally-based thesis about the need of peace finds its counterpart in the belief in the fantastic necessity of inevitable wars. A trend toward fighting and the agonistic in the principle human attitude towards life are supposed to be genetically coded in man's nature.

Third, together with the development of techniques, the opposition between the desire to increase prosperity, *i.e.,* to live in peace and happiness, on the one hand, and the menace connected with that increase, on the other, was disclosed. We have in mind the excessive excavation of raw materials, devices for destruction, and pollution.

Similarly, the development of the sciences gives as much

progress as it does fundamental dangers for mankind, in nuclear physics, chemistry, and genetic-medicine.

Finally the birth of so desirable an organization as the United Nations revealed at the same time the impossibility of common agreement in the matters most important for all people.

COMMENTS ON
"THE ROLE OF EUROPE IN CREATING A PEACEFUL WORLD ORDER"

Stanislav Andreski

Although both world wars began in Europe, there are good reasons for expecting no repetition. None of the European nations shows any traces of the warlike spirit which animated them in the past. Given the pacific consensus, no democratic European leader would be able to start a war. Only the Soviet politburo has the power to do it. Fortunately, there are good reasons for believing that this is not their intention. As nobody knows what they talk about at their meetings, we can only make inferences from their public acts in the past and from the circumstances which they must take into account if they make rational decisions. The evidence of the first kind suggests that caution is their enduring characteristic. Only Lenin and Trotsky have acted against the odds. Stalin (in contrast to Hitler) was neither a gambler nor a demagogue who intoxicates himself with his oratory. Despite his obvious lust for power, he always acted cautiously, invariably preferring a ruse to a confrontation which might entail a risk. The attack on Finland in the winter of 1939 seems an exception, but I suspect that he deliberately refrained from using the full force of his army in order to appear weak and unthreatening to Hitler, so that the latter would be less tempted to launch a pre-emptive strike. Now the USSR is a pure bureaucracy in which the top positions are reached through a long climb along the regular channels of promotion where impetuous or naive types have no chance. So long as this continues, the Politburo will consist of cautious calculators anxious to avoid risks. They have shown that they are ready to use force when there is no danger. So, they might decide to invade western Europe if they had good reasons for believing that it would be a safe pushover. It follows that only a unilateral disarmament of the West would create a serious danger of Soviet invasion.

Anyone contemplating an atomic war as a method of conquest must be a maniac incapable of rational judgement. In pre-atomic times war could be fun for the chiefs who lived comfortably in safe places while dispatching other men to die. The atomic missiles have put the rulers in the front line: they might die even before the soldiers in the field. This is the greatest deterrent. Moreover, a "nuclear winter" would spare nobody. Even a successful pre-emptive strike would be a dubious victory. The area to be conquered would be heavily contaminated, and therefore of no value. If targets in Western Europe were hit, the fall-out would soon reach the USSR, owing to the prevalence of westerly winds. The walls of the Kremlin would offer no protection from radioactivity. It would be like Chernobyl magnified several hundred times.

Not much better would be the consequences of a conventional invasion of Western Europe, in which many atomic energy stations would be bound to be blown up: instead of several hundred times, Chernobyl would be multiplied perhaps only fifty or sixty times, not to speak of the atomic energy stations in the USSR which might be bombed. Even if no atomic power stations were destroyed, the havoc would be much greater than in the Second World War, because the industrial economies have become much more vulnerable. Everything now depends on electricity and oil. Without it, only in Poland, where there are peasants who use horses, could some food be produced. The lack of pesticides and fertilizers would suffice to cause general starvation. And the import of food from across the ocean, which the USSR needs even in peacetime, would not be available.

A quick victory in a non-atomic war might also elude the invaders. A few non-atomic missiles would suffice to rupture the long pipelines which bring oil from the Urals. This would bring the Soviet tanks to a halt. In any case, small homing missiles have made tanks so vulnerable that they may already be out of date. So it is very likely that (even if it were confined to non-atomic weapons) an attempted *blitzkrieg* would lead to protracted mutual bombardment with various kinds of missiles which would cause utter ruin and starvation on both sides.

Given such prospects, only crazy fanatics can regard a large-scale war as a feasible method of imperial expansion. Fortunately, the present Soviet rulers give no signs of being fanatics. They do not even seem to believe in the fundamental dogmas of Marxism, one of which is the prophecy about the inevitable struggle unto death between socialism and capitalism. Lenin and Trotsky regarded it as beyond doubt, while Stalin and Krushchov probably still believed in it. So long as it was believed, it had a self-fulfilling character despite the lack of conflict of material interests between the USSR and the USA. On the other hand, there are economic grounds for a conflict between the USSR and China because of the contrast between the empty Siberia, full of valuable natural resources, and grossly overpopulated China. Indeed, it has often been reported (notably by members of the satellite parties) that the Soviet ruling circles fear China much more than the US.

If China and the USSR were controlled by one centre, its rulers might seriously strive for world domination. As they fear each other, neither has a chance of attaining such a goal. Being realists, the present rulers are unlikely to take it seriously. This does not mean that they will cease to try to extend their influence or control, if they can do it without a great risk or cost, but their recent actions smack much more of pure power politics than of a true believer's zeal to save the workers of the world.

Opportunities for expansion without much risk present themselves not in Europe but in the less developed parts of the world with corrupt and disorderly governments and dilapidated economies. There the population exploision maintains a vast miserable proletariat and a large class of white collar drudges and unemployed graduates to whom marxism appeals much more strongly than to the affluent industrial workers of Western Europe. Despite their wealth, the oil states are also vulnerable because of the greed, extravegence and indolence of their ruling classes. With Marxism as an unrivalled ideological weapon, expansion through subversion is safer, as well as enormously cheaper, than an invasion: subsidies for revolutionaries constitute a very minor position in the budget, while the weapons usually come from surplus stocks recently replaced by newer models.

The oil-producing states of the Near East constitute by far the most alluring field for Soviet imperialism. Their seizure would be enormously profitable. It would enable Moscow to compel Western Europe and Japan to supply goods (which the USSR lacks) on unilaterally dictated terms of trade, and thus to reverse the present difference in the standards of living. They would also come into possession of a powerful means for pressing for an installation of compliant governments. In view of these prospects, the only rational policy for imperialistically inclined Soviet chiefs would be to concentrate on this goal, and to treat distant dependencies like Cuba or Nicaragua as pawns which might be sacrificed. What has happened in Afghanistan, Ethiopia, Yemen, and elsewhere, fits such a strategy. Perhaps it is not impossible, however, that the Soviet rulers may abandon imperialism and devote themselves to internal reforms. Or they may try to establish a joint hegemony with the USA, which would not exclude attempts to extend their sphere of influence by bargaining.

Despite its industrial capacity and large highly skilled population, Europe is likely to play only a minor role in power politics because it lacks central direction and is short of space, which, in the age of missiles, is an essential ingredient of military power. China has both and, provided it acquires enough missiles, the primitiveness of its economy may be militarily advantageous, as it makes it less vulnerable to devastations. Any increment of China's power diminishes the likelihood of a war between NATO and the Soviet bloc.

A triangular balance of power is much more conducive to peace than a bilateral, because it depends much less on the peaceful inclinations of the players. The reason for this is that in such a constellation the best strategy for each player (even if his goal is eventual aggrandizement) is to stay out of the conflict and let the other two fight. By exhausting each other, the fighters are likely to ensure the neutral's dominance. With every player avoiding a direct engagement, a fight is unlikely to break out. If it does, the best strategy for the initially neutral is to prevent a decisive victory by coming to the aid of the weaker fighter. If this is to be expected, no rational player will launch an attack unless he feels that he can knock out the other two simulaneously, or that he will have enough strength after subduing the second to defeat the third. For this reason, a triangular balance of power, in which none of the players is stronger than the combined force of the other two, is less likely to lead to war than a constellation in which there are only two, or more than three, players. Together with the knowledge that an all-out war would end in joint suicide, a balance of power of this kind is likely to perpetuate peace — at least between technically advanced polities.

DISCUSSION ON SHTROMAS

Evanghelos Moutsopoulos

Thank you very much Mr. Chairman. I have deeply appreciated your paper, Professor Shtromas. I even admire its strictness and, I would say, scientific and logical character. However, first, it seems to me that its second part, as it is, strictly depending on the first is a corollary of a series of assumptions. One cannot prove that your propositions are necessary. They are only probable. Second, if you do not include European Russia, at least, then Europe remains. If you do include it, all of your other visions would be inadequate. I'm highly interested in how you react to my objections. I'm sure you could give us further reasons to appreciate your thought. Thank you very much.

José Delgado

I think that Professor Shtromas's paper is excellent. I really enjoyed it very much and my concern is whether we are not, all of us, thinking with old ideas about new and future problems; and what I think is that we should have, not a shortsighted, but a long-term idea about present problems: about how to solve them in the future. I think there are two aspects that must be taken into consideration. It is true that yesterday, I was watching the TV. Did you see the Dubvrovnik TV last night? It was "The Magnificent Seven", a film in English. Then I put the TV on just at lunchtime, and what I saw was rock music with a group that could be standing in the United States or any other country. What I'm saying is that there is a tremendous force in the world which will go over politics and over culture and over everything. This is, for several reasons, because we are in a new technological age, which must be taken into consideration. Through the TV, not today, but soon, all non-Western countries will communicate with our countries. It will come slowly, but I'm thinking in the future. Also, I think that military domination is unsatisfactory for the dominator and for the dominated. Look what happened with the military domination of the Soviet Union in the countries, even, well, not in Yugoslavia but in most of the countries that are dominated. It is not satisfactory. I am not talking about Afghanistan. It is unsatisfactory for both. Also it does not work very well. What I am saying is that we need to realize the reality to find new solutions, which is what we are missing today. Europe could play a role in this future world order. I should say, yes, but naturally I haven't studied this problem carefully. After all you have better ideas than I, but I was just thinking three points. Number one, just a few weeks ago, I think, a communications satellite was launched in Europe. That means that everybody can view the communications of this new satellite. Number two, Europe, England, France and the whole of Europe, Germany, are producing a very important new technology, a new science. This new science and technology are improving all human beings. When we find a new surgical technique, it's going to be used in the Soviet Union. When we find a new antibiotic, it's going to be used in Japan and in China, everywhere. Europe is very strong in that respect, and it is a role that must be considered and must be played. The third is, perhaps, the most difficult, and a group like ours could work on this idea. It is the possibility of the ideological improvement of social relations. This is difficult. I don't think that we should ask for sacrifices, not from the Soviets, not from the Europeans. I think that we should show them that some of our ideas are beneficial to their countries. I think that some of the ideologies, such as communism, have many limitations. I think that democracy does also. I think that our role is to think of a new ideology, to think about new possibilities. There should not be utopias there should be realities. And this is a great challenge which I think it is possible for us to meet. I have my own bias, my own bias is the biological unity of all human beings. What is common in blacks and whites? Well, biology. Psychology, naturally this is formed by the culture (in principle), but basically we share, and what we share is not ideology, it's biology. Somehow I think that biology unites. Sometimes ideology makes people apart. I would like to end just by quoting UNESCO. I don't remember very well, but it's something like this. The constitution of UNESCO says something like: "Since war begins in the mind of man, it is in the mind of man where the defenses of peace must be constructed." What I'm saying is that we should use these tremendous advances in technology by constructing a new ideology, and this would be the best contribution for the peace of Europe.

Gerard Radnitzky

Well, I want to thank Alex for the paper, especially the thesis about what follows from the clique nature of the Soviet regime at present. I think if this thesis would become common knowledge, we would have a far more rational discussion of international problems. But, fascinated as I am by your paper, I have some questions. The current international situation is one of anarchy. The problem of your paper is how the present international game of power can be transformed or can evolve into a sort of world order. You sketch one particular scenario, so we have now two problems: to clarify what we mean by "world order" and to spell out the way toward such an order. To make up my mind I would need some clarification, elaboration of many passages in your paper. I give just a few examples. With respect to the two Germanies, we are to guarantee the national security of a new state, of a unified Germany. Personally I think the will towards unification will recede with each generation. What about the enforceability of such a contract? Likewise for institutions created with a view to securing enforcement of international agreements. Again, if it is not secured, the "prisoners' dilemma" cannot be eliminated. You mention Europe as the protector of the rights and interests of non-Western nations. I have three questions here. How could Europe play this role? Do you intend that Europe could play it by means of military power? Then there is the question of what are their rights and interests. How are they legitimized and, again, how can they be enforced in practice? For instance, a property right means that you can use with not too great cost the police power of the state to enforce your decision. Then of, the non-western nations, what about Japan? Japan is about to surpass the Soviet Union in economic potential, and will soon be the number two world power after the United States, surpassing Soviets who would be classified as number three. Well, I have a lot of questions, and I think perhaps you can help me with a few of them to get more clarity.

David Gruender

I have a great many questions, too, but I'll just ask two of them, or make two comments in any case. I wanted to say as a citizen of the United States that I cannot imagine my fellow citizens being interested in running the world, either with or without the Russians. We have enough trouble running things in the United States. And since Professor Shtromas is interested in evidence for propositions, I would like to mention something that I had not heard mentioned here before. There is much talk about the European Economic Community on the one hand versus Comecon on the other hand. I wish to remind you that the United States is not a member of the EEC although it worked very hard to persuade the Europeans to establish such a community. I do not believe the same is true of Comecon. And so the situations are radically asymmetrical in that respect. Another point you comment on is very different. I happen to have been in Great Britain in 1978 and just at that point the issue of Scottish devolution came up, probably you remember, Alex. This was the proposal of Scotland that it remove itself from the United Kingdom. The discussion at that time I found enormously interesting. Being a foreigner one could look at it with a certain amount of dispassion. For one thing, the Welsh said, Well, if Scotland goes, we go, too. And then, Cornwall said to the Welsh, count us out; we have no interest in becoming part of Wales. We will become a separate nation of our own. And the Orkney Islands went to the trouble of sending a delegate to the United Nations to find out how they could apply for membership, because their population of 25,000 wished to have no part of the new nation of Scotland. So, I want to suggest to you that, if we are to take seriously all the historic reasons why this, that, or some other people, as a result of religion, language, or some other reason, needs to be a separate country there would be no end of new nations. Catalonia will have to remove itself from Spain. The Basques would, of course, also withdraw, so would the Gallegos, and I'm sure that, once they go, the Iberian Peninsula would have many, many Portugals in it, and I could not guess what the map of Great Britain would look like. And when I was in Tyrol, of course, I learned in no time at all that the Tyrolians had no higher aspiration but to remove themselves as a separate nation from the presents parts that they occupy of Austria, West Germany, Switzerland, and Italy — is there another nation there? They want to be independent, too. And they are willing to shoot people for this. As you know, the Armenians are busy shooting Turkish representatives all over the world because of the grudge they hold against Turkey for the events that occurred during the nineteenth century. But a free Armenia would require the cooperation of a number of countries. I think that is a totally hopeless direction for us to pursue. The last irony was that in that election in 1978 in Great Britain, the citizens, not only got a chance to vote on whether or not to remove Scotland from the kingdom, but also which representatives to send to the new Parliament of Europe in Strasbourg.

Nansen Behar

Well, the paper of Alex Shtromas was very fascinating, and it seems to me here that the road is narrow for the ideas of Alex: restructuring the world. But anyway, this is inspiring some thinking about these problems. The idea of having an independent Europe is not a new one. At the beginning of the century, the idea for a United European States arose. After that, several similar ideas occur. For example, I remember the idea that the small and the middle-sized countries in Europe unite and become a third superpower. They would counterbalance the power of the Soviet Union and the United States. But it seems to me, to follow the idea of Mr. Moutsopoulos, that to think about Europe without having in mind the role of the Soviet Union, and without having in mind that it is a European state, is unrealistic. The second point I would like to bring to your attention is that in the paper there is a serious underestimation of the real economic and social and political factors which affect the political distribution of power in the contemporary world. If Western Europe is so closely tied to itself and if we are living in the age of interdependence which is not only west-west interdependence, but also east-west interdependence, and which is enlarging that objective, how is it possible to have a sort of third independent entity which would counter balance the two other parties. I think that is a little unrealistic now. The third point to which I would like to draw your attention is that in the paper there is a very serious underestimation of the processes of change that take place now in the Soviet Union, because for Europe it is impossible to leave out any aspect of the great powers. The trick is to learn how to live with them, and how to create a secure Europe. There are several alternatives which would preserve its identity, and further this idea for a common European home. For example, one idea which was very underestimated was this recent idea in the Soviet official statement that we have to change the idea of our rival from being our enemy to being our partner, our real partner for solving some problems: problems of war and peace, ecological problems, development problems, and so on. Maybe that is just the beginning of some great change of attitude, but it seems to me that this has to be taken into account. And one point which will follow Mr. Andreski's point is that now in these days there is a change in the military doctrine even for conventional arms. I'm not speaking of the nuclear arms race, but for the conventional arms race. Now the doctrine is that the whole military structure has to be based on the so-called non-offensive defense, the non-offensive character of the new military doctrine. This also has to be taken into consideration. Thank you.

Tamás Kozma

Let me make three statements very briefly. One is coming back to reality. The last year showed us how vulnerable both of the superpowers in terms of military are. Think of the event of a young person who flew straight to Red Square, while the superpower was guarding the border. This is one. Think of the Iranians when they attacked the American warship. This was just in one month, and it shows us that while we're thinking in terms of political possibilities and forecasts and balance of power matters, the reality is that in terms of military force, the superpowers today are fairly vulnerable. This is one point that we should think of in terms of reality. Secondly, although I admire Shtromas's very informed paper and the thinking he's engaged with, I do not see any long-term aims or goals of the Soviet power to attack Europe. (Shtromas: I never said that.) I must confess to you. But I cannot see why in the long run they should attack. (Shtromas: They never will attack.) My third point is, don't forget that peace is the greatest challenge to that kind of war economies that even we sometimes have in Eastern Europe. So, in other words, following Prof. Behar's idea, that peace is the best way to make further peace and to lessen the danger of war, this is the reason why we all are engaged for peace. Thank you.

Andrzej Werner

Yes, thank you Mr. Chairman. I would like to ask Prof. Shtromas to elaborate a little bit farther how Western Europe could evolve to embrace the other part of Europe. I would like to say to Prof. Behar that there is no such thing as economic interdependence between Eastern and Western Europe. I tried to indicate in my paper that we are drifting apart, not getting together. Third, I think that (Behar: not only economic interdependence.) No, but, I could agree that the lack of that interdependence is the great threat to the ecology. There is another fact that we should be aware of, that puts some of the ideas of Prof. Shtromas in an even more dramatical dimension. I would like to end by saying that Professor Shtromas rightly pointed out the significance of sovereignty. I think that without that myth we would have trouble with increasing interdependence. In a world of growing interdependence we must preserve sovereignty. And this is something that now is very important, but since the last war, in the collapse of Western colonialism, we found a triumphant march of sovereignty with the perfect meaning of the French Revolution.

Jindrich Zeleny

I think that in the comments by Professor Golaszewski there was, after all, one deeply truthful sentence with which I have been greatly satisfied and this was the statement that he is not a Marxist.

To turn to the paper of Professor Shtromas, I have problems in understanding how the settlement between East and West can be attained. You speak about a settlement that would be mutually satisfactory. And then you list five or six points. The first is Russia's total withdrawal from Africa and Latin America. Would you agree that we have to qualify this notion of withdrawal? We can have influence through economic and cultural relations; however you speak not only about withdrawal, but total withdrawal. Do you mean that even these would be excluded? I think "total withdrawal" should be qualified. Second point: reliable guarantees of Russia's noninterference in internal affairs of respective countries. Well, I agree. I am for the policy of noninterference, but what I do not find here among these points is a requirement of mutual guarantees, for instance, for the United States' noninterference in the internal affairs of Nicaragua.

If you acknowledge self-determination as a generally valid value, you should put requirements of guarantees of noninterference for the United States and for the Western countries, too.

Alexander Shtromas

First of all I must state that at no point in my paper did I suggest that the Soviet Union could attack anyone or start war against any European country. I entirely agree with Professor Andreski that that is very unlikely, and when I was talking about expansionism I meant entirely different things. That means expansion by using groups of influence and political parties, minority political parties depending on Soviet support to get to power in their respective countries, and other means which could be termed as peaceful, without resorting to war. You see, the Soviet Union has the advantage: it can expand through various constituencies which are their sort of supportees and their supporters in each country without resorting to confrontation with any government at all. That is what makes the Soviet Union different, and maybe superior to Western countries who have no such constituencies and are unable to expand or pursue their interest in that particular way. So this point that Europe will not be the theatre of world war is my thesis, too, which does not exclude Soviet expansionism being pursued in other ways. However, I must say that as the record of Soviet history shows, yes, the Soviets never start any wars which could be risky. The few wars the Soviet Union started, against Georgia in 1921, against Finland in 1939, were safe wars. They were safe both internationally and because the power they attacked was a minor power. And here I agree, but if America withdraws, if a break between America and Europe could take place, Europe would be automatically penalised. That's why I said in my paper there is no need to undertake any action.

This connects me with the question posed by Professor Zeleny about interference in the internal affairs of other countries. You see, you could take this formula in a very abstract way in which it is used in many present international agreements. I am talking about a very particular and specific phenomenon: namely supporting brothers in ideas and arms in their pursuit of power in particular countries. That is the kind of interference I was talking about. This sort of interference works through constituencies in open societies which are subject to such interference. It could not be happening in closed societies, even if the West were to look for constituencies sympathetic to them in such countries, these constituencies would be prevented from acting by the absence of political freedom. But the West never looks to such constituencies. It deals with governments. As long as Stalin was a partner in the war, he was a wonderful Uncle Joe. And that's what matters for Western people: what Stalin did; what the terrorists did didn't matter. Stalin was a good business partner, and so was Somoza. That Stalin was a bloody dictator didn't matter. Because he was a dictator, the Soviets could use *their* constituencies very effectively to install *them* into power. Without Somoza's assistance that would be an impossibility.

Whether Russia is a part of Europe or not, I think is a bit abstract. Of course Russia is a part of Europe. Of course Russia shares in the culture of Europe; no doubt about that, the common destiny of Europe, too. But Russia is too big for Europe. Russia is a huge Euro-Asian continent. Russia's problems are actually not in

Europe. Russia's real problems are with China, with Japan, on its eastern borders. That's where Russia's problems lie. As a nation, Russia has no real problems or cleavages as far as European states are concerned. Of course it has some national interest: access to the Baltic Sea, maybe the Straits, there are some interests Russia has in Europe. Those could be easily settled and that's what I'm trying to say when I say: let's not really be too adamant about the opposition. You see, the problem is that Eastern Europe is in latent opposition to Russia, which is very unpeaceful. In the case of change, that could turn into a problem if nobody is going to feel that the political situation will settle mutually acceptable relationships in that area. That was the essence, so what I'm trying to say is that Europe, Eastern Europe — now your question — is a part of Europe. You see, I'm saying that Western Europe has to start consolidating and strengthening unity now. Now we have Western European unity, East Europe is on the other side. So again, this does not fulfill the concept of Europe, although it is a problem of political reality. What can be done now? As soon as Western Europe becomes consolidated, it will become a power; and, of course, Eastern Europe will come together, I'm sure, to create a parallel common market, as we discussed before, with the capital city being, perhaps, Vienna, for that unity and then it will all draw closer together. But, this was Professor Behar's notion, what kind of confrontation would Europe face with Russia and the United States? It would not be confrontation, but influence to be recompensed, cooperation for the evolution of a global authority which would be equally acceptable to all and not representing the dominion of the few, particularly of the powers such as Russia or America who have no idea what is going on in the world, and that is very well exemplified by Professor Gruender's remarks about the preposterous stand of the Scots and of the Cornish. That's not a problem, Professor Gruender. You see, that shows that America couldn't appreciate those things. Whatever the process of national self-determination in democratic countries, the Flemish in Belgium, the Catalans and the Basques in Spain, they are going on in the open. They are tested by referenda, they could be openly discussed. That's a different matter. And they are resolved in accordance with their significance, value, *etc*. The problem is not with those nations which live in democratic conditions and where cleavages of any national kind are open to everybody to observe, study, and test; the question is about those nations where there is no freedom, no democracy and where there is real national oppression. Actually, before democracy was established in Europe, there was very much oppression there. Now most of the states of Central and Eastern Europe are parts of the former Austrio-Hungarian Empire. Maps change, and to think that a nation like the Orkney Islands is an unviable proposition well, why not? If Trinidad and Tobago can be a nation, so could the Orkney Islands. Our units in the world are too big to be manageable. There are problems which could be solved either on the regional level or on the global level or on the district level. National units are only viable in so far as they represent a consistent interest of a national entity and, in that sense, not as managerial units, they should be preserved. And in the interdependent world, if that provides for it, they could also be economically sustainable as such.

But I would like to say that as far as the problem of European unity is concerned, I think it will be superseded by global unity. The problem whether Russia is Europe or not will stop being important because as long as Europe has this central role and awareness of the world's problems, we will move closer to one another, moving into an interdependent world in which Europe, America, and all the continents, all the nations will cooperate with one another, and in which conflict resolution could be really organised in a way in which it is organised within nations. That is the vision.

Last, I have to answer Professor Moutsopoulos. When I talk about the developments within the Soviet Union of today, I'm talking in definite terms. The postulate is what will be the result of such changes, and here, yes, I'm projecting the possibility — only a possibility — but I know that the world is not prepared for such possibilities. The world is short-sighted and looking only at today and tomorrow, but the day after tomorrow doesn't matter. That is the power of ideas, because if ideas get a currency, they become powerful vehicles in their own right. So my ideas about the possibility are aimed at spreading such ideas, and maybe contributing to making them into reality. Because there is no way, really, to say that this will happen. But if you say that it could, and would be good if it happened, then you have a chance that this idea would be picked up and then implemented in practice. That's how all developments in our history took place: first the idea, then the reality. Thank you very much.

Stanislaw Andreski

I would like to say that throughout this discussion there is a confusion between 'peace' and 'harmony'. 'Harmony' means that people really have no conflict, no grudges against anyone, whereas 'peace' means, simply, that they don't fight. I don't think the world has progressed all that much towards harmony, but peace can be preserved because, nowadays, fighting is so dangerous that the consequences of it would constitute gain to nobody. I think that the situation between the two blocs is, say, like two men in a small canoe in a sea full of sharks. They may hate each other's guts but they know if they start fighting the canoe will overturn and they will be eaten by sharks. The major powers may not quite like each other, but if they know that the war would lead to utter devastation and a loss to everybody, they may think on it and I'd just like to add here one point, and that is that even in conventional war, and I won't go into detail, the devastation would be much greater than in the Second World War. Already the Second World War was much worse than the first, even in conventional war, because of the dependence of the economy on electricity and oil.

As far as any kind of aims of global domination on the part of the USSR are concerned I think that the crucial factor here is China. If the USSR got involved in a war with NATO, China would gain from it, and, in the long run, perhaps the tension between the USSR and China might be much greater than between the Soviet Bloc and NATO.

Alexander Shtromas

The problem I posed in my paper was not harmony, but world order, peaceful world order as different from absence of war. That's why we discussed at cross purposes.

EMERGENCE OF A WORLD CULTURE AND THE FUTURE OF EUROPE

Heinrich Beck

The fundamental requirement for a world culture is the creation of an active, ethically responsible consciousness, by which we respect nature and men — not only as useful objects for certain purposes, but fundamentally in their being as values in themselves. Only on this basis could we bring about liberating creative peace, which is the nucleus of a future world culture.

But here there arises the philosophical question: what does such a peace mean in its deeper onto-anthropological essence. 1) What are the general and principal conditions of its possibility as a *unity* of *different* peoples and cultures, and 2) What is especially the place and the *positive* function of the European-Occidental mentality and culture, in contrast to the Asiatic-Oriental one, which both have to integrate themselves — not in their negative and destructive, but in their positive and constructive dispositions in an integral world culture? This shall be the topic of the following commentary, which we divide in the mentioned two steps.

1. World peace and world culture mean fundamentally that all peoples and all beings must come together and form a certain unity. Unity, today reveals itself as the first condition for the possibility of existence: in the same degree as mankind is in disagreement, as peoples isolate themselves and fight each other, the continuation of their existence is endangered.

   But if a plurality — a plurality of peoples and cultures — must necessarily form an unity in order to be able to exist, it follows logically, that this plurality can only exist in an *order*. For order means plurality that is intrinsic unity. Order means neither an unsegmented unity nor a disjointed plurality and variety: order means a plural-unity. Every part of a plurality has its solid position and task in it.

But under which connecting, unity-creating point of view could the different peoples come together, forming an universal order? It is no other aspect than their basic human being and humanity, in the totality of attributes which distinguish Man from other beings, and in which all races, peoples, and cultures participate and have their position. They differ, however, in the way they embody it; the eastern peoples, for instance, show another kind of humanity than the western peoples. Within the bounds of human existence the peoples are neither absolutely equal nor absolutely different; they are only similar or analogous.

It is now of the highest importance that both aspects of this "analogy of being", the aspect of community and unity, as well as the aspect of variety and plurality, be taken into consideration equally; only if this is done, can the order which enables the existence and the continuation of the peoples be fully realized.

If we really comprehend the whole of mankind as an analogous unity of plurality of peoples, it will become clear that the peoples intrinsically are created for mutual completion and partnership. If the same human nature realizes itself in the different peoples and cultures in a different way, it follows clearly that a single people for itself can never realize the possibilities of humanity completely, but only in a limited manner. However, it may liberate itself in a high degree from the limitations of its own viewpoint of the world by establishing close participating contacts with other peoples who have exactly those qualities which this people itself does not have. Therefore, rightly understood, order does not mean something rigid, but an enrichment of being and life by mutual participation and partnership. This is the task of history and peace.

2. The role a certain people has to play in these mutual relations is defined by this aspect of order which characterizes that people, for instance the aspect of unity or the aspect of plurality. An

order as a "plural-unity" is only possible if both aspects are taken into account in the proper proportion. Therefore it is quite all right that one part of mankind is more inclined to differentiating and analysing the unity into the plurality, and that another part is more inclined to integrate the plurality of parts into the unity of the whole. In the first inclination there is — if we have a deeper look into it — a relation to the significance of truth, in the second an inclination to the significance of the good. For, by unfolding in its parts, a unity reveals its intrinsic substance, but, by funding together, the parts come to completion and they also complete the whole in the being.

It turns out that the so-called West of mankind inclines to the truth, the East to the good; for the West has always shown a more differentiating and analyzing basic attitude, while the East, however, shows a more integrating and synthetizing basic attitude towards the being. That means: the East and the West both have the ability to analysis as well as to synthesis, yet not in the same, but in a similar, analogous way, that is in an exactly reverse accentuation. This can be shown by a comparative reflection on the several departments of culture, and we take three examples: the political and social department, science, and religion.

In the *West,* in Europe and in America as it emerged from European civilization, in this West the *individual* character, the individual rights and the freedom of the various peoples and parts of peoples against the whole have been accentuated since time immemorial; you may think for example of the symptomatic wars of liberation and other struggles for emancipation. The *"East"* on the other hand, that means, above all, the continent of Asia, has always shown a tendency towards integrating mankind into continental or global empires, from Attila and Genghis Khan to the China of later ages, India, and czarist Russia up to communism, which is expanding from the East over the whole world. In the stricter social and economic sphere, the West has developed a combative sense of individual rights and freedom against the higher entity of the people that was exaggerated to Liberalism; whereas in the East the person, the individual, demanded fewer rights of free development, and the safety in tradition was stressed, as we see in the dominating position of Confucianism in China throughout a long period of history.

Or look at another example: The development of the *sciences* is a typically western phenomenon. For science is directed to the analysis and dissection of entities which are originally experienced in a more intuitive way. This scientific attitude increased even to the extreme by splitting off from the whole of life and proclaiming its autonomy. Similarly, also the other departments of culture such as art, economy, and politics did not want to find their fundamental sense in the whole, but in themselves, and declared comprehensive ethical norms to be invalid; think of the slogan *"L'art pour l'art"* for instance. In contrast with that, the way to understanding in the East shows fewer analytic and more synthetic or even meditating traits.

In the dimension of *religion,* finally, the West-East polarity culminates: Whereas the West emphasized towards God the attitude of free *partnership* which was even exaggerated to religious individualism, the East, on the contrary, has always accentuated the connection of the individual to the unity of being and its divine center, with the immanent inclination into a pantheistic and monistic exaggeration of fusion with the whole.

From all that we can recognize now in the entire order of mankind, East and West are intrinsically called to mutual correction in their negative aspects, and completion in their positive dispositions, and so could not even exist without each other. The being as a well-ordered unity can be realized only in the adequate rhythmical complementary relationship of West and East, of revealing outwards movement of truth and completing inwards movement of the good — and that is its *beauty.*

This integration of mankind is a unique chance to survive. And so, the evolution of life nowadays is about to do a new creative step, to create the unity of One World. This means an integrative world culture in which the occidental and the oriental parts have their indispensable place and task. That requires basically a new type of human being and consciousness, which is more communicative and more integral. It is evident, that such a step of evolution cannot succeed anonymously, according to impersonal laws of nature, but includes a challenge to our will and to our heart, to which we have to respond.[1]

NOTES

1. *Cf.* Heinrich Beck, *Kulturphilosophie der Technik. Perspektiven zu Technik — Menscheit — Zukunft.* Trier 1979; *ders.: Beitrag der Ontologie zu einer sinnvollen und friedlichen Ordnung der Völker. In: Zeitschrift für Ganzheitsforschung 23* (1979) 85–91, *und ders.: Entwicklung zur Menschlichkeit durch Begegnung westlicher und östlicher Kultur.* Bern-Frankfurt a.M. — New York 1988